THE BETTERMENT OF MAN

A Rational History of Western Civilization

THE BETTERMENT OF MAN

A Rational History of Western Civilization

by **G. L. OWEN**

Capricorn Books

G. P. PUTNAM'S SONS

NEW YORK

In Memory of
C. B. WORTHEN,
who introduced me to Western history

SBN: 399-11140-9
Library of Congress Catalog
Card Number: 72-97306

Contents

PART III
The Triumphant or Modern Phase

PART IV
The Uncertain or Contemporary Phase

PART V

Illustrations

FIGURES

MAPS

Preface

My purpose in writing this book has been to provide readers with an account of Western history which, unlike the great majority of those already available, emphasizes its meaning and achievements rather than its details and shortcomings. My fundamental premise has been that Western Civilization's history is, on balance, one of rational progress. In keeping with that premise, I have viewed our past primarily in terms of Western mankind's conscious organization, direction, and advancement toward goals of its own definition—the majority of them rational goals tending to improve the human condition. Furthermore, in presenting this view, I have tried to be as concise as possible—at the risk of underspecifying and overgeneralizing.

Evidently, then, what follows is not an effort to make a further contribution to historical scholarship, but rather a synopsis and interpretation thereof, intended to extend the range of history's influence and increase the degree of its utility. Above all, the book is meant to remind readers that present-day Western Civilization is a preeminently rational way of life, having developed in the course of a preeminently rational history.

A Note On The Data

The data presented in the figures and the text are based on estimates made by the author from available historical evidence, which is for the most part fragmentary. The reader will therefore appreciate that the statistics offered are indicative of probable trends rather than descriptive of certain facts.

Broadly speaking, these statistics refer to the Western world—herein taken to include Europe, European Russia, the Near East, North Africa, and all these regions' settlements and colonies (whether contiguous or overseas) as they were founded or acquired. However, reference is also made to other regions and the world as a whole for comparative purposes; and in the treatment of medieval and modern economic affairs, attention is concentrated on the increasingly predominant area of western Europe—herein taken to include Scandinavia, the British Isles, and all the lands in Europe proper west of a line from the Gulf of Trieste to the Gulf of Danzig.

Whatever region or time they refer to, the valuations offered reflect then-and-there current prices uniformly expressed in their equivalent in gold or pre-1913 U.S. gold-backed currency ($20 currency = 1 ounce gold). They take no account of fluctuating money supplies, inflationary trends, or the like, and are therefore indicative of nominal, marketplace values that actually prevailed rather than of so-called real or constant ones such as economists prefer to employ.

For comparative purposes, the nominal values presented may be roughly converted to their real equivalents by multiplying them by the appropriate factor derived from the following table (interpolating as required):

Year	Factor	Year	Factor
1500 B.C.	1.5	A.D. 1500	1.2
500 B.C.	1.0	A.D. 1750	.73
A.D. 500	1.2	A.D. 1910	.33
A.D. 1000	1.3	A.D. 1970	.10

To convert either nominal or real valuations (expressed in pre-1913 U.S. dollars) to their approximate equivalent in 1970 U.S. dollars, multiply by 3.3.

Introduction

Imagine, if you will, a scene five thousand years ago and half a world away. Night has just fallen, and a full moon is rising over the desolate landscape of ancient Mesopotamia. A lone man, clad only in a skirt of rough homespun, is visible in the moonlight, standing before one of a dozen rude earthen huts. He is looking out at the fields before his village and wondering if it is time to let the waters of the nearby Euphrates River in upon them, wondering if the crop will grow, if his toil will be rewarded, if the spirits will be lenient and permit him to survive yet another season. Lifting his eyes upward, the man begins to pray to the moon—to Sin, creator of all things and father of the gods.

Now recall a second, kindred scene only a few years ago but a quarter million miles away. The sky is black, and an unfamiliar earth is rising over the desolate landscape of the timeless moon. A lone man, heavily clad in a self-sustaining space suit, is visible in the sunlight, standing before one leg of a spider-like spacecraft. He is looking about him at sights never before seen by man and wondering if it is safe to proceed with the lunar excursion as planned, wondering if everything will work as expected, if his stamina will hold up, if all will go well and permit his safe return home. Lifting his eyes to the spacecraft, the man begins to speak to his companion inside it, to his base, and to a waiting world—to mankind, master of the earth and explorer of the universe.

From moon worship to moon walk—such has been the progress of the race across the span of Western Civilization's history, the most recent and most important segment of the whole of human history. At the present juncture in that history, Western man remains, as he was at its outset, a solitary figure confronting the unknown—still a worried, wondering contestant for survival, seeking solace in communication with the presumed arbiters of his fate. But he has nonetheless taken giant strides ahead from where he began, managing to move in his mental quest for wisdom from exploration of the familiar world to the unfamiliar, and to advance in his material quest for sustenance from an attitude of submission to nature to one of dominance over it—to pass, via the persistent application of reason to human affairs, from the twilight of barbarism into the daylight of civilization.

This epic journey up from savagery, this odyssey of self-improvement is our heritage; and to recount it is to describe the formation of the world we live in today—a world far richer, much wiser, and somewhat less bellicose than the world was five thousand years ago when Western Civilization first began.

Part I

The Formative or Ancient Phase

CHAPTER 1

The Near Eastern Origins, 3000-500 B.C.

The Emergence of Civilization

   Western Civilization first began to develop in Mesopotamia, an inhospitable region thinly populated by warlike nomads, more than five thousand years ago. It was there that the requisite circumstances first combined with the requisite incentive to initiate the widespread rational organization of human affairs for human betterment, a process which gradually became the basis of Western life, and which has since transformed not only the West but the entire world. Likewise, it was in Mesopotamia and the territories surrounding it—the present-day Near East—that Western Civilization passed through the first two thousand years of its development and acquired many of its enduring characteristics.

   That development was originally set in motion by the sharp spur of hunger, the fundamental condition of human life in

3

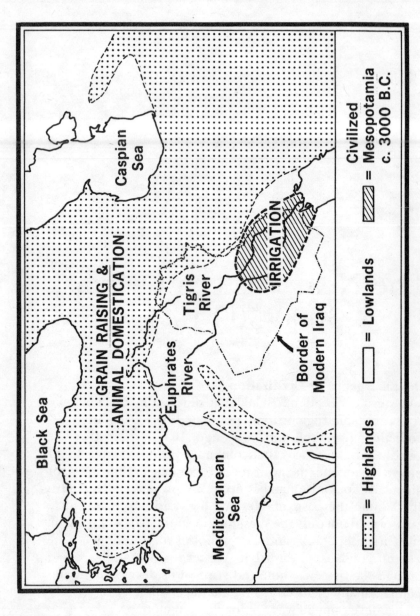

Map 1. The Ancient Near East: Birthplace of Western Civilization

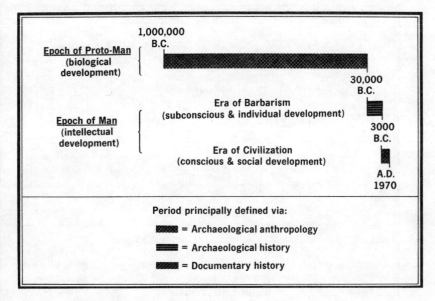

Fig. 1. The Span of Human History

precivilized times—nowhere more so than in the semidesert expanses of Mesopotamia before 5000 B.C. There, in that primeval period, hunger slowly drove the barbarians then dwelling along the region's mountainous northern fringe to begin domesticating animals, because they could no longer get enough meat by hunting, and to begin cultivating cereals, because they could no longer get enough grain by foraging. Subsequently, in the course of incessant migration and raiding, such practices were diffused southward into the Tigris and Euphrates river valleys running through Mesopotamia proper. And in these river valleys, across countless further generations down to 3000 B.C., they were combined with a local discovery—irrigation—to create a system of sedentary agriculture which afforded revolutionary increases in food production and thereby laid the foundation for the estab-

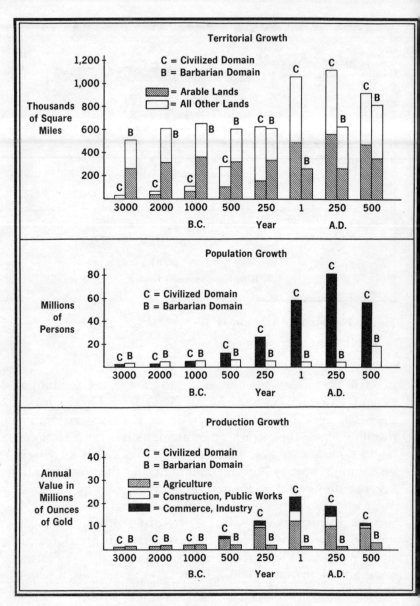

Fig. 2. Indexes of Development in the Ancient West

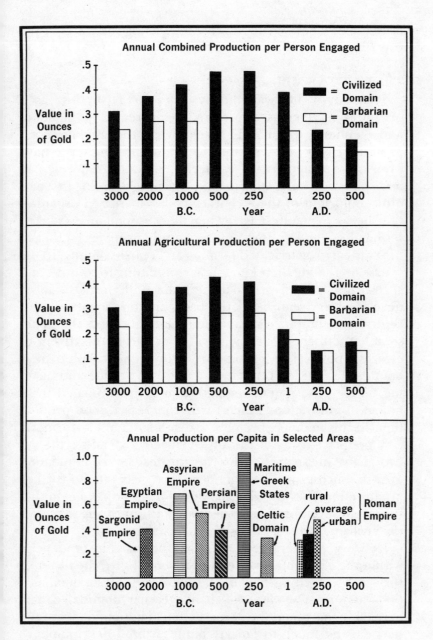

Fig. 3. Productivity in the Ancient West

lishment of a new, civilized way of life along the banks of the two rivers.

The First Two Millennia

That way of life was initially characterized by increased organization, increased production, increased population, and a tendency to continue developing in the same direction at an increased rate—all traits which, in the long term, have proven to be hallmarks of Western Civilization and which, in large measure, have come to define its progress. The first and most important of these characteristics, increased organization, began to manifest itself when the Mesopotamians started settling in fixed locations and cooperating with each other in order to carry on irrigated farming and reap its bounty. In the course of pooling their know-how, submitting to routine, and specializing their efforts to achieve that end, they also slowly developed and embraced the basic organizational tenet of central direction or centralization. Once adopted, that tenet soon led to the establishment of towns and to the advent of effective political organization or government within their bounds. The steady refinement of both urban life and farming under government regulation in turn stimulated technological innovations which further increased food production. In this manner, premature death by famine—formerly commonplace—was drastically curtailed, extending the reproductive life span and fostering unprecedented population growth. Such growth, for its part, soon necessitated further organization to cope with the additional people, beginning the whole developmental cycle anew, and appearing to render the civilizing process robustly self-sustaining.

However, the persistence of powerful barbarian tendencies within the emerging civilized order soon dulled the luster of that prospect. In particular, the survival in Mesopotamia of the warrior-priest elite, which had earlier dominated barbarian life there, and the perpetuation of its dominance in the new era did much to quickly blunt civilized development's

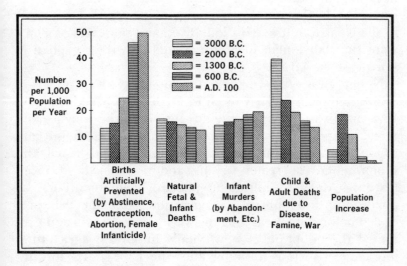

Fig. 4. The Demography of the Ancient West

initial forward thrust. Concerned only with the preservation of its own position and the pursuit of its own selfish interests, this archaic elite soon managed to pervert every aspect of civilization's increased organization to serve those narrow ends. Quick to usurp control of the new forms of government and reshape them along authoritarian lines, the elitists then hastened to employ the formidable instrument thus created to appropriate the bulk of the new agricultural surplus unto themselves. Ere long, they succeeded only too well, monopolizing the budding power and wealth of Western Civilization for their private purposes, robbing the new order of both its sense of direction and means of growth, and thereby slowing its pace of development from a run to a walk.

Such retardation and the greedy elitism inducing it continued to prevail for the duration of Western Civilization's first two millennia, perpetuating relative economic stagnation and fostering political pandemonium throughout the civilized domain. The history of the period therefore found its principal expression in the incessant wars and intrigues carried on by the numerous warrior-priest regimes that arose in the Near East, the most long-lived and powerful of which were the Babylonian in Mesopotamia and the Egyptian in northeastern Africa.

Nonetheless, the further development and spread of civilization—particularly its elitist aspects—proceeded apace. In arms, this resulted in the advent of chariot warfare and metal weaponry. In religion, it produced monotheism and organized pantheons. In culture, it improved visual and monumental art, created writing, and dramatically advanced learning. And in the mundane sphere of economic affairs, the onrunning development of civilization simultaneously produced new commercial methods such as accounting and promoted the adoption of new, vitally important agricultural implements such as the plow and wheel. In short, notwithstanding all the pointless spilling of blood, hurling up of pleas to the gods, and hurling down of cities into the dust that outwardly characterized it, the period from 3000 B.C. to 1000 B.C. witnessed significant, measured civilized advance across a considerable portion of the spectrum of human affairs (see figs. 1-4).

Unfortunately, most of the benefits of that advance were monopolized by the dominant elite, forcing the population at large to live in relatively unchanged circumstances once the Mesopotamian agricultural revolution had been completed and its benefits widely diffused. Thus, for the common man tilling the Near East's soil, there probably was no more to eat, no more security from his real or imaginary fears, and no more respite from the burdens and monotony of his days in 1000 B.C. than twenty centuries before. Indeed, by that time, the initial promise of Western Civilization must have faded altogether in the eyes of the common people. For, although long since freed from nature's ruthless grip by the development of irrigated farming, they were still being squeezed by a set of perhaps even harsher artificial forces—forces dictated half by the new agriculture, half by the new authoritarianism—two thousand years later. Thrust into close quarters, sentenced to endless manual drudgery, bound by an ever stricter sense of community, and overawed economically, socially, politically, and religiously by self-serving cliques and their invented deities, the people of the Near East had escaped from an onerous barbarism only to be reenclosed within an equally onerous civilization.

In other words, the further progress of civilization once it had been firmly established and subjected to elite dominance only slightly influenced the multitude. Once the effects of the Mesopotamian agricultural revolution had been broadcast throughout the Near East, civilized development touched the entire population of the region chiefly only as did war and politics, the main spheres of elite activity. The sweep of plundering armies and the vicissitudes of domineering regimes continued to affect large numbers of people; but for the rest Western Civilization tended to be an elitist phenomenon from not long after its genesis down to the first millennium B.C.; and selfish elite interests in arms, religion, culture, and the exercise of power tended to dictate the character and pace of its advance throughout this period.

The First Unification

This epoch of elite predominance was climaxed by the establishment of the Persian Empire during the sixth century B.C. The last and greatest of the Near Eastern warrior-priest regimes, it unified virtually the entire civilized West under a single political system for the first time. In doing so, it not only culminated two millenia of elitist development but also Western Civilization's Near Eastern development as a whole, thereby preparing the way for the onset of the Mediterranean or classical period to follow.

The engineers of this unification, the Persians, were the last in a series of militant peoples who burst forth from the high-

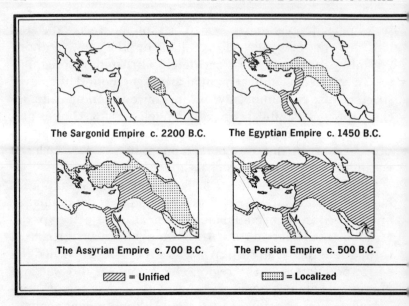

The Sargonid Empire c. 2200 B.C.   The Egyptian Empire c. 1450 B.C.

The Assyrian Empire c. 700 B.C.   The Persian Empire c. 500 B.C.

▨ = Unified   ▦ = Localized

Map 2. The First Consolidation of Western Civilization

lands northeast of Mesopotamia in the centuries just after 1000 B.C. to overrun the civilized heartland. However, unlike their predecessors, the Persians did not stop there, but rapidly extended their conquests in every direction until they had become masters of virtually the entire civilized West. The empire they created stretched, at its maximum extent under Darius the Great about 500 B.C., from the Nile to the Indus and from the Persian Gulf to the Black Sea.

Yet for all its size, the Persian Empire was little more than the epitome of the Near Eastern warrior-priest regime which had first appeared many centuries earlier; and as such, it offered mute testimony to the relative stagnation of overall civilized advance, in spite of what had been achieved in arms and politics—the primary spheres of elite endeavor—during the long period of elite hegemony. Likewise, the existence of severe poverty and oppression throughout the Persian domain demonstrated that elite-inspired economic and social development across the same span of time had also been superficial in character. In fact, the Persian Empire was nothing more nor less than a monument to the drastic constriction of Western Civilization's general development after its initial leap forward under the Mesopotamians.

For the history of such development was not one of robust, self-sustaining, popular advance toward a better life such as the Mesopotamians had begun, but rather one of sluggish, self-interested, elite improvements, principally in culture, religion, warfare, and politics. The end result of this regrettable turn of events, as summed up in the Persian Empire, was a Western-wide system of predominance by a few, based on armed might and political-religious contrivance, an exploitative, elitist status quo hardly better than barbarism so far as the multitude was concerned. In other words, notwithstanding the revolutionary transformation of agricultural production by the Mesopotamians and all that ultimately followed from it, the initial promise of civilized life had not been realized more than twenty-five hundred years later.

Nor did it seem likely that it ever would be unless the stultifying predominance of the Near East's warriors and priests could somehow be terminated. Indeed, if the West was to advance much further in the direction in which the Mesopotamians had initially thrust ahead, then the Persian Empire and much of what it stood for would have to be destroyed. Fortunately, hardly had the Persians completed their conquests than a quarrelsome people arose on the western periphery of their domain who were determined to do just that—to challenge the Persian Empire's might, overthrow it, and snatch the further control of civilized development from the Near East and its elite. These people were the Greeks.

CHAPTER 2

The Greek Transition,
500-200 B.C.

The Greeks and Their Legacy

Inhabitants of a rough, mountainous peninsula jutting out into the eastern Mediterranean from its European shore, the Greeks were descendants of primitive nomads from the Eurasian steppe and of more advanced seafarers from nearby islands like Crete. Their way of life, Hellenism, therefore incorporated elements from both Indo-European barbarism and Near Eastern civilization, a combination which served to stimulate the rise of a distinctive Greek branch of Western Civilization, and, through it, to initiate the transition from an essentially elitist Near Eastern phenomenon into an essentially popular Mediterranean one.

The Greeks thus ushered in the classical period of the West's ancient development by pioneering fundamental changes in almost every significant aspect of Western life; but

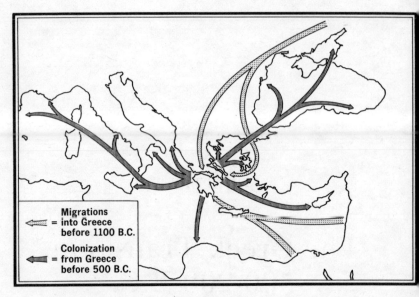

Map 3. The Origins and Diffusion of the Greeks

they overtook and outstripped their predecessors most notably in culture, and it is for their culture above all else that they
are remembered today. A consolidation of and improvement
upon all its Near Eastern antecedents, Greek culture organized, refined, popularized, and thereby preserved the
fruits of over two thousand years of prior civilized development in aesthetic endeavor. What is more, it did so in so
masterful a manner as to remain a potent influence for
another two thousand years, as long as culture itself endured
as a significant factor in Western Civilization. As late as the
nineteenth century A.D., surviving Hellenic masterpieces
such as the Venus de Milo and the Parthenon still elicited
widespread recognition and admiration; and the artistic style
of the period in which they were created continued to find
imitators throughout the Western world. Indeed, many facets
of Western culture—e.g., monumental architecture, statuary,

coinage, poetry, and philosophy—retained a distinctly Greek flavor until only a generation or two ago, offering vivid testimony as to the strength and duration of the Hellenic cultural consolidation's impact.

The Greek Achievement

The majority of Hellenic achievements, however, made no such indelible impression across the ages. Rather they signaled the end of the Near East's hegemony and prefaced the shape of things to come under the Romans. In arms, politics, society, and economics alike, the Greek improvements upon the Near Eastern heritage were less significant in and of themselves than as consolidations of prior accomplishments and harbingers of coming ones—as causeways connecting the Near Eastern past with the Roman future.

The archetype of such interim Hellenic improvements was the hoplite phalanx, a new military formation that the Greeks developed. Derived from both Near Eastern and barbarian antecedents, it consisted of nothing more than a force of heavily armed foot soldiers arrayed several ranks deep along a single frontal line of attack. However, it differed significantly from earlier military formations in that it was manned via universal service and was far better organized for greater striking power. Given that power, its primary short-term effect was to make Greek arms predominant in the eastern Mediterranean region during the fourth and third centuries B.C.; but its long-term effect was transitory, for with the rise of the Romans, military hegemony throughout the Mediterranean world passed to them and their even more powerful formation, the legion.

Naturally, the influence of the hoplite phalanx was not merely military; but the political ferment Greece experienced in the wake of its development—chiefly due to the Greek custom·that linked citizenship with armed service—had an equally short-lived impact. The hectic experimentation with various new forms of government that ensued when the Hellenic armies were expanded to meet the extraordinary manpower requirements of the phalanx bore little lasting fruit. Rule by one (tyranny), by a few (oligarchy), by the privileged (aristocracy), by the wealthy (plutocracy), by the citizenry (republicanism), and by the multitude (democracy) were all tried, but without conclusive result. Indeed, until the Romans conquered the entire Hellenic world and forced it to adopt their political system, Greek political life remained hopelessly chaotic, scarcely more than a microcosm of the preceding Near Eastern order in spite of the phalanx-induced mania for political innovation.

Likewise, in the realm of social affairs, Greece experienced drastic upheaval after the phalanx was introduced, but once more without producing durable results. To be sure, the extension of citizenship gave common men status for the first time; the fortunes of war redistributed wealth throughout the Hellenic world, often enriching the poor; and various political movements further stimulated equalitarian tendencies. But in spite of such stimuli, little genuine, lasting social change ensued either within the bounds of the Greek city-states themselves or elsewhere in the Hellenic sphere.

Much the same was true of parallel Hellenic economic innovations, whose full impact would not be felt until they were applied throughout the Mediterranean world by the Romans (see figs. 2 & 3). Such innovations evolved chiefly from piracy and the hunger for luxury, both commonplace in early Greece. The pursuit of the former in order to satisfy the latter eventually led to regular, sustained maritime trade, and that in turn to the development of naval power, colonization (see map 3), and the specialization of both agriculture and handicrafts. From these components, a comprehensive economic system interlinking the trade, state finance, and production of the entire Greek domain was gradually constructed; and that system considerably increased the available surplus of wealth, chiefly by organizing output and distribution more efficiently.

Even in its most advanced stages, however, (as at Athens in the fifth century B.C. and in the later Hellenistic kingdoms), the Hellenic economy remained largely confined to Greek-ruled areas. Elsewhere in the civilized West, men still depended upon backward, local agricultural economies little improved over the pioneer Mesopotamian model. In sum, although the Greek maritime economy represented a significant advance in civilized economic development and enabled the Greeks to elevate their own standard of living considerably, (see fig. 3), it had only a very limited Western-wide influence upon economic endeavor prior to the incorporation of its practices into the Roman imperial economy.

The net effect of Hellenic noncultural development as a whole was equally restricted. Confined largely to the eastern Mediterranean region during the period of Greek hegemony, it did not become a general influence throughout the West until Roman times; and for that reason, its significance was largely transitional. In spite of being both a summary of and an improvement over its Near Eastern antecedents, the Greek achievement—except in culture—was simply too limited in scope relative to Western Civilization as a whole to serve as anything more than a harbinger of things to come. Far more than it altered the West's present, it pointed the way toward its impending future—toward the quest for a more equitable social order, the search for a more prosperous economic order, and, above all, the establishment of a more effective political order under Roman auspices.

The Greek Wars

The first definitive step in this general redirection of Western Civilization away from the narrow elitist goals of its Near Eastern period of development was the Greek rebuff of the

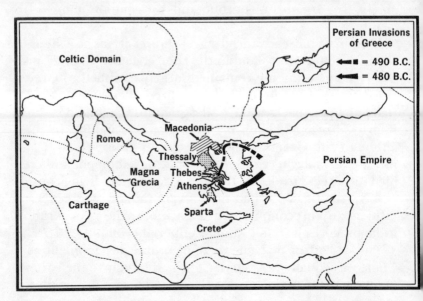

Map 4. The Hellenic Domain

Persian Empire's attempt to conquer and assimilate them. That rebuff was effected by force of arms just after 500 B.C. at the now legendary battles of Marathon, Thermoplyae, and Salamis, in which the Greek city-states defeated two successive Persian invasions of their homeland.

Having once decisively checked the Near East in this manner, however, the victors were so quick to resume quarreling among themselves that they lacked the combined strength to make other than token retaliations against the invaders. Consequently, although Persian strength ebbed steadily thereafter, the Persian Empire and the Near Eastern order it upheld were not actually overthrown for generations to come. Instead, having successfully blunted the threat of engulfment from that quarter, the Greeks spent the next century and a half trying to engulf each other.

The resultant fratricidal warfare culminated—but by no

means ended—toward the close of the fifth century B.C. in the Peloponnesian War between the two leading Greek city-states of Athens and Sparta and their respective allies. The conflict lasted thirty years and ended in Athenian defeat and subsequent decline, a hard blow to the Hellenic cultural genius that city had done so much to nurture, and a victory for Spartan discipline and martial fervor. It was a triumph of war over peace, one whose only fruits were further wars, further dissipation of Greek strength, and further delay of their ultimate reckoning with the Persian Empire.

For having once defeated their Athenian adversary, the Spartans soon undertook to reduce the remaining independent city-states of Greece to their will in the same manner. Regrettably, the resources of their inherently poor and underpopulated homeland, already nearly exhausted by the struggle with Athens, proved unequal to so ambitious an undertaking. Not many years later, therefore, Sparta went down to resounding defeat at the hands of Thessaly and suffered an internal collapse from which it never fully recovered. Thessaly in its turn embarked on an equally futile mission of unilateral conquest and was shortly overthrown by neighboring Thebes. Ere long Thebes, too, set forth on the same path and succumbed to Macedonia. But here the familiar sequence broke down, for the new victor was able to succeed where all its predecessors had failed—first in conquering Greece, and then in destroying the Persian Empire.

The Macedonian Conquest

Macedonia actually was not a Greek city-state but a semibarbarous kingdom situated on the northern fringe of Greece proper—a halfway house on the land route from there to the Near East. Able therefore to borrow from both civilized camps as well as from the barbarian hinterland to the north, it was armed with a hoplite phalanx better than any in Greece, was ruled by a king more absolute and ruthless in his power than any Near Eastern monarch, was possessed of a gloss of

Hellenic culture sufficient to pass as a civilized country, and yet was still in many respects a land on the borderline of savagery. In short, it combined the foremost military, political, and cultural developments of civilization up to that time with a semiprimitive way of life devoted to martial activity, and had only to await an opportune time to embark on an unprecedented career of conquest.

That time came in a few brief years toward the end of the fourth century B.C. under the leadership of the Macedonian king Philip and, after him, of his famous son, Alexander the Great. With Philip at its head, the Macedonian army first overran Greece, consolidating Hellenic power. Then, wheeling eastward with the maritime and economic support of that power, the same army under Alexander overwhelmed the Persian Empire in a lightning series of campaigns—a blitzkrieg of antiquity. Before Alexander stopped, he went on to conquer Iran and the Indus River valley, thereby unifying not only Greece and the Near East, seats of Western Civilization, but the homeland of the Indian civilization as well.

It was a dazzling feat of arms, the son's contribution in particular, one which generals have striven to emulate ever since. But that was all it was. When Alexander died unexpectedly, either of alcoholism or fever, his subordinates immediately fell to quarreling over the spoils of his conquests; the frail political structure he had only begun to frame to replace the Persian system crashed in ruins; and the unity of his domain disintegrated as abruptly as it had been forged.

The Hellenistic World

After a generation of warfare, the partition of the Alexandrian heritage was completed—and with it the establishment of a new Hellenistic international order to succeed the Persian Empire, an order that summed up Near Eastern and Greek civilized achievement and spanned the twilight of Greek hegemony. In Greece proper, it was characterized by a return to the status quo, the city-states there having freed themselves

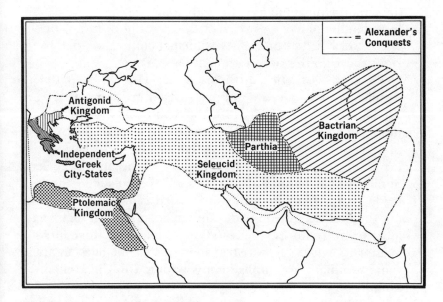

Map 5. The Hellenistic Domain

of Macedonian control in the wake of Alexander's death only to resume fighting each other and thereby continue accelerating their own exhaustion and decline. Elsewhere, the victorious heirs of Alexander's generals had established the so-called Hellenistic kingdoms from which the period derived its name—the Antigonid in Macedonia, the Ptolemaic in Egypt, the Bactrian in Iran, and the Seleucid throughout the remainder of the Near East—as the dominant political units.

It was in these same kingdoms rather than in Greece itself that Hellenic civilized achievement was climaxed. In all of them, a gloss of Greek arms, culture, and urban life overlay the indigenous economic, social, and political patterns upon which the regimes were actually based; and the gradual fusion of this veneer to the underlying structure created the version of the Hellenic heritage passed on to later ages. The last phase in the Greek consolidation, refinement, and improvement of

Near Eastern civilization, this Hellenistic amalgam solidified the Greek achievement sufficiently to serve as one of the main foundations of Western Civilization for the duration of the ancient era and as one of its principal cultural cornerstones right down to the twentieth century A.D.

Thus, in aesthetic endeavor, it was Hellenistic patterns, distilled from generations of prior Greek creativity, that were used as Western standards for the next twenty centuries and more. In arms, it was the Hellenistic rather than the Spartan or Macedonian hoplite phalanx that served as the basic Western military unit until the Roman legion became prevalent. Similarly, in economic affairs, refined Hellenistic methods of trade, finance, and manufacture served as models in developing the Mediterranean-wide Roman economy. In fact, virtually the entire impression the Greeks made on the course of Western Civilization was transmitted to later ages by these same summary accomplishments wrought in the Hellenistic kingdoms.

As already pointed out, the strength of those accomplishments and of that impression was cultural: in the three centuries of their dominance, the Greeks did more to consolidate, refine, and elevate Western Civilization's aesthetic standards than any other people have before or since. But for the rest, their achievements served chiefly to facilitate the transition from Near Eastern to Mediterranean civilization, to consolidate the work begun by the Mesopotamians and prepare the ground for the work yet to be done by the Romans in the ancient era. In spite of their innovations in warfare, their experimentation with a variety of political modes, their development of a relatively prosperous maritime economy, and their spasms of social reform, the Greeks came to the end of their ascendancy without bringing unity, better government, increased material well-being, or greater equality even to their own Hellenic homeland, much less to the West as a whole. Perpetually absorbed in fratricidal strife, they only succeeded in elevating such objectives into common view, in suggesting by their own example that the further development of Western Civilization need not be a continuation of the age-old elite struggle for privilege. It remained for the Romans to act decisively upon that suggestion and so redirect the course of Western development.

CHAPTER 3

The Roman Hegemony, 200 B.C.-A.D. 200

The Roman Achievement

Of the two major periods of Western Civilization's ancient or formative era, the Near Eastern and the Mediterranean or classical, the contemporary West probably owes most to the latter. In particular, we are indebted to the Romans, who conquered the better part of the ancient civilized West, imposed a durable political unity upon it, and then endeavored within that context to fulfill the promise of the West's civilized heritage by seeking to render Western mankind's existence more prosperous, more equitable, and more purposeful.

The Romans thus consummated the ancient phase of Western Civilization's development primarily by giving practical confirmation to the new direction in which the Greeks had already inclined the West. Having conquered the entire Mediterranean world and simultaneously evolved a political system to govern it, they then proceeded to implement and maintain a general peace—the famous Pax Romana—for over two hundred years. Within that context, they also began to grope their way toward the establishment of a life without fear or scarcity for the mass of men, such as the Greek departure from Near Eastern elitism had already prefigured.

Furthermore, in doing so, the Romans gave the West a mystique of civilized development. By making the pursuit of civilization the fundamental objective of Western life rather than the mere pastime of a select few, they conjured up an enduring and alluring interpretation of mankind's future and destiny, which in time became the supreme civilized ideal, the paramount goal toward which the proponents and practitioners of Western Civilization have striven ever since—namely, the dream of progress.

Nevertheless, the Romans' material creations rather than their dream of progress were what gave them an enduring reputation. The Roman legions, the Roman roads, the Roman cities, and, above all, the Roman Empire established the lasting impression that they were basically pragmatists and that their accomplishments were essentially physical ones. In fact, the idealism and strength of character that inspired and infused such creations and ultimately superseded them provided a far more reliable index of what the Romans truly were—the first civilized people (as opposed to a regime or class). Similarly, the ideological foundation for mass civilization which, as a civilized people, they laid down, rather than the roads and cities and the empire they constructed, was the essence of the Roman achievement.

The Republican Political Order

The Romans commenced both their material and ideological achievements with the formation of their republican political order in the fifth century B.C., at the very outset of Rome's thousand-year history. Amid circumstances akin to those concurrently prevalent in Greece, they established a republic at Rome quite similar to certain of the Hellenic city-states. Then, in contrast to the Greeks, they kept it in being, eschewing further experimentation with other forms of government. Having once embraced republicanism, they held fast and sought to make the best of it. Accordingly, during the next five hundred years, down to the time of Christ, the development of the Roman Republic proceeded apace, enabling it to grow from a simple municipality into a complex, almost continental empire encompassing virtually the entire civilized West.

In the course of that growth, Roman government underwent a fundamental transformation from a relatively casual mode of political organization to an extremely disciplined one—a transformation that not only rendered the Republic capable of unifying the West politically but also of overseeing great works of material accomplishment and preparing the way for the popularization of Western Civilization. Constitutionally, this metamorphosis became apparent with the advent of an increasingly elaborate array of increasingly sophisticated political institutions to replace the crude, semitribal ones of the early Republic. Functionally, it was manifested in the transfer of political power from a rustic hereditary elite to an ever more cosmopolitan, more professional corps of civilian and military leaders, the foremost of whom were elected officials. But above all, the transformation of the Republic was reflected ideologically, in the gradual substitution of law for custom as the dominant standard of Roman behavior.

The principal agents of this transformation—especially of its crucial ideological aspect—were Rome's magistrates, the consuls, censors, praetors, and the rest, who from earliest times served not only as judges but also as the chief administrative officers and military commanders of the Republic. Elected periodically by one of the several popular assemblies at Rome, their primary duty was to execute the rulings those assemblies made; and in order to do that, they were compelled

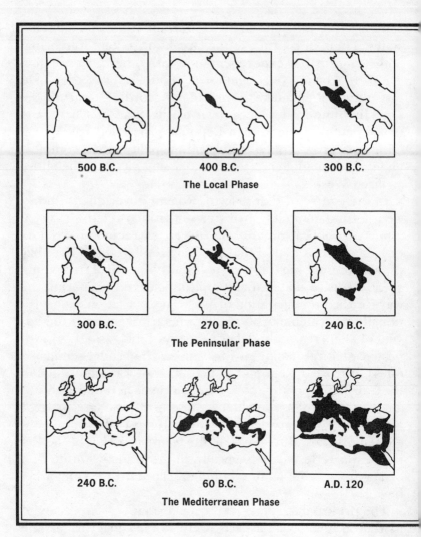

500 B.C.   400 B.C.   300 B.C.

The Local Phase

300 B.C.   270 B.C.   240 B.C.

The Peninsular Phase

240 B.C.   60 B.C.   A.D. 120

The Mediterranean Phase

Map 6. The Expansion of Rome

not only to interpret, but also administer and enforce the whole Roman code of conduct. Consequently, they gradually came to exercise a more and more dominant influence upon both the functioning and reshaping of the Roman state and Roman life, overshadowing the very assemblies they nominally served.

That burgeoning influence was most acute in the ideological realm, since it was the Roman magistrates, in their capacity as overseers of the entire apparatus of state, who were primarily responsible for displacing custom with law as the governing credo of Roman behavior—both in politics and everyday affairs. The magistrates initiated this far-reaching ideological facet of the republican political transformation because, in the course of attempting to rule by custom, the majority of them gradually became convinced that the customary system was unreasonable, unjust, and inefficient. Concluding that it therefore must be based upon an improper, unnatural code of conduct, they sought to devise and implement an alternative system based upon so-called natural law: that is, upon sensible tenets of behavior conducive to the general betterment of mankind, tenets suggested by both logic and experience.

Their sustained efforts in this direction eventually produced Roman law, a blend of natural law and custom that became the cornerstone of the ideological foundation for mass civilization, which would ultimately prove to be the Romans' greatest achievement. A rational, righteous, comprehensive system for guiding the conduct of men's affairs, the new jurisprudence not only enabled the Romans to expand and reorganize their republic from a city-state into an empire unifying almost the entire West, but also prompted them to subsequently undertake the fulfillment of Western Civilization's initial promise of a better life for all men.

The development of Roman law was, in short, the essential ingredient in the commencement of Rome's civilized achievement via the formation of its republican political order. It was the primary accomplishment without which all succeeding accomplishments would have been impossible —the mortar and stone that Rome employed not only to construct the Republic but also to begin building the first mass civilization in the history of the Western world. All that the Romans ultimately achieved and that endured was based upon their legal code; and the code itself proved to be one of the most important and long-lived of Roman achievements, lasting right down to the present as the core of most Western legal systems.

The Triumph of Roman Arms

In addition to the law, armed force was a fundamental ingredient in the Roman success story. Repeatedly at war from the time of its birth, the Republic developed and expanded to Western-wide predominance not only due to its legal resource but also in very large part due to sheer military might. At nearly every crucial juncture in Rome's history, battles were fought to determine its fate; and in almost all the decisive ones, Roman soldiers were victorious. The history of Rome under the Republic was not, of course, a merely military one, as has already been seen, but one of its principal themes was the triumph of Roman arms.

The chief instrument of that triumph was the legion, the basic unit of Roman military organization. In its composition, the legion closely resembled the phalanx, consisting essentially of heavily armed foot soldiers enlisted by means of universal service and arrayed in several ranks along a single frontal line of attack. It differed decisively from its Greek counterpart, however, in that it was better organized and better disciplined for greater tactical mobility and striking power and became progressively more so. Indeed, organization and discipline were the principal characteristics of the legion and of Roman arms as a whole for the lifetime not only of the Republic but of the Empire to follow as well. They were the qualities that gave Roman troops the staying power and tenacity that won Rome so many of its battles. Consequently, for centuries on end, whether well led or ill led, those troops withstood the blows of every adversary they met, responded with more powerful counterblows, and then irresistibly and remorselessly drove the enemy from the field. On battle-grounds all the way from Scotland to Arabia and from Spain to Rumania, the legions time and again proved invincible —too well drilled, too well disposed, and too well directed to be defeated.

Consequently, the Romans won a series of victories never before or since equaled in duration or number; and on the strength of those victories, they conquered an area larger than any acquired in the West before them or since until the advent of mechanized warfare in the twentieth century A.D. To be sure, making such a conquest took almost five hundred years (the better part of the Republic's life span and beyond), but it was still an extraordinary military accomplishment. For, with combined forces that never numbered more than a few hundred thousand men and a supporting population that probably never exceeded five million, Rome eventually de-

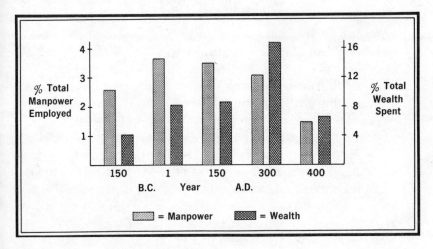

Fig. 5. Rome's Military Effort

feated and subdued the armies of virtually the entire civilized
Western world and its environs, an area peopled with fifty
million or so inhabitants by the time they had established their
hegemony over it.

The Romans began this unprecedented career of conquest
early in the fifth century B.C., having barely founded their
republic, by defeating their neighboring city-states and at-
taching them to Rome either by alliance or annexation. During the next two hundred years, they successfully consolidated these early gains and thereby created a base from which
to conquer all of Italy. Thus prepared, they swept over almost
the entire peninsula in less than half a century, setting the
stage for a third and final phase of expansion across the
Mediterranean and beyond the Alps after 250 B.C. (see map
6).

At this juncture, Rome faced formidable rivals in almost
every direction: the Greeks to the south and east in Sicily,
Italy, and their Balkan homeland; the Carthaginians to the
south and west in Sicily, Africa, and Spain; and the barbarian
Celts and Germans to the north, beyond the Po River and the
Alps (see map 4). All were opposed to further Roman expansion; all were potentially quite as powerful as Rome; all therefore had to be overcome by military conquest if Rome was to
continue such expansion.

During the next half century, from 250 B.C. to 200 B.C.,
they were overcome. In one of the most crucial periods of its
history, Rome fought and defeated all three of these rival
powers, thereby rendering itself preeminent throughout the
West. The Romans initiated the struggle by abruptly overrunning the long-established Greek colonies in southern
Italy. Their domination of the Italian peninsula thus made
complete, they next struck across the Mediterranean to contest for control of its western half with the Carthaginians; and
in three conflicts—known as the Punic Wars—they checked
them, then after much difficulty subdued them, and finally
destroyed Carthage altogether. Between the second and third

of these wars in the west, they also reengaged and defeated the Greeks—the Hellenic city-states and the Hellenistic kingdoms alike—by invading Greece and the Near East.

Consequently, by about 180 B.C., the Romans were everywhere victorious along the shores of the Mediterranean (even though desultory fighting continued for some time to come); and by their victories, they had become predominant throughout the region. But along its northern border they still remained at war with the Celts and Germans—the barbaric inhabitants of continental Europe.

Fighting on this front had begun in earnest in 390 B.C., when a tribe of Celts swept down from the north to annihilate the Roman army and sack the city of Rome itself, a nightmare occurrence that haunted the Roman memory ever after. To prevent its repetition and to extend their domain northward as they were extending it in every other direction, the Romans during the next two hundred years mounted a relentless series of ruthless campaigns to drive the barbarians back north of the Alps from whence they had come or else compel them to embrace civilization.

Having all but achieved these objectives with a last major effort from 250 B.C. to 200 B.C., they undertook to simultaneously conquer the Celtic homeland—Spain, France, and Britain—and to curb the growing strength and aspirations of the Germans. After several generations of sporadic but intensive warfare, this mighty enterprise was finally climaxed by that most famous of Romans, Julius Caesar, in one decade of strenuous effort midway through the first century B.C. In that brief span of time, he resumed the piecemeal conquest of Spain, subdued virtually the whole of Celtic France, invaded Britain, and broke the power of the German tribes in France, driving their remnants back into Germany, beyond the barrier of the Rhine River.

In the wake of Caesar's campaigns, the Romans, after nearly four centuries of warfare, had finally reduced the menace of northern barbarism to manageable proportions.

By conquering the Celts and their continental domain, and by thoroughly chastising the Germans, they had made their predominance quite as absolute along the West's European frontier as in the Mediterranean basin. For the next four centuries, thanks to the triumph of Roman arms, virtually the entire Western world would be subject to Roman rule.

☐ = The Republican Empire	
▨ = Annexed by Julius Caesar	⊙ = Rome
▨ = Annexed by Augustus Caesar	○ = Other Major Cities
▨ = Annexed by the Good Emperors	—— = Primary Roads
▨ = Contested Territory	------ = Sea Routes
▨ = Parthia (Civilized)	⋀⋀⋀ = Fortified Frontiers
■ = Barbarian Domain	

Map 7. The Roman Empire

The Roman Empire

The initial fruits of that triumph and the first steps in establishing Western-wide Roman government were to be seen in the formation of the republican Roman empire—the first truly international state in Western history. Just as the development of the law's supremacy in Roman domestic affairs found its principal expression in the creation of the republican political order at Rome, so did the development of force's supremacy in Roman foreign affairs find its principal expression in the extension of that political order throughout the West. As the Romans conquered the Western world, they imposed their own forms of government upon it rather than preserving its many existing regimes; and in so doing, they created a new kind of political organization—the republic-as-empire.

The Romans chose this unique unitary method of territorial-political consolidation not only because the more multifarious alternatives available had already been tried without lasting success by the Persians and Greeks, but also because their growing preference for law over custom urged them to do so. In effect, they had developed a sense of mission concerning the law and were determined to spread its benefits—especially its Romanizing and civilizing influences—as far afield as possible. So, when their conquests provided the opportunity, they seized it without hesitation and commenced to expand the Republic from an ethnic to an imperial government.

The chief means by which they carried out the expansion was through lateral extension of the extant Roman administration into the newly acquired, non-Roman territories. That is, simply by multiplying the number of magistrates and assigning some to carry out their familiar duties in the new domains, the Romans found it possible to extend their versions of law and government quickly, without significantly altering the Romanness of either, into conquered areas.

Once this had been done, the inhabitants of the conquered

areas were more or less fully exposed to the Roman system; and any beneficial results such exposure could produce were soon forthcoming. The conquered peoples generally responded by embracing Roman ways, imitating them assiduously, and eventually becoming Roman citizens themselves. Thus, in time, both peoples and territories were permanently attached to Rome as integral members of the Republic-empire, permitting the withdrawal of all but token military forces and contingents of imperial officials from their midst.

In this way, with a minimum of manpower and expenditure (see fig. 5), the Romans were able to introduce in relatively rapid succession first order, then Roman law, and finally semiautonomous local government of the Roman sort into their new domains, thereby firmly binding such territories and their populations to Rome and placing their resources at its disposal. Indeed, empire-building in this manner more than paid for itself in the long run, not only by facilitating the spread of Roman ideals and customs and fostering the growth of Roman dominion and power, but in a strictly monetary sense as well.

The empire that resulted was an enduring union of diverse regions and peoples unlike any previous Western political system. Balancing the unprecedented mass influence enabled by lawful government against the customary elite control secured by superior armed force, and pitting the forces of local self-interest against those of central efficiency, the republican imperium successfully fused the major disparities of the most promising modes of government that had preceded it. Building upon the heritage of both the small, politically oriented Hellenic city-state and the large, territorially oriented Near Eastern monarchy as they pursued justice and dominion with ever-increasing zeal, the Romans ultimately produced an almost civilization-wide regime more cohesive and powerful than any the West had ever seen.

As such, the republican empire was one of Rome's supreme

pragmatic achievements—the first great monument to the establishment of Roman hegemony in Western Civilization. Unfortunately, the empire also proved to be the Republic's undoing, for in the course of its formation the magistrates became so strong and the assemblies so weak that the former began to vie for absolute control, plunging the Republic into a fatal political crisis near the end of the first century B.C.

This most famous—or perhaps notorious—period in Roman history had its beginnings in the last, abortive efforts at popular reform made just prior to the onset of the first century B.C. When these were frustrated, the continued growth of magisterial power became rampant, particularly among consuls endowed with military commands. This trend was confirmed when compulsory armed service was abolished, making the legions semimercenary units loyal principally to their commanders. Thereafter, it was only a matter of time until some consul employed this unshackled military power to seize control of the government; and once the precedent had been established—in 88 B.C.—Roman political life rapidly degenerated into a free-for-all contest among the leading magistrates for supreme power. After decades of armed strife and intrigue toward that end, Julius Caesar, just after mid-century, appeared to have won out; but when he was assassinated at the peak of his power, the strug- gle for supremacy broke out anew and raged for another twenty years, culminating in the destruction of the Republic.

In the wake of its downfall, a new, avowedly imperial re- gime, the Roman Empire of historical repute, quickly emerged. Perpetuating all the essential features of the repub- lican empire, this regime consummated Roman political de- velopment by completing the conquest of the West and its territorial-political consolidation. Then it climaxed the estab- lishment of Roman hegemony as well by imposing a general peace—the so-called Pax Romana—throughout the Western world for the next two hundred years.

The Roman Peace

The Pax Romana lasted from the end of the Republic in 27 B.C. to the end of the early Empire in A.D. 180—from the reign of the first Roman emperor, Augustus, to that of the last of the so-called good emperors, Marcus Aurelius. Its principal characteristics were growth of government, stability, and the pursuit of greater equality and prosperity, the cornerstones of the new Roman imperial order established at the beginning of the period. Likewise, its principal shortcomings were those of that same order. In fact, the Pax Romana and the early Roman Empire were inseparable phenomena—the two foremost manifestations of Western Civilization at the climax of the classical age.

The architect of both was Augustus Caesar, nephew of Julius. Tireless, methodical, and pragmatic to his fingertips, Augustus came to the fore during the final years of the Republic as one of the several powerful magistrates who were the last to vie for unilateral control of the Roman state. Shrewdly exploiting his assassinated uncle's name and fortune as his rivals occupied themselves destroying the Republic and each other, he emerged eventually as the lone victor. Having done so, he set about creating a lasting peace and a new imperial order based on the republican experiences of the past and the exigencies of the moment.

His principal tool was compromise—the balance of opposing forces by the partial conciliation of each; and his principal assumption in using that tool was that, for the first time in the history of Rome or any other large Western state, the mass of the people had to be conciliated as well as the traditional elite forces of the army, the aristocracy, and the wealthy. The multitude wanted greater social equality, material prosperity, an end to civil strife; and Augustus knew that he must supply all three in some measure if he was to succeed in putting Rome's affairs in order. In addition, he knew that he must satisfy the wealthy's desire for a larger role in a more efficient

government, the army's quest for an assured future mission
and sphere of action, and the aristocracy's longing for stability
and a republican restoration. Beyond that, he had to defend
Rome's imperial domain from external enemies. And, as Augustus well realized, he possessed only limited funds and
manpower to do all this.

Hence he made not only compromise but also efficiency a
hallmark of his regime. The Augustan Empire was to be a
system not only of conciliation but of economy as well. Peace,
established at the outset and prerequisite to any new Roman
order, had to be maintained by minimizing the causes of
conflict as well as those of extravagance. It was necessary to
create a regime which, in the best republican tradition, was
not only an amalgam of its predecessors and an improvement
over contemporary alternatives but also more efficient than
any other.

Augustus set about instituting such a government by first
establishing himself as absolute head of both the army and the
imperial administration. Then, behind a façade of republican
restoration, he reformed both institutions completely. The
army he transformed from an unruly collection of large field
units into a single, compact frontier defense force of 300,000
men. The administration he transformed from a tangled,
overburdened extension of the old republican city-state into a
tightly knit, centralized imperial bureaucracy run by his own
slaves and loyal freedmen. This done, he had the necessary
means to undertake the remainder of his program by the
gradual but steady promotion of greater social equality and
prosperity, a monumental task to which he devoted himself
for the rest of his long life.

Augustus' successors emulated his example for the duration of the Pax Romana, giving the order he had created its
desired stability. Embracing his policy, they sought to implement it in the same manner he had—by preserving their
absolute authority via control of an efficient army and

bureaucracy, and by using that authority to foster greater material well-being and social equality throughout the Roman Empire.

In the maintenance of their authority, those who donned the purple after Augustus were generally successful; but in its exercise on the multitude's behalf, they generally were not.

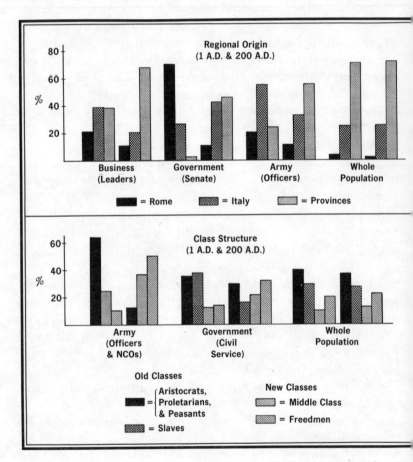

Fig. 6. Composition of Elites and Masses in the Roman Empire

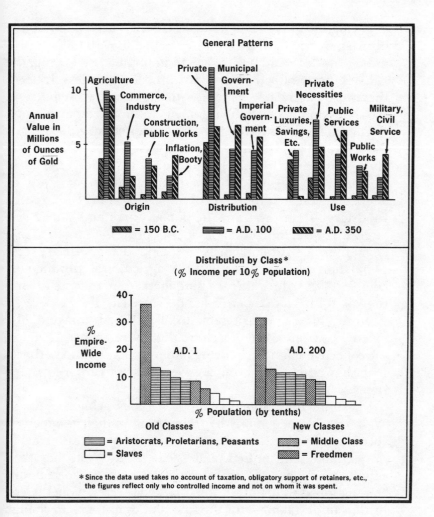

Fig. 7. Income in the Roman Empire

Laboring to transform a nascent, barely perceived mystique of mass civilized advance into an actual but undefined program of widespread improvement in popular well-being, the early emperors for the most part proved powerless. Indeed, they were barely able to cope with unfolding economic and social developments in their domain, let alone reshape them.

Consequently, the social (and geographic) stratification of the overall population of the Empire—if not of its ruling elite—remained relatively unchanged under the Pax Romana. So did its economic stratification, in spite of wholesale state manipulation of imperial income resources to fund large-scale programs of public works and public services. Likewise, individual prosperity proved no more than a chimera to the rural majority of the population, since excess population growth and stagnant agricultural productivity combined to reduce the absolute increase in income during the Pax Romana to a per capita decrease (see figs. 2, 3, & 4). Even the urban minority able to take full advantage of the extensive system of state welfare did not really prosper; and the collective standard of living under the early Empire therefore showed no improvement over those of earlier Western states.

In sum, the Romans capped their achievement of Western-wide hegemony by foundering in their pioneer efforts to promote Western-wide material progress. Having once conquered, unified, and pacified the West, they then sought to initiate the transformation of its socioeconomic foundation as well, but without marked success. Nonetheless, by thus undertaking—for the first time in history—to change civilization from the pastime of a few to the purpose of many, they culminated the Roman consolidation of Western Civilization and climaxed that civilization's development in the ancient era.

CHAPTER 4

The Roman Collapse, A.D. 200-500

After the Roman Peace

The Augustan order climaxed classical Western Civilization but it failed to prepare the way for further civilized advance in the wake of the Pax Romana. Quite the contrary, the shortages and stresses it generated throughout the Mediterranean world initiated the gradual decline of the Roman Empire during the third and fourth centuries A.D., and this in turn led to the Empire's disintegration and fall during the fifth century—a catastrophe that not only destroyed the fruits of the Pax Romana but also precipitated the collapse of Western Civilization in much of the Mediterranean world, thereby terminating the ancient era and submerging its heritage for centuries to come.

Rome first entered upon the decline implicit in the Augustan order when Marcus Aurelius, the last of the good emperors, died in A.D. 180. During the ensuing decades, rival claimants to the imperial scepter arose and began battling for supremacy, ending the golden age initiated by Augustus in the same kind of civil violence from which it had been fetched forth. Such violence persisted for the next hundred years, prompting increased neglect of imperial affairs, particularly those relating to defense and the economy, and ushering in the period of the so-called later Empire. Then, for the better part of the fourth century, a series of capable but despotic emperors succeeded in restoring peace and retarding decline by reconstructing the imperial regime along lines of absolute social, political, and economic rigidity, i.e., by completely institutionalizing the status quo. But not even this desperate expedient sufficed to preserve the achievements of old for long.

By the last quarter of the fourth century, the economic foundations of Mediterranean civilization had begun to crumble and its frontier defenses against revived northern European barbarism to collapse. Ere long, therefore, the barbarians seized their opportunity and started to invade the Roman Empire in force, further accelerating its already rapid decline. Soon it split asunder into eastern and western halves; the tempo of civilized activity within its bounds slowed even more; and a generation later, it was gone, the western half altogether overrun and plunged into anarchy by the Germans and the eastern half driven back upon its Greek and Near Eastern inner resources, permanently cutting it off from the mainstream of Western Civilization's development.

The Causes of the Decline and Fall

The causes of this disaster, of the decline and fall of the Roman Empire, have long been debated among historians. How the destruction of so mighty and long-lived a regime as the Empire came to pass, terminating the formative or ancient phase of the development of Western Civilization in catastrophe, and what the reasons for it were are necessarily among the principal questions that must be asked and answered in recounting the history of the classical period.

A variety of answers have been given to these questions. The Roman Empire's demise has been attributed to such divergent causes as slavery, Christianity, class conflict, soil exhaustion, racial degeneracy, historical cycles, and diminished rainfall. The surviving evidence as presently interpreted, however, discounts such monolithic explanations in favor of more comprehensive alternatives that focus upon the Empire's military and economic failures in the face of a resurgent barbarian menace and the demands of an impoverished, growing population. In other words, imperial Rome's downfall was apparently caused primarily by insufficiency under stress—by a dearth of the manpower and materiel required to defend civilized life from savagery and scarcity.

What in turn caused these shortages and stresses, these fatal insufficiencies and strains, has yet to be definitively resolved. Historians continue to debate whether they were more the product of unfortunate human choices or of unfavorable natural circumstances. Evidently, then, neither factor can presently be discounted. The Roman Empire's collapse must be attributed at bottom both to the human choice of an extremely difficult path of imperial development leading toward permanent Western-wide peace and prosperity, and to the formidable natural obstacles that thrust up to block that path—namely, the unexpected resurgence of northern European barbarism, the unprecedented growth of the Empire's population, and the irremediable stagnation of its agricultural technology.

The Roots of Roman Failure

The onset of the Roman catastrophe was initiated by the basic decision made by Augustus at the outset of the Empire to adopt a defensive stance in foreign affairs, particularly toward the northern barbarians, so as to concentrate Rome's energy and resources upon the domestic pursuit of mass material prosperity and the corollary development of greater equality. This decision, which permanently fixed the character of imperial policy, was based on two grave miscalculations regarding the circumstances in which that policy would have to be carried out, miscalculations that made the failure of Roman policy all but certain and set in motion the Empire's eventual downfall.

The first such miscalculation was the assumption that, by the time of Christ, Rome's few surviving external enemies had been sufficiently cowed to permit the imperial government to concentrate its attention upon internal affairs. Unfortunately, once this became policy and the legions accordingly took up more or less permanent defensive positions along the Empire's frontier, the unconquered Germanic tribes still opposing them in Europe quickly began to recover their former strength and bellicosity. Furthermore, as the Roman forces settled into the routine of garrison life, their effectiveness gradually deteriorated, compounding the danger of the barbarian resurgence (see fig. 5). As a result, the Germans ere long had once again become a serious threat to the Empire's safety, starkly contradicting the presumption of barbarian weakness implicit in imperial policy.

The other faulty element of that policy was the assumption that mass material prosperity could be readily achieved. To their distress, Roman officials soon discovered that this simply was not so, that the creation of widespread and lasting popular well-being was a task quite as complex and difficult as the conquest and political consolidation of the Mediterranean littoral had been, and likely to take quite as long or longer to complete. They also soon discovered that the persistent effort and intensified organization which had served Rome so well in unifying the West would no longer suffice to implement its policy, given that policy's increasingly economic bias. In short, mass material prosperity simply was not within easy reach, official promises and programs notwithstanding.

One of the most important specific reasons for this was Rome's failure to spur the development of agrarian technology and thereby increase farm output, the mainstay of the Western economy. For the inhabitants of the Empire, just as for all their predecessors since the Mesopotamians, agricultural improvement proved to be an impossible task. In fact, farm production seems to have declined throughout the Mediterranean world under Roman rule, both per acre and per farmer. For reasons that elude the historian, the Romans—like the ancients as a whole—were never able to devise the new methods required to increase farm yields significantly beyond the levels to which the Mesopotamians had lifted them at the outset of civilized history in the West (see figs. 2 & 3).

Nor were the Romans much more successful in increasing the returns from nonagrarian economic endeavor beyond the levels to which the Greeks had already raised them. Rather they adopted as their own the Hellenistic system of commerce, industry, and construction that incorporated all the major Greek economic innovations, and then proceeded to extend it throughout the Mediterranean world as part and parcel of their imperial order. Naturally this expansion and the improved organization that necessarily accompanied it increased nonagrarian production substantially, but not enough to increase the overall standard of living decisively. Furthermore, such commercial and industrial gains peaked when the process of empire-wide organization had been completed; and thereafter, as agricultural stagnation, population growth, and misuse of the available surplus curtailed the supply of fluid capital, the nonagrarian sector of the economy rapidly began to atrophy. In sum, Rome's nonagricultural economic development under the Empire was ephemeral at best; and the nonagrarian sector therefore contributed no more to the establishment of lasting prosperity than did its agricultural counterpart (see figs. 2 & 3).

Thus the Augustan order's domestic program of mass

material prosperity utterly lacked bona fide economic support. Even so, the program was not abandoned. Instead,
efforts were made to underwrite it by falling back upon the
time-tested, time-worn Roman political technique of administrative efficiency—i.e., by resorting to the proceeds of strict
government economy, adroit financial manipulation, and
uniformly heavy taxation. In effect, the attempt was made to
finance the wholesale elevation of popular living standards
throughout most of the Western world with the monetary
fruits of the Roman political consolidation—with the revenues to be derived from the more efficient operation of
Western government along highly centralized, imperial lines
(see fig. 7).

Needless to say, this endeavor to create prosperity by fiat
did not succeed. The proceeds it netted barely sufficed to
create a façade of prosperity in the cities of the Empire, where
a mere 10 percent of the population resided. Elsewhere,
among the rural 90 percent of the population, poverty remained the norm. Indeed, as the stagnant imperial economy's
small surplus was increasingly diverted away from the rural
majority into the hands of the urban minority and increasingly spent upon luxuries such as baths, circuses, and statuary
rather than upon necessities such as food, clothing, and fuel,
the overall economic output—especially nonagrarian
production—began to decline for lack of markets and essential capital investment, causing rural poverty to grow progressively worse.

The continued proliferation of the farm population
throughout the Empire only accelerated this descent into the
abyss of want. To be sure, the rate of population growth was
not large and it continued to decline rapidly toward zero, but
the effect was still serious—the more so since it came in the
midst of deepening economic distress (see figs. 2 & 4). By the
time the civilized community's numbers had been checked
under the later Empire, the consequences of too many people
had already combined with those of too few goods to reduce

the Western standard of living back to the bare subsistence level of early Mesopotamian times, making a mockery of the imperial domestic program for the promotion of mass material prosperity—just as the Germanic resurgence had nullified Rome's plans for perpetual peace in foreign affairs.

Here then were the principal roots of Roman failure. The unalterable material circumstances of overpopulation, underproduction, and barbarian recovery had rendered the mutable ideological objectives of permanent, Western-wide peace and prosperity unachievable just when these objectives were being made the basis of imperial policy. Imperial officials nonetheless persisted in their efforts to implement that policy, largely through purely political and administrative means. By doing so, they only succeeded in making patently excessive demands upon not just the imperial order's extant available physical resources but also its institutions and people, thereby giving rise to that condition of perpetual insufficiency under stress which finally destroyed not only the Roman Empire but classical Western Civilization as a whole.

The Onset of Collapse

The impending failure of the Roman imperial system first began to become manifest early in the fourth century A.D. By then, the façade of urban prosperity erected during the Pax Romana had become so expensive to maintain that the municipal and imperial governments were expropriating virtually the whole of the Empire's economic surplus for the purpose. Government officials struggled to support the ruse with whatever share of the Empire's now predominantly agricultural output they could direct into the state's hands. In doing so, they found themselves reduced to squeezing the last iota of substance from the already impoverished rural 90 percent of the population simply to maintain the urban 10 percent in the semiprosperous style to which they had become accustomed (see fig. 7).

In the course of this grim endeavor, farm taxes were first

maximized and then transformed into exorbitant fixed rents, prompting the widespread reintroduction of single-family plots to maximize rent yields. This in turn revived small-scale farming, further curtailing an already minimal production and spurring the government to invoke still more drastic measures to ensure itself the necessary agrarian revenues. These measures culminated in freezing the farm population on the land, thereby isolating it in rural backwaters and permanently eliminating it as a source of imperial vitality.

But not even this forlorn expedient sufficed to maintain agricultural output or the state's income therefrom. Both declined even more markedly in the fourth century than they had in the third, as did popular support for the imperial government. During this twilight period, officials of the later Empire sought to counteract such trends by the arbitrary creation of wealth through monetary inflation and of loyalty through compulsory service, but they were not notably successful in either endeavor. Consequently, although the imperial regime became increasingly despotic, it also became progressively and ever more apparently weaker. Inadequately financed and lacking the necessary popular support any longer to govern effectively within its borders or to maintain the integrity of those borders, it threatened to succumb momentarily either to invasion or to disintegration from within.

The former eventuality materialized when toward the end of the fourth century A.D. the German tribes along virtually the entire length of the Empire's European frontier became restive and began to cross it in force. These onslaughts, although they pitted no more than three million savages against a civilized community of at least sixty million, nonetheless placed heavy new demands upon Roman arms and upon the fading wealth and loyalty required to sustain them (see fig. 5). Unable to withstand so severe a strain for long, the Empire finally cracked. Its northern border repeatedly violated and its richest territories in Europe overrun, it split in two, the eastern half eventually being consolidated as Byzantium and the western half degenerating into a chaos of petty, ramshackle, transitory, German-dominated regimes, in which the only reasonably stable economic, social, or political unit was the self-contained rural estate with its population of land-bound, small-plot farmers paying fixed rents to a dominant landlord. By the mid-fifth century A.D., it can be said that the Roman Empire had fallen and the medieval world had begun to emerge.

The End of the Roman Empire

The Romans' nightmare of barbarian triumph rather than their dream of progress had come to pass. Their empire, almost a thousand years in the making, and ancient Western Civilization itself, more than three thousand years in the making, had been superseded by Germanic savagery. It was a disaster without parallel in the history of the West.

The Romans tried valiantly to prevent it but failed. Successful in their efforts to consolidate the civilized West politically and territorially, they also undertook to permanently stabilize its foreign relations and transform its economic and social structure as well, but they could neither find nor develop the means to do so. Nor could they bring themselves to abandon these unattainable new objectives once having adopted them. The intertwined dreams of Western-wide order and progress, once conjured up, could not readily be dispelled; and the Romans sought to realize their promise of enduring peace, prosperity, and equality with all the bulldog tenacity for which they were famous—but without success.

Nonetheless, their effort was prodigious; and it paradoxically proved to be both their greatest achievement and the cause of their ruin. By trying to render life more peaceful, prosperous, equitable, and purposeful for all of Western mankind, the imperial Romans not only made the pursuit of mass civilization the fundamental objective of Western development thereafter: they also destroyed most of that development's extant material achievements by precipitating the decline and fall of the Roman Empire.

Fortunately, ancient Western Civilization's most important creations, its ideas and ideals, especially Roman ideals, survived that awful collapse, although buried for a time in the rubble. Eventually they were unearthed and served to guide the revival of Western Civilization along its former lines, saving men from the necessity of making a new start from scratch. In time, the dreams of international order and progress which the Romans had first dreamed full-blown were rediscovered, and the quest for their fulfillment was once again made the ultimate purpose of human life in the West. In time, the endeavor to create a truly rational, all-encompassing mass civilization, which the Romans had first undertaken, was resumed, and, once the classical economic impasse had been overcome, was carried forward swiftly. In time, Western Civilization recovered and resumed that course toward the material, the equalitarian, and the just upon which Rome had irrevocably set it, thereby placing the contemporary West forever in the debt not only of Rome but of ancient Western Civilization as a whole, of which Rome was but the culmination.

Part II

The Resurgent or Medieval Phase

CHAPTER 5

The Germanic Regression, A.D. 500-800

After the German Invasions

In the centuries following the end of the Roman Empire, western Europe sank into a state of anarchy unlike anything experienced in the civilized Western world for more than fifteen hundred years, since the last great barbarian upsurge around 1000 B.C. That upsurge had probably been Celtic; the one that brought the Roman Empire down was certainly Germanic; but in most other respects, they were not dissimilar—save in the degree and kind of civilized regression they produced.

In neither case was that regression fatal to Western Civilization, although each retarded the course of its development for about five hundred years; but in the latter instance of the German invasions, only the strength of the civilized community, developed during the long period of Roman hegemony,

enabled that civilization to survive at all, even at the cost of
severe retardation. The bases of that strength were two: on
the one hand, the Romans had begun to transform Western
Civilization into a mass phenomenon rooted deeper in society
than the barbarians' influence could reach; and on the other
hand, they had reoriented it about a few enduring ideals
that barbarian ravages could not destory.

Certainly the material trappings of the civilization founded
by the Romans—the roads, the cities, the magnificent build-
ings, and all the rest—did not survive the Germanic onslaught. As commerce expired and urban life ended throughout western Europe under the barbarian impact, their great
works of empire, already robbed of political support by the
collapse of the imperial government, were deprived as well of
the last vestiges of financial and social support, and were no
longer undertaken. Likewise, the already extant creations of
empire that were not destroyed outright by the Germans'
initial pillaging soon fell into disuse, disrepair, and decay once
the imperial system which had built and maintained them had
been swept away.

In the absence of that system's order and direction, men
were compelled to fall back upon the land to survive; and,
having once done so, they were also compelled to abandon the
civilized amenities in order to meet the stringent demands of a
still-backward Mediterranean agricultural system upon their
time and energy. Seeking to endure the anarchy and chaos
created by the Germans, the people of the hardest-hit areas of
the West—particularly of western Europe—regressed completely to the patterns of self-sufficient rural village life that
had begun to reemerge under the later Empire; and those
patterns were unable to support the kind of material civilization that the Romans and their predecessors had created.

As the manifestations of this regression became steadily
more apparent after A.D. 500, the rational quest for human
betterment, which the Mesopotamians had first initiated

more than three millennia earlier, ceased to be undertaken almost everywhere the Germans established themselves. Faced with fewer and fewer material vestiges of Western Civilization, men remembered that civilization with less and less clarity and strove for its objectives with less and less vigor. As even kings forgot how to read and write, the imitations prompted by a fading civilized heritage became increasingly unauthentic and increasingly uncivilized, permitting western Europe to sink ever deeper into the shadows of northern savagery which the Germans had cast across its length and breadth.

The Germanic Kingdoms

Nowhere were the depths of these shadows blacker than in politics, the sphere in which Roman accomplishments had been most brilliant. Once they had overthrown that long-lived masterpiece of international political organization, the Roman Empire, the barbarian invaders had no means of replacing it that could compare even remotely in scope, effectiveness, or durability. Instead, having exhausted their impulses for pillage and migration, the German tribes one by one settled more or less within the bounds of former Roman administrative units and then tried to rule the native population by imposing their own savage political traditions upon the surviving remnants of the old Roman machinery of government.

Needless to say, the crude kingdoms that resulted left much to be desired; they were nonetheless one of the major institutional achievements of the early medieval era and, as such, set the pattern for large-scale political organization for the next millennium. The Roman concepts in that pattern—of the territorial state; of central administration; and of government as an instrument of law, efficiency, and public service—rested at the base of the governmental pyramid, where the conquering Germans' influence barely penetrated, and consequently they were forced to rely largely on the manorial vestiges of

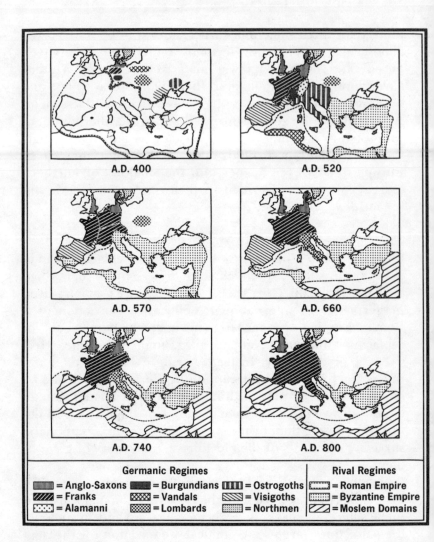

Map 8. The Post-Roman West

Roman local government. For the rest, the traditions and agencies of Germanic tribalism were chiefly responsible for the character of western Europe's new political system.

The foremost of these was the dominant warrior's household, which was utilized as the principal component in constructing the upper echelons of all the Germanic kingdoms. Composed not only of personal servants but also of a group of advisors and a retinue of soldiers, all bound to the dominant warrior by ties of individual loyalty, the institution of the household combined the familiar elements of Western barbaric government—the ruling warrior, the advising-judging elder council, and the approving warrior host—into a peculiarly Germanic amalgam typified by the individual leadership, bonds of personal loyalty, and martial prowess.

The preeminent household was that of the foremost warrior or king of the tribe; it served as the central government. Beneath it were arrayed all the lesser warriors' households in descending order of importance, and beneath them all the nonmilitary, non-Germanic manorial households that had survived from Roman times—the lot of them being interrelated by a sequence of protofeudal lord-vassal, vassal-lord pledges exchanged by their heads. These pledges, which promised allegiance and aid (in service or in kind) in return for military protection, law enforcement, and land grants, were the sinews of the primitive Germanic kingdoms. Through them, tribal leaders were able to establish and exercise at least a semblance of authority over the lands and peoples they had conquered, as well as over their own tribesmen; and through such authority, they gave their regimes sufficient permanence and value to render them the prototype for the post-Roman political reorganization of western Europe.

The Frankish Hegemony

One of the first and doubtless the foremost of these Germanic kingdoms was that created in what is today northern

France by the Franks, a German tribe from the lower Rhine River valley. The Franks invaded the Empire late in the fourth century A.D. and thereafter steadily expanded their domain, both southward within the empire's borders and eastward within their German homeland. Often ably led, they gradually forged the largest territorial state to be created in early medieval western Europe, either absorbing or sharply reducing all their neighboring rivals until, by A.D. 600, their holdings stretched from the Pyrenees in northern Spain to the Bohemian Forest in central Europe (see map 8).

But the pace of the Frankish conquest outstripped that of the Germans' post-Roman political and military evolution alike; and so, for want of the means to hold so extensive a realm together for long, territorial disintegration threatened almost as soon as the conquest was completed; and an interlude of chaos ensued in Frankish affairs. It was finally terminated almost a century later by Charles Martel, leader of one of the three principal tribal-territorial factions into which the Franks had by then split. By force of arms, he reunified them and began to reconstruct the formerly tribal Frankish state along the household lines described above, preparing the way for its further expansion and refinement by his descendants into the Frankish Empire, the greatest of the Germanic kingdoms. At the same time, unfortunately, he so transformed western European military practices as to ensure the subsequent disintegration of all these kingdoms—including the Frankish Empire—and their replacement by smaller, if otherwise quite similar, feudal states.

Martel wrought these contradictory changes principally by adopting the stirrup, a Chinese invention that reached German Europe just as he was about to embark on his drive to reunite the Frankish realm. The stirrup greatly improved a mounted warrior's ability to resist being unhorsed in combat; and by combining it with better arms and armor, Martel made his cavalry capable of shock tactics similar to those upon which the earthbound Roman legions of old had relied, tactics that soon rendered Frankish arms supreme in western Europe and made elite cadres of heavily armed and armored horsemen or knights the mainstay of warfare throughout the West for centuries to come.

The temporary military advantage the Franks derived from introducing knightly warfare enabled them not only to reunify their divided kingdom but to expand it into an empire uniting most of western Europe under a single government. Under the protection of that government, the Germanic regression was finally halted and a semblance of order restored. To be sure, little or nothing was done to ameliorate prevalent conditions of economic depression, but a roughshod rule of law was restored and clumsy efforts were made to revive the Roman heritage and resume civilized development along similar lines.

Charles the Great (Charlemagne), the most famous of the Frankish kings, climaxed these endeavors just after A.D. 800, raising the Frankish Empire to a level of supremacy and civilization unequaled since Roman times. But hardly ere this had been done, Charles died; his sons divided up the empire; and the nonmilitary consequences of adopting the stirrup began to transform the power structure of western Europe, destroying the basis of Frankish hegemony.

The foremost such consequence was the emergence of a new warrior class whose members were sufficiently wealthy and skilled in arms to behave as independent polities. The extraordinary expense, in both time and money, of service as a knight was what brought this class into being. Since only the wealthy could afford the special mounts, arms, armor, and incessant training that knighthood required, the Franks, once having established their military superiority by adopting the stirrup, had to create and maintain a wealthy class in order to preserve it. This they did by the reallocation of land, the reassignment of vassals, and the reinterpretation of the law in favor of their warriors. Unfortunately, the Frankish knights were so favored and enriched in the process that they gradually became powers unto themselves and could no longer be subjected to any higher authority, not even that of their kings. This transformation sealed the fate of the regional Germanic kingdoms, and they soon began to disintegrate into thousands of lesser regimes, many of them the petty bailiwicks of individual knights.

Simultaneously, western Europe was invaded anew from every side: in the north by the barbaric Scandinavians or Norsemen, in the south by the semicivilized Moslems from the Near Eastern hinterland, and in the east by the savage Hungarians or Magyars from the expanses of Eurasia. These renewed onslaughts from without only served to speed up the collapse of the Germanic order from within, already set in motion by the rise of the knights; and so, by the mid-ninth century A.D., western Europe had resumed its regression from the heights of Roman civilization into the throes of medieval manorialism.

Charles the Great and his predecessors' effort to transform Frankish military hegemony into a stable, far-flung, post-Roman political order had failed; and hardly a generation after his death, not only the Frankish Empire but all the major Germanic kingdoms had vanished. In their wake, they left only a plethora of similar but far smaller, far weaker feudal states; a comprehensive tendency away from equalitarianism toward elitism; and a few refreshed memories of Rome. In effect, their net contribution to the development of Western Civilization constituted less than a halt—hardly more than a pause—in its continuing regression.

The Christian Church

Although the Franks failed to revive or even maintain civilized development in western Europe on a long-term basis, they did succeed in helping to preserve and develop a formidable civilizing institution: the Christian Church.

Christianity, one of several Near Eastern religions that had spread into Europe in the days of the Roman Empire seeking to replace the increasingly unattractive classical modes of belief, initially found a role there only as a fanatical cult of persecuted dissidents. But with the passage of time and the ebb of Roman glory, it became more sophisticated and more popular until, midway through the fourth century A.D., it was made the official religion of the Empire.

Even then, however, its influence remained limited. Outside the cities, conversion to Christianity was largely nominal; and even in urban areas, because its doctrines were still in flux and its institutional structure was still ill-defined, it exercised less authority over the lives of the people and the affairs of state than it did over developments in the cultural sphere, where Christian motifs—especially in art and literature —became increasingly predominant.

As a result, the Christian Church, particularly its western branch, was hit quite as hard by the barbarian invasions as were the other civilized institutions around it; and in order to survive them, it had to devote virtually all its energy to the rudimentary tasks of preserving its learning and institutional forms from the Germans' ravages on the one hand, and stopping those ravages by converting the Germans to Christianity as rapidly as possible on the other hand. It achieved success in both instances because it consolidated its power and focused it upon these same tasks, chiefly by means of institutional innovation and reform. This was done first, as necessity demanded, at the hard-hit local level during the chaotic fifth and sixth centuries; and it took the form of developing a system of self-sufficient havens or monasteries for the clergy. Next, church administration was centralized in the hands of a few leading officials in each province, often men drawn from the monasteries. Finally, during the seventh and eighth centuries, the government of the entire western branch of Christianity, in affiliating with the predominant Germanic tribe of the Franks, broke free from its eastern counterpart and focused at Rome. Consequently, church power was not merely preserved but increased; and by the time of the Franks' decline,

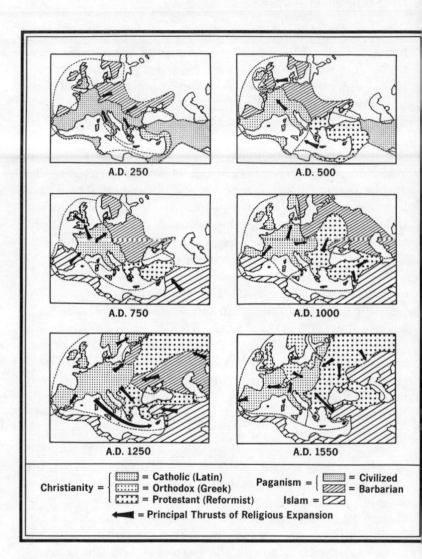

A.D. 250

A.D. 500

A.D. 750

A.D. 1000

A.D. 1250

A.D. 1550

Christianity = { ▦ = Catholic (Latin)
                ⋯ = Orthodox (Greek)
                ⋯ = Protestant (Reformist) }

Paganism = { ▨ = Civilized
             ▨ = Barbarian }

Islam = ▨

◀━ = Principal Thrusts of Religious Expansion

Map 9. Religious Spheres in the Medieval West

Christianity in western Europe had become sufficiently strong to stand alone.

The most appropriate symbol of this self-sufficiency was the monastery. At first way stations along the institutional road to survival which the western church followed, they were nothing more nor less than clerical equivalents of the lay manors. Widely scattered and often secluded, they provided sustenance and sanctuary, thereby ensuring to the church in western Europe the necessary wealth and manpower to keep its activities alive during the darkest days of civilized decline. Indeed, monastic efforts in cultural conservation were so successful that the church soon became the universally acknowledged repository of the West's civilized heritage and remained so for the duration of the medieval era. Likewise, the success of monastic missions in making converts to the faith began to expand the Christian sphere markedly about A.D. 600, and continued to do so for centuries to come, spreading not only the gospel but also the heritage of classical Western Civilization among the northern barbarians in the process.

At the same time the monasteries played a key role in fostering the centralization of church administration, the second major step in Latin Christendom's saving institutional reform. The lay equivalent of this process was the formation of the Germanic kingdoms; and just as certain warriors used the manors as a springboard to dominion, so did certain clergymen use the monasteries. The principal result was the diocese, which concentrated the religious affairs of an entire province in the hands of a single churchman, the bishop, and his household.

Through this device, the church was able to attach itself to the various Germanic kingdoms, the Frankish Empire in particular, and prosper accordingly. As these regimes flourished, they patronized the bishops with lands, privileges, and support for their efforts at conversion. The bishops in return blessed the Germanic rulers' actions, helped manage their

affairs, and brought a modicum of culture into their households.

Thus assured of powerful lay support, the western branch
of the church undertook to disaffiliate itself from its increasingly unsympathetic, alien eastern counterpart. As friction
between the two camps intensified, Christianity gradually became permanently divided into two distinct factions—one an
eastern, Greek-speaking, so-called Orthodox branch headed
by the Byzantine emperor-bishop of Constantinople, known
as the Patriarch; and the other a western, Latin-speaking,
so-called Catholic branch headed by the bishop of Rome,
known as the Pope.

Initially, the papal faction, by far the weaker of the two,
counted on the several western bishops' alliance with the lay
German governments to offset the Patriarch's formidable
temporal power as Byzantine emperor. But as the schism
widened and even the mighty Frankish Empire began to
disintegrate, emphasis was shifted to self-sufficiency in lay as
well as religious affairs; and the government of Latin Christendom was accordingly concentrated more and more in the
hands of the Pope's own household at Rome.

Consequently, by the mid-ninth century A.D., the Latin
church had become a formidable power in its own right. In a
period when many Western governments were too weak even
to impose let alone gather taxes, it collected a general levy or
tithe throughout much of western Europe; it maintained
agents and representatives at all levels of society in the same
domain; it installed important lay officials in the region's
secular governments; it owned and ruled rich if scattered
territories all over western Europe (in particular, the district
immediately surrounding Rome); it ran perhaps the most
sophisticated administration then extant in the Latin West
from that city; it preserved, promoted, and elaborated upon
Western culture almost single-handedly in the region of the
Germanic conquests; and it exerted a claim on men's loyalties
quite as strong as any the lay regimes of the day could make.

Not unexpectedly, therefore, once the Frankish Empire vanished from the scene, the Latin branch of the Christian Church became the most important civilized institution in western Europe; and thereafter it proved strong enough not only to survive further regression there, but to serve as the cornerstone of civilized life throughout the region for the duration of the medieval era.

The Byzantine Empire and Islam

In the wake of the Germanic political order's collapse in western Europe, the focus of Western Civilization's development shifted back toward its fountainhead, east and south of the Frankish domain and Latin Christianity's seat at Rome. And in that direction, on all the opposing shores of the Mediterranean, the Franks and the Latin church alike faced active and powerful rivals bent on placing their own imprint on Western Civilization, namely the Byzantine Empire and Islam (see map 9).

The Byzantine Empire, the older and more powerful of the two, was the heir to the Roman Empire in what had been its eastern provinces. There the Greek-Near Eastern branch of Western Civilization had survived virtually unscathed the German onslaught that had all but destroyed its predominantly Roman counterpart in western Europe; and thereafter it reorganized itself into a rich, powerful, imperialistic, Orthodox Christian despotism—the Byzantine Empire.

Throughout the early medieval period, that empire stood in the first rank of Western states, at once the foremost object of rival regimes' envy and the chief potential threat to their survival. The Germanic kingdoms in particular, lagging far behind Byzantium in nearly every field of civilized endeavor, were both awed by its splendor and cowed by its strength. Even as they struggled to prevent the loss of their Mediterranean territories to its armed forces (based, like theirs, on the stirrup-equipped, heavily armed and armored knight), their citizens became increasingly reliant upon its culture for guidance, imitating and copying it in arts and letters, in trade, in government, and in law. In Byzantium, western Europeans perceived the lost glories of Rome still extant; and when they sporadically sought to recover those glories, it was not so much by resurrecting or re-creating the originals as by emulating their Byzantine survivals. Generation after generation, the peoples living under Germanic rule looked to Constantinople and the empire of which it was the capital, much as their barbarian ancestors before them must have looked to Rome and its empire, at once envious of its civilization and covetous of its advantages, yet also afraid of that civilization's power and responsibilities, and unwilling or unable to shoulder its burdens and adopt its ways.

Nowhere was this more apparent than in the increasingly intertwined spheres of religion and politics: western Europe steadfastly refused to follow Byzantium's lead, preferring its own crude rituals and policies to the far more sophisticated ones of its would-be mentor. Indeed, after about A.D. 600, the rough regimes of the Latin West—both the Germanic kingdoms and the Papacy—openly began to resist Byzantine pressure and pretensions to hegemony throughout Christendom. Thereafter, such independent attitudes led to increasing antagonism and, finally, to outright hostilities between the two regions. As a result, by Charles the Great's time, their formal relationship had degenerated to one of incessant quarrels and wars—a relationship whose acerbity was only slightly mollified by their continued informal, cultural, and commercial intercourse.

Moreover, just as in the case of the earlier conflict between the Roman Empire and the Germans, this enduring state of antagonism between the Byzantine Empire and Germanic western Europe eventually redounded to the latter's favor, doubtless because Byzantium's resources, like Rome's, simply proved unequal to its pretensions. Whatever the reason, the ongoing religious strife between the Catholic and Orthodox branches of Christianity finally resulted in a permanent schism in the church (made official early in the eleventh century); and the Papacy emerged from it far stronger than the Patriarchate. Likewise, the extended military contest between Byzantium and the Latin West ended in the latter's favor, an outcome symbolized by the final ouster of Byzantine armed forces from the Latin sphere (notably Italy) in the eleventh century.

Thereafter, the Byzantine Empire passed into eclipse, and never again did it rival western Europe or vie with it for control of Western Civilization. In fact, Byzantine decay signaled the permanent ascendancy of the Latin sphere in Western affairs until the twentieth century, for western Europe's only other potential rival for mastery, Islam, had preceded the eastern empire in decline.

Islam was born in Arabia early in the seventh century A.D., when the restless, nomadic tribes of the region adopted a new missionary religion first proclaimed by the prophet Mohammed. Militant from the outset, the movement shortly burst forth from its homeland to attack the Byzantine Empire and the Germanic kingdoms and to overrun sizable portions of both, as well as the entire Near East. By the eighth century, it stretched from the Pyrenees in southwestern Europe to the Hindu Kush in south-central Asia and comprised the largest territorial regime seen in that quarter of the globe since the Roman Empire.

Under the protection of that regime, elements of Greek and Near Eastern culture long native to certain of its districts were suddenly catalyzed by the Arabic infusion and combined to produce a new, highly developed hybrid Islamic branch of Western Civilization. Most notable for its abstract and aesthetic achievements in such fields as mathematics and poetry, this startling amalgam unfortunately produced few parallel economic, military, or political innovations, forcing the Moslems to rely instead on the long-since-outdated practices of the kind already employed within their conquests. Consequently, by the beginning of the tenth century, the Islamic empire, for want of organizational cohesion and direction, had already passed its peak and entered into rapid decline. Thereafter, beset by internal unrest, territorial fragmentation, and cultural atrophy, it presented no serious threat to western Europe.

Yet, like Byzantium, Islam continued to exercise a significant cultural influence upon the Latin West for some time after its political, religious, and military eclipse. In fact, the net contribution of both to the course of Western Civilization's development proved to be largely cultural and was for the most part made after their heyday had passed. For, although they were eventually exhausted and destroyed by their efforts to succeed the Romans as arbiters of the entire Western world's fate, they nonetheless retained a degree of cultural affinity to classical Western Civilization that western Europe, caught up in the throes of continuing Germanic regression and preoccupied with the elemental problems of survival, did not. Both therefore continued to serve as repositories of ancient Western Civilization's heritage long centuries after their bids for Western-wide dominion had failed; and western Europe did not hesitate to borrow heavily from what they had preserved to make up its own deficiencies.

During the ninth century, however, the inhabitants of western Europe were less concerned with self-improvement than with self-preservation. Having come to grips with both Byzantium and Islam in what would eventually prove a successful struggle to assert their predominance abroad, they still faced the abiding problem of the onrushing Germanic regression at home. The Frankish Empire had come and gone in vain, and the Latin church was devoting the greater part of its energy merely to saving itself, permitting the descent from Roman heights to continue unabated.

For even though the military mastery of the Germans had

long since been confirmed and the far-reaching civilized objectives of the ancient era's Roman heyday had long since been abandoned, the third cause of the classical collapse—the economic crisis of underproduction—persisted in the wake of Frankish decline, perpetuating western Europe's regression.

CHAPTER 6

The Economic Transformation, A.D. 800-1100

The Medieval Economic Achievement

Medieval western Europe finally halted the Germanic regression and began to solve the West's abiding crisis of underproduction by initiating an economic transformation of Western Civilization comparable to the cultural and political transformation earlier effected by the Greeks and Romans. Indeed, this accomplishment ranks with the continuation of Roman tradition in its ultimate influence upon the course of civilized development, and as such represents medieval Europe's foremost original contribution to that development.

The western European economic transformation was of such consequence because: (1) it finally gave a semblance of unity and direction to a fragmented and seemingly rudderless economy; (2) it provided a bond sufficiently powerful to nip the Latin West's persistent trend toward further disintegra-

tion during the crucial three centuries after the collapse of the
Frankish Empire; and (3) it laid the basis for the kind of mass
prosperity upon which depended a successful revival and
fulfillment of Roman ideals. In other words, the inhabitants
of western Europe from the ninth to the twelfth centuries
devised and set about effecting a cure for the fatal malady of
economic insufficiency that had destroyed the material manifestations of ancient Western Civilization; and in doing so,
they not only forestalled the complete collapse of that civilization in their own time, but also made possible its eventual
regeneration along previously established lines.

The Genesis of Manorial Agriculture

During the period in question, from A.D. 800 to A.D. 1100,
the consolidation and innovation that formed the substance of
Western economic advance was initially restricted for the
most part to local developments in western European
agriculture—to changes effected on individual manors, but
on enough of them so as to constitute a general phenomenon
throughout the entire region. The majority of those changes
hinged upon unifying the agricultural systems formerly prevalent in the northern and southern sectors of western Europe;
and in order to understand the nature of those changes, it is
first necessary to understand these systems.

The more familiar of the two is, of course, the southern or
Mediterranean one—the agricultural configuration born of
the civilized Western world's efforts at farming since its very
beginnings, the mode of cultivation prevalent throughout the
Mediterranean littoral during the declining years of the
Roman Empire and right down to the twentieth century A.D.
Contrived for the tillage of the area's infertile soil in its typical
climate of intense summer heat and sparse winter rainfall,
and based upon the hidebound utilization of the most commonplace agrarian techniques of the age, it was essentially

primitive, semiarid, hard-grain farming such as the Mesopotamians had first developed before 2000 B.C.

In keeping with its practices, half the arable land was planted each autumn to a single crop—usually wheat—and the remainder was left fallow, the whole of it having previously been prepared for seed or dormancy by cultivation with the crude wooden stick plow (also developed by the Mesopotamians). Because it could be readily fabricated and required little power to pull (that of a single scrawny ox or of two humans ordinarily sufficing), this implement was almost universally employed in Mediterranean agriculture. Unfortunately, it was incapable of turning much earth under the best conditions; and so its use made cross-plowing a necessity and tended to limit tilling to easily turned hillside or floodplain soils, thereby not only drastically reducing the amount of land that could be farmed but also rendering much of that which was the least fertile of the available acreage. However, in spite of such grave shortcomings, the Mediterranean two-field system was prevalent throughout the southern sector of western Europe at the beginning of the medieval period.

To the north, in the civilized portion of what had been the barbarian domain, a more diversified system obtained. The basic technique of cultivation it employed—cross-plowing of easily turned ground with the stick plow, half the acreage tilled to be planted and half to be left fallow—was akin to that used in the Mediterranean; but northern Europe's wetter, cooler climate and richer soil encouraged spring rather than fall planting, the sowing of a greater variety of crops (rye, barley, oats, and beans, as well as wheat), and more reliance on livestock (since more natural pasture was available). The resulting amalgam was known as the Celtic two-field system; and it had become the dominant mode of farming throughout the Celts' former territory as well as the Germans' homeland long before Rome fell.

In the wake of that catastrophe, the patterns of husbandry

everywhere in the Latin-speaking half of the West changed relatively abruptly (that is, within a few centuries). Western European agriculture, like western European politics and society, was disrupted by the chaos of the times and had to adjust in order to survive. Agriculture, like politics and society, did so by the twofold expedient of: (1) falling back upon the self-sufficient unit of the manor; and (2) fusing barbarian and Roman practices. The most important creation of the medieval period resulted—the manorial agricultural system of western Europe.

The manor, as has already been seen, was the primary mode of political, social, and economic organization evolved in the period of the Roman Empire's decline as a substitute for increasingly ineffective imperial institutions. It was, in essence, no more than an autonomous, self-supporting, local agricultural unit centered about the residence or manor of a dominant landowner or warrior, called a lord. The majority of manorial inhabitants—the peasants or serfs—were small-plot subsistence farmers bound to the land and the lord both by Roman precedent and their own dependence. Accordingly, they cultivated the soil to sustain not merely themselves but also the lord and his household, in keeping with the terms of their bondage or serfdom, and in return for the lord's protection and governance. Their lives were thus given over to unremitting agrarian toil, enclosed in the relatively inflexible bounds of the seasons and of manorial custom, in particular, agricultural custom.

Those customs were born of the fusion of the Mediterranean and Celtic agricultural systems of Roman times into a new manorial agricultural system, which became prevalent in western Europe during the forepart of the medieval era. The principal trait that distinguished the new mode of farming from those that preceded it and gave rise to many of its basic customs was more efficient utilization of the available arable land.

This efficiency resulted from combining both of the old

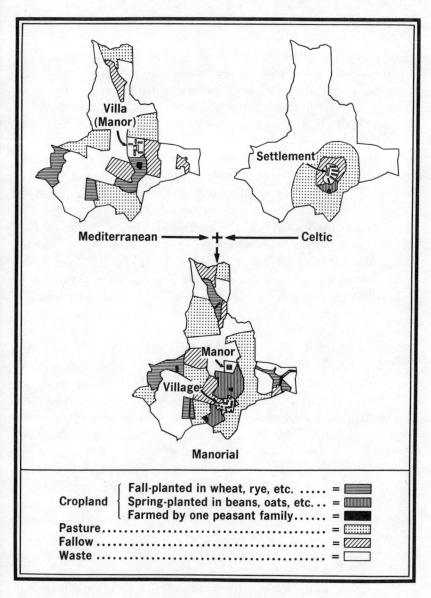

Map 10. Early European Agricultural Systems

two-field systems into a new three-field system. Under the new system, one-third of the arable land was planted in the fall to wheat or rye in keeping with the Mediterranean practice, and another one-third was planted the following spring to oats, beans, or the like in keeping with the Celtic practice, leaving the remaining third fallow. By rotating each cultivated plot through each of these uses on a three-year cycle, it was possible to increase the amount of arable land in crops during each growing season by about 15 percent without clearing new acreage, undertaking more intensive cultivation, or making any appreciable reduction in the period each plot was let lay fallow. In addition, such rotation helped replenish the soil's fertility by varying the crops raised on it from year to year; and the yields obtained in the process tended to provide a more varied and nutritious diet. In short, the three-field system made possible not only a sizable increase in farm output but also an equally effortless improvement in the quality of that output within the bounds of existing agricultural effort and technology.

The other outstanding characteristic of the new manorial agricultural system, its dependence on livestock as well as crops (an imitation of the Celtic system), had similar ramifications. A simple matter of utilizing the pasturage which the climate in much of western Europe produced on the extensive tracts of uncultivated land on each manor, livestock farming required little effort and produced a food supply valuable for adding further nutritional variety to the peasants' fare and for being relatively independent of natural vicissitudes. Thus, if the crop yields faltered or failed, milk and cheese were still available, and in the last resort, animals could be slaughtered for meat. As a result, large herds of cattle, sheep, and hogs were raised under the new system; and in combination with the three-field system, this served to maximize the productivity of the land within the limits of the crude agricultural practices prevalent in the wake of Rome's fall. Such was the

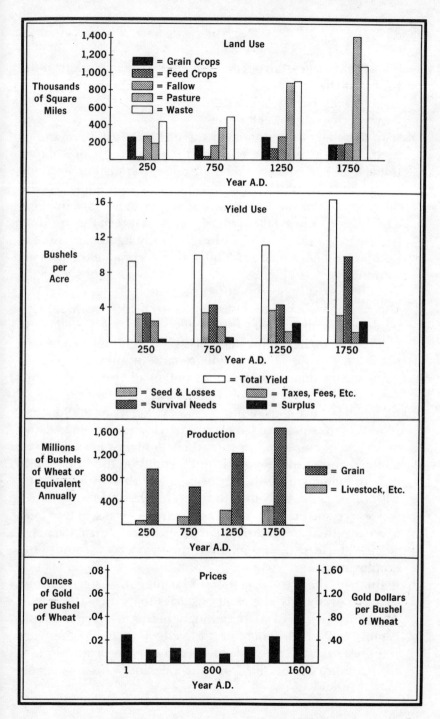

Fig. 8. The Conditions of Medieval Western Agriculture

bounty of western European agricultural consolidation, of the fusion of the Mediterranean and Celtic farm systems.

New Agricultural Techniques

In the chaotic conditions of the day that fusion, in and of itself, was not sufficient to maintain overall agricultural output at a level adequate to feed the entire population, let alone to keep the fires of civilization burning. Consequently, the development of the manorial system per se was not the only agricultural improvement carried out in western Europe during the medieval era. Before long, equally significant innovations were being made in cultivation techniques, especially plowing.

As has already been pointed out, the light stick plow was almost everywhere employed in western European agriculture down to about A.D. 500. But it was not really suited to the cultivation of heavy or wet soils, such as those in most of northern Europe. Accordingly, reliance upon it in these regions meant that a great deal of potentially productive land could not be farmed simply for want of the proper means to till it. To be sure, such a means did exist: a heavy moldboard plow that the northern barbarians had long since devised and occasionally employed to turn their domain's lowland soils; still it required eight oxen to pull, could be used efficiently only in elongated fields, and was slower than cross-plowing with the stick plow. Naturally, therefore, so long as livestock was scarce and cooperation among farmers was scant, so long as square fields remained the rule and easily turned acreage sufficed to feed the population, the heavy plow found little employment.

But with the transformation of farming in western Europe to a manorial basis, the chief obstacles to its use—the lack of draft animals and of cooperation in their use—were suddenly removed. With the increase in livestock farming, the oxen required to pull the heavy plow became readily available; and with the advent of serfdom, the peasantry became accustomed to cooperating in farming the lord's land and in sharing out their own, which was held in common by the manor's entire farm population but worked in periodically redistributed individual parcels by each peasant household.

At the same time, the concentration of virtually the entire population upon the manors and the curtailment of the amount of land that could safely be cultivated produced a powerful incentive to adopt the heavy plow. In fact, such was the fear-induced reduction in the quantity of land available for farming that not even the increased yields of the manorial system or the overall decline in post-Roman western Europe's population sufficed to prevent widespread local overpopulation in relation to the food supply being produced with the stick plow. Nor were prevalent population controls, either natural or artificial, adequate to solve the problem. Therefore, in order to prevent wholesale famine, it became imperative to bring into cultivation a larger share of the islands of

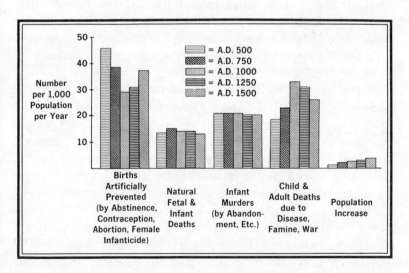

Fig. 9. The Demography of the Medieval West

territory defensible from the manors; and this could best be done by bringing the heavy plow into more general use.

As a result, the peasants began pooling their oxen and employing the heavy plow extensively to strip-farm both new, previously untilled bottom land and a portion of that already under stick-plow cultivation (usually large plots belonging to the lord). In this manner, the total number of acres being farmed in early medieval western Europe was sufficiently maintained (in spite of the reduction in accessible land area), and per acre yields were sufficiently increased (due to the more intensive cultivation of heavy plowing), both to feed the population and to begin providing a surplus (see fig. 8).

Nor did the technological improvement of western European agriculture end with the adoption of the heavy plow. As the locus of farming shifted northward, more plentiful supplies of leather, wood, and iron were made available to medieval peasants by the herds, forests, and forges inherited from their Celtic predecessors; and they utilized these means to experiment incessantly and widely with the implements of agrarian life. Perhaps the most significant inventions that resulted from this activity were the horse collar and the horseshoe, both of which began coming into general use around A.D. 1000. Together with the growing of spring-planted oats or other feed grains and the raising of large numbers of domestic animals, which resulted from the Celtic heritage, these two devices made possible the adoption of the horse as a draft animal. This in turn had the effect of making it possible to plow almost as rapidly with the heavy plow as with the stick plow and for a lesser consumption of feed, rendering horses increasingly popular for farming. And as they replaced oxen throughout western Europe, the increases in overall productivity realized were quite as substantial as those that had followed the introduction of the heavy plow. Together, therefore, these two essentially technological innovations were almost as important as the fusion of the Mediterranean and Celtic farm systems to form the manorial in transforming the nature of western European agriculture during the medieval era.

The Second Agricultural Revolution

When viewed whole, that transformation must be regarded as revolutionary in character. For in the period from A.D. 800 to A.D. 1100 the monumental problem of scarcity which the Romans had been unable to solve and which had subsequently caused the collapse of ancient Western Civilization was solved—agriculturally. By means of consolidation and technological advance, western European agriculture was changed from an amalgam of timeworn, inefficient, no longer adequate farming practices into a more intensive, more productive system of cultivation, not merely equal to the nutritional and economic demands of the medieval population, but, in fact, destined to remain the Continent's basic mode of farming—and overall economic production—right down to the last century of the modern era. Just as the Mesopotamians prior to 2000 B.C. laid the economic basis of Western Civilization for the next two thousand years and more by the invention of civilized farming, so did the Western Europeans after A.D. 500 lay the economic basis of Western Civilization for the next thousand years and more by the reform of civilized farming. Just as the Mesopotamians combined grain cultivation and animal domestication to create a system of sedentary surplus agriculture, so did the western Europeans combine Mediterranean farming practices with Celtic ones and adopt the horse-drawn heavy plow to transform the Mesopotamian system of agriculture into the far more productive manorial one. In short, they revolutionized Western agriculture a second time—the supreme achievement of the medieval era.

The Revival of Trade and Urban Life

Nevertheless, the medieval economic achievement was not an entirely agrarian phenomenon. Once agricultural revival had gotten under way, commercial enterprise was not long in

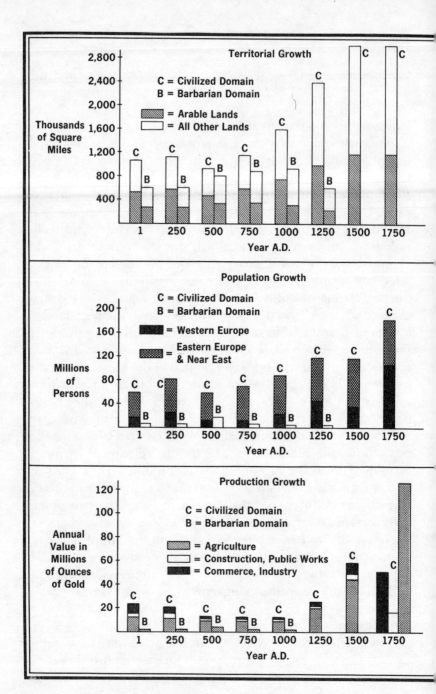

Fig. 10. Indexes of Development in the Medieval West

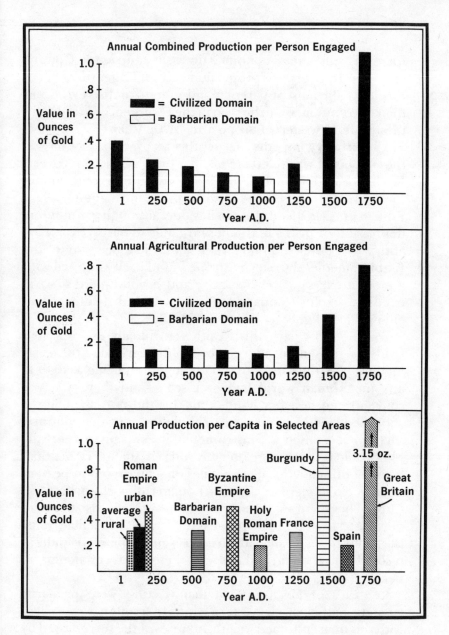

Fig. 11. Productivity in the Medieval West

following suit; and as in Roman times, its contribution toward economic recovery was proportionately far larger than that of farming. The most apparent manifestation of this revival and this contribution was to be seen in the resurgence of trade and urban life in western Europe after A.D. 1000.

The primary impetus that set this recovery in motion was the surplus of wealth created by the prior agrarian recovery. For by the end of the first millenium A.D. the second agricultural revolution had raised farm output to the highest levels of Roman times in quantity if not in value, although a continuing depression of prices in the period tends to obscure the fact; and with a population no larger than it had been under the Empire, medieval western Europe found itself endowed with a modest excess of wealth above and beyond mere survival needs, a surplus comparable to that which the Romans had enjoyed (see fig. 8).

For the most part, this wealth was initially expropriated from its peasant producers by their overlords—the early medieval tax rates in labor, goods, and kind being as high as any the Roman world had ever seen—and thereby it was concentrated in a few hands; but this did not, as might be supposed, tend to restrict its circulation. On the contrary, such concentration was instrumental in assuring that the surplus would be put into reasonably wide circulation rather than being confined to local economies or sequestered in peasant hoards. No sooner had the post-Roman ruling elite in western Europe begun to accumulate this bounty than it also began to demonstrate what was to prove one of its most indelible traits: the ability to spend such unearned revenues quite as rapidly as it could collect them, and to spend them chiefly on nonessentials.

Luxuries of Near Eastern manufacture were primarily what the half-civilized Western elitists first sought to purchase with this unaccustomed wealth, luxuries of the sort enjoyed by their peers in Byzantium and Islam. Envious of the level of civilization that produced such goods, yet unable to induce a

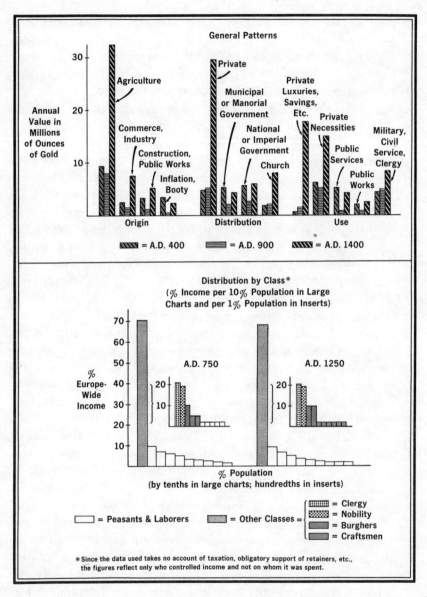

Fig. 12. Income in Medieval Europe

recovery of their own branch of Western Civilization to such a level, the feudal lords of medieval Latin Christendom sought to satisfy that envy by aping their eastern cousins' trappings—by endeavoring, via their newfound agrarian riches, to surround themselves with similar paraphernalia. In doing so, they created a demand for Near Eastern luxuries that formed the basis for the revival of the entire nonagrarian portion of western Europe's economy.

Prerequisite to such a revival, however, was the sudden decline of Islam and of barbarian incursions into the civilized West, both of which fortuitously occurred just prior to A.D. 1000. Not only did this turn of events relieve western Europe of the expense and strain of defending itself from powerful adversaries on every side, but, even more important, it transformed the Mediterranean from a contested sea ranged by rival Norse, Moslem, and Byzantine fleets into a Christian sea dominated by the vessels of Byzantium and Italy. This was a crucial development because it opened to Latin merchants the only feasible trade route from western Europe to the Near East of the age (alternative routes overland being about five times slower and ten times more expensive), at precisely the moment when they first began seeking the wares of oriental bazaars. From that happy juncture onward, the revival of western Europe's trade was assured and, with it, the revival of the entire nonagrarian portion of western Europe's economy.

Since this revival was based on the luxury trade with the Near East, it first became manifest in the coastal towns of Italy, which, as centers of the Latin region closest to the Near East by sea, pioneered such trade and soon acquired a virtual monopoly of it. Venice, situated at the head of the Adriatic Sea, led the way and became predominant in such commerce, not only on account of its favorable location but also because of its long-established ties with the Byzantine Empire (of which it had previously been a part), under whose aegis Latin Christians first ventured in numbers into eastern waters, and to whose capital, Constantinople, they went for the widest selection of the finest goods.

After Venice came Genoa, situated in almost identical proximity to continental western Europe on the opposite side of the Italian peninsula. Next the inland towns of northern Italy prospered and began to renew themselves on the proceeds of the same East-West luxury trade. Then, as that traffic expanded with the advent of the crusades (see Chapter 7) to include a brisk business in military transport and supply, its arterial routes spread north over the Alps into the Rhine River valley and thence to the North Sea. From the mouth of the Rhine, they soon extended east and west along the coast to reach both Britain and the Baltic, thus completing a comprehensive commercial network linking the heartland of western Europe, fountainhead of new agricultural wealth, with the bazaars of the Near East, repository of old aesthetic treasure.

Nor was this the only aspect of commercial revival. A corresponding resurgence of local trade, a flow of such mundane commodities as foodstuffs and clothing between town and country, soon followed the revival of international trade throughout most of northern Italy, the Rhineland, and the North Sea littoral. Indeed, it was upon this simple domestic commerce in necessities rather than the East-West traffic in luxuries, pilgrims, soldiers, and their supplies that medieval nonagrarian prosperity eventually came to rest. The wool trade and its allied industries, for example, had by the twelfth century become almost the sole basis for nonagricultural economic activity in some of the most prosperous areas of England, the lower Rhineland, and the Low Countries in between. Elsewhere the production, processing, and exchange of truck, leather goods, and spirits as well as woolens gradually came to account for the bulk of trade and industry. In other words, once its growth had gotten well under way, the nonagrarian sector of the medieval western European economy became oriented to the production and distribution of staples rather than to the import of luxuries.

Nonagrarian economic activity also became increasingly a function of urban life, which had revived and spread in direct proportion to the growth of trade and industry. The initial and perhaps crucial step in the rise of the medieval towns, however, was their early achievement of political autonomy. This was generally accomplished when a few prominent townsmen or members of the bourgeoisie simply made a place for themselves in the feudal hierarchy by corporately simulating joint lordship over their community and becoming vassals of the dominant warrior in their locality, promising to furnish him goods, money, and manpower in return for a relatively free hand in ruling the urban population.

Once having acquired such status and authority, the bourgeois elite generally comported themselves creditably (at least in comparison to their rural overlords); and in so doing, they not only fostered the recovery of the towns but also attracted a flood of refugees from manorial serfdom. This influx, together with the growth of trade and industry, spurred urban economic growth, greatly enriching the towns and their leaders alike, and soon rendering both quite as powerful in every respect as their older, rural counterparts (see fig. 12). Consequently, from the eleventh century onward, the bourgeoisie and their municipalities were factors to be reckoned with in western Europe; and they accordingly exercised a formidable influence on the subsequent revival of Western Civilization's overall development.

The emergence of this bourgeois-urban influence and the creation of a vigorous, widespread nexus for the production and distribution of staple goods were the principal results of the medieval revival of trade and the rise of towns. They were both significant factors, in part for their impact on the course of medieval Western history itself, in part for their impact on the future; but they were not comparable in importance with the consequences of the medieval agricultural revolution.

Throughout almost the entirety of the medieval period, the rural population remained twenty times that of the towns, and the magnitude of agricultural production remained more than three times that of its nonagriculgural counterpart, rendering the influence of events in the countryside overwhelmingly dominant.

The Medieval Economy

Because of the limited influence of commerce, industry, and urban growth; and because of the equally limited exploitation of the improvements made in agriculture through consolidation and technological discovery, the medieval economy, in the wake of its transformation and revival, still remained essentially a backward agricultural system not unlike the ancient economy that had preceded it. It was a system much improved in A.D. 1100 over what it had been in A.D. 800 (particularly for being more intensified), but nonetheless one in which farming remained the preeminent means of production and in which farm output per farmer had been restored for the time being only to about what it had been in Rome's heyday (see figs. 10, 11, & 12).

The reasons for this were in part circumstantial, in part volitional. Circumstances were especially important in curbing manorial agriculture's potential output, because they severely restricted both the amount of land that could be farmed and the amount of produce that could be marketed. Requirements of physical safety were the culprit in the former instance, since they made it dangerous to work fields far from the protection of the manor, a limitation only partially compensated for by more intensive cultivation of the fields safely within reach. Likewise, the isolation and stagnancy of manorial life tended to minimize any demand for farm products above and beyond local needs.

An additional consequence of these natural restrictions was the deemphasis of grain cultivation, the kind of farming whose productive potential had been most significantly increased by the new technological discoveries of the early medieval era. Knowing that they could not safely bring much new acreage suited to grain under the plow or readily sell any surplus grain they raised, farmers instead concentrated their efforts at additional output upon lower-yield products such as livestock, feeds, legumes, and wool, products more suited to the safely exploitable lands, to the peasants' own needs, and to agrarian consolidation.

A more willful factor in curbing the development of the medieval economy was the misuse of the surplus wealth it produced. This was chiefly the result of its acute concentration in the hands of the ruling elite—as ignorant and irresponsible a dominant clique as the West has ever been subjected to. Having enriched themselves even more than the puny political regimes and crude social institutions of the day by purely selfish, largely intuitive means, the lords of medieval western Europe spent their wealth—in effect, the region's entire surplus—in much the same way, a way often inimical to economic well-being and economic growth.

In a private sense, this was most aptly reflected in the rise of the luxury trade with the Near East; and in a public sense, it was best revealed by the foolish bellicosity and adamant conservatism that increasingly typified elite behavior. Thus that portion of western Europe's surplus that was not splurged on oriental extravagances was wasted on petty, futile wars or squandered in attempts to ossify medieval life, leaving nothing to nurture the productive processes that supplied the elite with its wealth. The end result of these follies, and of the restrictive circumstances that paralleled them, was to keep western Europe poor, if no longer penurious, for long centuries after it had devised the means to make itself rich.

Even so, the second agricultural revolution and the region's economic achievements were remarkable; and without question, they constitute the hallmarks of the medieval era. Through them, the Germanic regression was finally halted; the perennial crisis of underproduction that had so long plagued Western Civilization was finally solved; and a foundation was laid for the future revival of civilized development in the West along Roman lines of mass material prosperity and general well-being.

These were formidable achievements, comparable to those of the Greeks and Romans; but the new civilized era they anticipated still lay centuries in the future. More immediately, western Europe had managed to save itself from total collapse and to recover to Roman levels of economic achievement from A.D. 800 to A.D. 1100; but for the rest, the accomplishments of Rome continued to stand supreme, still unexcelled half a millennium after the Roman collapse. During the remainder of the medieval era, the Latin West would struggle to match or surpass those accomplishments, a struggle that began with efforts to reunify the entire Western world.

CHAPTER 7

The Christian Mission,
A.D. 1100-1300

Papal Supremacy

The foremost effort to reunite the West in imitation of the
Romans was made by the Papacy at the height of the medieval
era. By declaring themselves, on behalf of the Latin church, to
be the supreme mortal authorities in spiritual matters and
simultaneously taking an active hand in secular politics, a
series of Popes during the twelfth and thirteenth centuries
attempted to consolidate Western Civilization religiously, just
as the Romans had consolidated it politically. They succeeded
in uniting Latin Christendom for a time; but they could not
bring the remainder of the Western world under their control
or influence, not even by force of arms. Instead, the sustained
effort to do so—the crusades—combined with the Papacy's
secular machinations within the bounds of Latin Christendom
itself to thrust the West into a pandemonium of religious and

97

political discord after 1300, which eventually shattered even the degree of religious unity that had been established, and which altogether destroyed the possibility that Western Civilization might be reunified along pseudo-Roman lines, frustrating the Christian mission.

The origins of the policy of papal supremacy, which lay at the root of all these developments, were to be found in the church's dependence upon secular regimes during the troubled first few centuries of the medieval era. In the Latin sphere, that dependence soon proved to be unsound, since the Franks first sought to exploit the Latin church in return for protecting it, and then defaulted upon their obligation to provide such protection when their empire began to disintegrate. Papal officials therefore early began making preparations—chiefly ritualistic, administrative, and financial—in anticipation of eventually establishing Latin Christianity's complete independence. Then, at the appropriate juncture, a succession of Popes declared themselves supreme to lay rulers and set about transforming the Latin church into an international European state, a state fundamentally religious in character, a state under which it was hoped the consolidation of Western Civilization could be carried forward successfully by religious rather than political means.

Pope Gregory VII formally launched the enterprise about 1075 when he first made the papal policy of absolute supremacy explicit. Having done so, he then set about asserting the authority the Papacy claimed for itself by wresting the power to appoint the clergy from the secular states, which had held it since Roman times. His weapons in this struggle were threefold: (1) a well-organized, well-funded, capable church administration—perhaps the most efficient administration then extant in western Europe; (2) a widespread desire among the clergy to free the church from secularism; and (3) most important of all, control of Latin Christian ritual and hence of the presumed way to salvation.

An extended struggle ensued, principally between the Papacy and the so-called Holy Roman Empire, a loose-knit regime encompassing the whole of Germany and northern Italy. The primary issue of the struggle was control of the many church lands and offices in the Germanic empire and, through them, effective control of the empire itself. That is, in order to make good their claim of secular supremacy, the Popes set out to refute a like claim by the most formidable regime then extant within its own territory.

The ruling house of the Holy Roman Empire sought to combat this seemingly foolhardy undertaking by expropriating the church's holdings and continuing to dispose of its offices as of old, in the belief that the Popes themselves were relatively powerless. So they were, too, at least in a strictly material sense. But the religious power they had long been centralizing in their grasp soon proved to be a highly formidable weapon, the more so when exercised by an administration as skilled as the church's had become, and in a society as steeped in Christian belief as medieval western Europe had become.

In the end, the Papacy won out, reducing the greatest of the Holy Roman emperors to groveling, contrite submission via excommunication—i.e., by denying him access to Christian society and the prospect of salvation. By 1200, papal supremacy had become an established fact throughout western Europe; and the union of Latin Christendom under papal auspices had become a real possibility. The dawn of a pseudo-Roman revival, of a new international order based on religion seemed at hand in Western Civilization.

The Crusades

Unfortunately, the day promised by that impending dawn never came to pass. For, in spite of the Papacy's success in asserting its supremacy in lay as well as spiritual affairs and thereby opening the way toward a genuine unification of Latin Christendom, the Western world as a whole remained sharply divided into rival religious spheres, just as it had been since the advent of Christianity (see map 9). To be sure, the papal sphere, once well-established, was the most formidable of the lot, but it hardly comprised a civilization-wide commonwealth on the Roman order, papal pretensions notwithstanding. Nor were the prospects for expanding it into one at all promising, given the antagonism that uniformly characterized its relations with the West's other religious spheres —pagan, Moslem, and Orthodox. Indeed, those prospects were so dim that the Papacy very early began resorting to force in order to effect such expansion, launching religiously inspired military expeditions or crusades against Latin Christianity's sectarian foes abroad.

The first such crusade was proclaimed by the Pope in 1095 against the Moslems with the avowed objective of capturing the holy city of Jerusalem from them. Doubtless, papal officials also hoped that the expedition would demonstrate the extent of their influence over the population of western Europe, in particular the military elite; and that it would simultaneously deflect that same elite's untrammeled greed, ambition, and armed might away from the Latin church and toward its enemies. When over thirty thousand men answered the Pope's call to arms and marched forth into the Near East to seek promised absolution from sin and probable wealth and glory, these unstated objectives were more than fulfilled; and when the expedition not only took Jerusalem but also established several petty Christian states in the vicinity, its stated purpose was also more than achieved.

This resounding if rather surprising initial success ensured that more crusades would follow; and it also established their pattern for a time: that of international volunteer armies raised by the Papacy's call to arms and dispatched far afield from western Europe to do battle with the principal foe of Christendom, Islam, on its home ground in the Near East, Spain, and North Africa. Unlike the first crusade, however, the later expeditions spent themselves without producing the results expected. Jerusalem, lost in 1187, was not retaken;

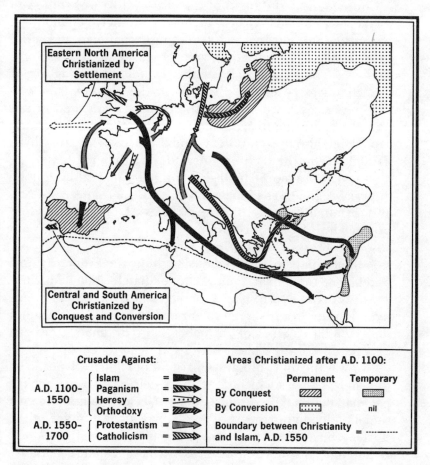

Map 11. The Christian Crusades

the Christian states established near it were not preserved; the Moslems were not expelled from Spain; and Islam was not defeated and brought into the papal sphere, either in whole or in part. The first phase of the Papacy's forceful attempt to unify the West on a religious basis therefore failed decisively: Islam, even in decline, had proven too strong and too far away to be subdued.

Consequently, the focus of the papal effort was shifted to weaker opponents closer at hand, namely Orthodoxy, paganism, and heresy; and armies more national and more professional in composition were raised to attack these new foes. The first crusade of this sort was carried out by a force of French warriors against Byzantium, the champion of Orthodoxy, early in the thirteenth century. It resulted in not only the capture and sack of Constantinople, the Byzantine capital, but also the temporary establishment of a Latin Christian empire in the territory surrounding the great city. The blow was all but mortal to the Byzantine Empire; although the imperial regime was soon restored, its former power was not, and terminal decay set in. Nevertheless, Latin Christendom profited little from the condition it had precipitated, for Islam absorbed most of the Orthodox sphere.

A similar papally inspired onslaught by the French against heretics in their own country, immediately following their attack on Byzantium, likewise failed to further papal objectives. Rather it only served to enrich the participants, extend their feudal spheres of influence, and decimate southern France, one of the richest regions in western Europe.

Nor was the unity of Latin Christendom much advanced by the later crusades which the Papacy helped instigate against pagans, such as those undertaken by German knights against the Slavs living northeast of the Holy Roman Empire in the thirteenth century. In short, even against relatively impotent rival religious spheres within easy striking distance, crusades proved ineffective in furthering either papal supremacy or the establishment of religious unity in the West.

In its endeavor to effect by means of force a Christian religious consolidation of Western Civilization, the Papacy had failed utterly. The crusades, rather than enhancing the prospect of a civilized recovery along pseudo-Roman lines during the medieval era, dealt it a mortal blow, not only because they eventually negated the Christian ideals upon which such a recovery might have been based, but also because they helped discredit, exhaust, and finally divide the Latin church, the one institution through which a medieval recovery on the Roman pattern might have been carried out. Instead of unity, the crusades promoted only discord, helping speed western Europe on its way toward the holocaust of religious, civil, and nationalistic warfare that would rack it during the sixteenth and seventeenth centuries, a holocaust that would destroy not only medieval society per se but also virtually all faith in the notion of a Christian commonwealth, upon which that society had been based.

In short, the papal attempt to impose religious unity on the West via the crusades was instrumental in discrediting both religion and unity as means of civilized advance in the West, and in rendering secularism and dissension perennial features of latter-day Western Civilization.

The Church and Temporal Power

The first indications of these dour consequences appeared as soon as the Popes started to narrow their view of the church's role, from seeing it as a way to salvation to using it as an instrument of authority. Once thus inclined, they became more and more secular in outlook and turned increasingly to force as their chief instrument of policy, not only beyond the borders of Latin Christendom but within them as well, a tendency that before very long hopelessly embroiled them in the unending struggle for temporal power in western Europe.

This embroilment initially manifested itself in a long and sordid conflict between the Papacy and the Holy Roman Empire during the twelfth and thirteenth centuries. As discussed above, this encounter resulted in a victory for the Papacy, but only at the cost of a severe depletion in its resources and a major devaluation of its prestige. Soon thereafter, it compounded this erosion of stature by moving its headquarters from Rome to Avignon in southern France to seek the protection of the increasingly powerful French and thereby submit itself to their domination for over a half century. Then, in

1378, as if bent on altogether destroying the church's moral influence, papal officials presided over the simultaneous election of two Popes, ushering in the so-called Great Schism in the Latin church. This debacle so hopelessly discredited the Papacy that it gave way for a time to conciliar rule of the church by assemblies of leading clergymen from all over western Europe; and it was a council that finally healed the schism and put papal affairs back in some semblance of order.

But to little avail, for so low had the Papacy's stock fallen in the interim that their claims to mere authority within the church itself, to say nothing of supreme authority throughout the West, were now openly disputed by religious reformers. Denying clerical control of the presumed way to salvation, the cornerstone of such authority, these reformers in effect repudiated not only the Papacy but the church it headed as well; and when lay rulers, long at odds with both institutions in the struggle for temporal power, began to listen to them, the fragmentation of Latin Christendom quickly followed.

Thus, the Papacy's entanglement in secular affairs, like its recourse to the crusade, bore bitter fruit in the end, and for much the same reason: obsession with force and with the objective of Western unification seemingly attainable only by force. This growing fixation gradually so dimmed the vision of church leaders that they repeatedly engaged in sterile conflicts with both the lay regimes of the day and the rank and file of the clergy itself, conflicts that not only sapped the Latin church's resources—moral and material alike—but also aroused mortal enemies in the guise of ambitious monarchs and zealous reformers. And eventually, as their strength increased and that of the church waned, they were able to defeat it and thereby dash both papal pretensions and all prospects for the Christian-led union of the West.

The Church and Culture

Yet if the Latin church failed to achieve its central objective of a civilization-wide Christian religious consolidation under supreme papal authority, it did at least succeed in retaining the cultural leadership of western Europe, which it had first established in the period of Roman decline. By concerted effort, it kept a small educated class in being, while also preserving a portion of the ancient world's heritage and developing new means of cultural expression suited to the medieval era—no small set of achievements in so turbulent, unlettered, and destructive an age.

The foremost single manifestation of these same achievements and of the Latin church's cultural leadership was the Gothic cathedral: haven of the educated, repository of ancient manuscripts, and epitome of medieval cultural expression. Historically, these structures, built throughout northwestern Europe at the height of the medieval era, were a further development of the Roman basilica or public hall. Religiously, they were centers of Christian worship and monumental statements of Christian ideals. Aesthetically, they were fusions of all branches of medieval art. And technically, they were tributes to medieval engineering ability. In short, they were tangible expressions of medieval civilization in toto and of its potential union in Christianity—soaring, massive, brightly illuminated, elaborately decorated, lovingly constructed monuments in stone and glass and space to the age and its aspirations.

At the same time, the cathedrals of Paris, Chartres, Reims, Winchester, Exeter, and dozens of other medieval towns were also impressive strictly as material edifices; this is what made them truly representative of medieval culture. Logical in their arrangement, accomplished in their architecture and decor, durable in their construction, and notable for their technical advances in masonry structure, they were an expression of and a tribute to the era's pervasive religious fervor, as well as its equally pervasive, equally important, but often unheralded practical capabilities. Their spires, reaching for heaven, aptly symbolized medieval western Europe's spiritual dedication to Christianity; but their foundations, rooted firmly in the earth, just as aptly symbolized medieval western Europe's secular dedication to materialism. And since both elements—the concern for material well-being as well as for spiritual redemption—were essential components of medieval culture, the Gothic cathedrals were indeed apt expressions of that culture and of the Latin church's role in nurturing it.

Medieval Christendom

By the same token, they were appropriate symbols of the medieval era as a whole, a millennium during which Christianity was undoubtedly the predominant influence in the Western world. Throughout Europe, in both the Catholic and Orthodox spheres, it permeated civilized life from the highest councils of state down to the lowliest peasant's workday. Men lived and breathed religion, existing at a pace and in a manner prescribed by the church. Even beyond the bounds of Christendom, in Islam and the pagan domain, Christianity made itself felt through its missionaries and crusaders. Indeed, for a time its Latin branch seemed about to unify not only Christendom but the entire West and thereby transform the course of Western Civilization's development. Cloaked in the robes of Christ, the ghost of Roman unity briefly walked abroad in Europe, only to be exorcised by the very institution which had conjured it up, namely the Papacy.

In the history of medieval Christendom, no single institution can compare with the Papacy in its influence. In a sense, the Popes both created and destroyed Latin Christendom almost unaided. They made the Latin church an administrative marvel in its day; they introduced clergymen into every hamlet; they sponsored and encouraged the preservation of cultural life; they launched the crusades; they entangled the church in the struggle for secular power; and they discredited, weakened, and finally fragmented it. Christendom, the predominant influence in the medieval world, was in effect papal Christendom in western Europe; and when the Papacy brought itself to ruin, it likewise brought to ruin not merely the Christian order it had sought to create, but the whole of the medieval order in the Latin West.

Not unexpectedly, therefore, as the failure of the papal mission of unification began to make itself manifest toward the end of the thirteenth century, men started to sense that the medieval era and the medieval way of life were drawing to a close; and they began to cast about in search of some alternative. Perceiving that the ideals of the Christian life and Christian unity were expiring, along with the Papacy's dream of a Western-wide Christian commonwealth, western Europeans commenced to hunt anew for direction; and in so doing, they finally initiated the revival of the West's ancient heritage (particularly its Roman heritage) and began to lay the ideological foundations—just as the second agricultural revolution had begun to lay the economic foundations—for the revival of Western civilized advance.

CHAPTER 8

The Cultural Renaissance, A.D. 1300-1450

Rediscovering the Ancient World

Western Europe's search for a new, postmedieval direction began in earnest early in the fourteenth century in Italy. At the outset, it was principally an intellectual endeavor; but before long it bloomed into a full-scale cultural revival, whose consequences would be felt throughout the entire West for centuries to come. Both the initial search and the subsequent revival sought some alternative to the religious and political formulas already applied in vain to revive Western Civilization's advance in western Europe, some solution to the dilemma of the medieval order's impending collapse, which the failure of those formulas had precipitated; and both did so by harking back to the ancient past, by probing amidst the ruins of classical Western Civilization for clues to its long-lived vitality.

This backward-looking search for new direction manifested itself primarily in a rediscovery of the ancient world, a rebirth of awareness in the Greco-Roman heritage upon which Western Civilization, in particular Western culture, was so largely based. The first evidence of this so-called Renaissance became apparent in western Europe just after 1200 when, as part of a general popularization of culture, medieval scholars for the first time gave concrete literary form and repeated expression to what had long been a commonplace belief: namely that the classical era, particularly in its terminal Roman or Latin phase, had been a golden age, a period in nearly every way more civilized and more advanced than the medieval era.

Once this viewpoint was made explicit and fashionable, educated western Europeans—especially those seeking to shore up the crumbling unity of Latin Christendom and to counteract the influence of feudal fragmentation and dissension—began to invoke Greco-Roman precedents with increasing frequency. More and more often, this class (most of whom were clerics) drew upon the residue of ancient culture preserved by the church, in both its Latin and Greek branches, in an effort to demonstrate that unity and cooperation had been characteristic of the lost golden age of antiquity and would therefore certainly benefit their own era. This tactic in turn prompted closer study of the classical era; and by the fourteenth century in Italy—where medieval decay was most advanced, where the clergy was most populous, and where the Roman heritage was most evident—such study had developed into a full-scale investigation of the ancient world.

By then, however, the purpose of the inquiry was no longer simply to muster historical arguments against the worsening medieval dilemma of drift and disintegration, but rather to discover a solution for it. Faced with an increasingly apparent breakdown of not only the Christian commonwealth but also the medieval order as a whole, Italy's scholars began to ransack the remains of the classical era in search of some alternative, some means of transcending or perhaps consolidating western Europe's seemingly incompatible Roman and Germanic heritages so as to fully revive civilized development within the region. Their study of classical Western Civilization was intensified in the hope of ferreting out the secrets of its enduring unity and apparent sense of direction, and then somehow bringing these discoveries forward to apply in their own day. By rediscovering the ancient world, they planned to revitalize the medieval world and thereby save it from impending collapse.

Scholasticism and Humanism

Precisely how such a rescue was to be effected was not at all clear at the outset of the Renaissance; but as it continued, the participants became increasingly convinced that the only possible solution to western Europe's difficulties was the reestablishment of its ideology on classical rather than Christian lines. From their study of the classical era, particularly its Roman culmination, they correctly concluded that the basis of ancient Western Civilization's development and direction in its latter phase had been largely ideological; and this in turn suggested to them that the requisite foundation for the revival of such development and direction in the Latin West during their own time was the widespread restoration of belief in classical ideals. Consequently, by 1400, they had initiated such a restoration via the transformation of western European thought from the increasingly stagnant, increasingly didactic, medieval mode of Scholasticism to the more robust, pseudo-classical, postmedieval one of Humanism.

The fruits of their labors were initially reflected in the Humanistic reinterpretation of the classical heritage, particularly the surviving corpus of classical literature. Refusing to accept the traditional Scholastic or Latin church evaluation of the ancients' writings as little more than unsanctified verbiage, or to adopt the established Scholastic intellectual method of conclusion by preordination, the Humanists instead looked to the ancients for guidance. They became critical rather than pious in their approach to the evidence of the past; and they endeavored to evaluate it by relying on practical experience and good sense rather than canonical tradition and syllogistic pseudologic, that is, to assess it rationally rather than dogmatically. By doing so, they began to give the classical heritage they were so assiduously studying an air of both historical validity and contemporary relevance, at once redefining its details and reevaluating its purport in terms the ancients themselves might have used and understood.

This assessment, in addition to abruptly altering the basic methodology of western European thought, soon succeeded in its avowed purpose as well by beginning to reestablish a progressive, Roman-like ideology, based on the principles of comprehensive organization, equalitarianism, justice, and mass material prosperity, as the predominant one in the Latin West. By reviving and embracing the entire classical heritage, both its physical remains and its mental attitudes, the Humanists made the already discredited medieval heritage they were seeking to transcend look so pale and inadequate by comparison as to firmly and finally expunge its lingering spirituality and prompt men to start thinking once again chiefly in worldly terms. Forsaking their predecessors' obsession with salvation and the afterlife, the citizens of the Renaissance began fully to concern themselves instead with the here and now, and, like the Romans they imitated, to recognize and try to exploit the many possibilities for human betterment.

This perception and this striving culminated the intellectual upheaval symbolized by the transformation of western European thought from Scholasticism to Humanism. The upheaval as a whole opened the way out of the dilemma posed by the impending failure of the medieval order; and by doing so, it helped set in motion the comprehensive revival of Western Civilization in the Latin West, which had been the goal of Renaissance scholars from the outset.

Italy and the North

The first steps taken in the course of this revival outside the scholarly community were aesthetic and artistic; and they produced a burst of cultural achievement such as the Western world had not seen since the heyday of Greek creativity. It began in Italy, where during the fourteenth and fifteenth centuries a host of still-famous artists such as Raphael, Leonardo da Vinci, and Michelangelo executed a collection of masterpieces in painting, sculpture, and architecture never before or since excelled; and then it spread beyond the Alps throughout western Europe, renovating the entire region's culture and thereby consummating the Renaissance.

In Italy, where the preparatory triumph of Humanism over Scholasticism had been most complete, this climactic cultural metamorphosis expressed itself in works whose themes were predominantly religious (like those of medieval cultural artifacts), but whose execution was generally pseudoclassical, in keeping with the new spirit of Humanism. These same works also incorporated masterful innovations in technique and revealed great interpretive originality and vitality, transcending the limitations of medieval tradition in every way and establishing new Humanistic standards of creativity for the entire Latin West.

These standards had less effect beyond the Alps than in Italy. Because the triumph of Humanism over Scholasticism in the north had been less than complete, medieval influences persisted to some degree in both intellectual and artistic endeavor, weakening the overall impact of the Renaissance. In painting, for example, although northern subjects were as original as in Italy—if not more so—and perhaps more secular, and while northern artists became even more proficient technically than the Italians, their treatments often remained bound by the limits of convention and seemed more expressive of rigor than vitality. In sculpture and architecture, the residual weight of medieval tradition was even heavier, perpetuating the close affiliation of both with the construction and decoration of cathedrals. Even in letters, the dead hand of the medieval past made its grip felt, somewhat retarding classical study in favor of a continued emphasis on Christian literature and church history. In short, the Renaissance in northwestern Europe failed to transcend completely the post-Roman heritage.

Consequently, when toward the middle of the fifteenth century Italy abruptly began to decline due to economic depression and political exhaustion and the northern Renaissance became characteristic of western Europe's intellectual-cultural revival as a whole, so did a residuum of medievalism. In other words, the survival of a significant medieval tradition throughout the Latin West became assured once its transalpine sector started to eclipse Italy. And because of that tradition's survival, the new culture that had just begun to emerge in western Europe as the first step in the general revival of Western Civilization there would prove to be neither Gothic nor classical: rather, like the new era of which it was the harbinger, that culture would prove to be modern, an amalgam of ancient and medieval, of Roman and German.

Even so, having once pioneered the resumption of civilized advance in western Europe, it was rapidly displaced as a predominant influence by the more powerful new economic, social, and political forces set in motion by that revival. Already beginning to generate during the fourteenth and fifteenth centuries behind the façade of intellectual-cultural transformation, these forces rather than the more immediately apparent fruits of the Renaissance would prove to be the decisive factors in setting the course of the development of western Europe and the entire West during the modern era.

By harking back to the ancient world and instituting an ideological and artistic Renaissance, the Humanists had saved western Europe from impending medieval collapse as they set out to do; but the revival of Western Civilization that they initiated in the process did not long remain a function of ideological and artistic development. Instead, it ushered in a new era whose dominant tendencies would soon either shatter the basis for further cultural advance—as they had already done in Italy by 1500—or transform it into a mere auxiliary of themselves while proceeding to alter Western life drastically in other ways. The impending onset of that new era first became manifest in western Europe's political arena, even before the Renaissance had run its course.

CHAPTER 9

The Dynastic Revival, A.D. 1450-1550

The Undoing of Feudalism

The end of the medieval era in western Europe was most aptly symbolized, and the character of the succeeding modern era was most accurately forecast, by the destruction of feudalism and its replacement by dynasty as the region's primary mode of political organization in the period from 1450 to 1550. This change initiated a political revival along prenationalistic lines that restored state power to Roman levels in much of western Europe; and that revival in turn established the direction of further political development throughout the West for the duration of the modern era. In short, the transition from crude, weak, local government to relatively complex, powerful, regional government—from the manorial domain to the prenational dynastic state —vividly illustrated the manner in which western Europe managed to resolve its medieval dilemma and recommence its civilized development once the Renaissance had given it the necessary start.

The origins of this political revival lay well back in the medieval era, chiefly in a variety of developments that undermined manorial feudalism sufficiently to initiate its overthrow and the creation of alternate means of regulating western Europe's affairs. Undoubtedly, one of the foremost such developments was the region's economic revival. For not only did it generate and diffuse enough new income to break the feudal elite's monopolistic control of wealth, but it also introduced new techniques for implement manufacture, which sufficiently transformed weaponry to break the feudal elite's monopolistic control of force as well.

Wealth, in the context of the manorial economy, was essentially equivalent to land, with the result that feudal overlordship of the latter constituted effective control of the former. But with the agricultural revolution and the subsequent revival of trade and industry, the exchange and manufacturing of goods once more became important sources of wealth, ending the landed elite's unilateral control of it. Likewise, the gradual readoption of money as the medium of exchange and the first small steps toward the development of mass material well-being contributed toward the same end.

On the technical side, the medieval economic revival so encouraged the use of new implements, such as the heavy plow and the horseshoe, that the manufacture of cheap implements from iron and wood became commonplace throughout western Europe. Predictably, given the age's bellicosity, this capability and the inventiveness that brought it into being were before long enlisted to devise and make new weapons as well. The less predictable result was a flood of armaments that destroyed the feudal elite's monopoly of force: hand implements such as the longbow, crossbow, and pike, which, when used en masse, were murderously effective against knights; and a revolutionary heavy weapon, the gunpowder cannon, which was equally effective against feudal fortifications when used in concentration.

In addition to being thus undercut militarily and economically, feudalism simultaneously suffered a dangerous erosion of its political foundations. This occurred as western Europe's once restive population became increasingly stable and began to manifest the first traces of nationalism. For as the region's inhabitants became permanently settled in fixed locations and began to evince common bonds of language and tradition throughout sizable territories, they also began to develop vague new political notions. From England to Sicily, the masses began to think of themselves increasingly in ethnic rather than feudalistic terms—as Anglo-Saxon or Norman or Flemish rather than as this or that lord's serf; and in doing so, they began to eradicate the basis of feudal political power.

Thus feudalism—that crude, clumsy political system calculated to meet the needs of an archaic warrior-priest elite and an ignorant, impoverished, terrified populace—slowly passed from the western European scene. Commencing to decline about A.D. 1000, it had all but vanished as a significant force by 1450. With the return of relative economic health and sociopolitical stability, with the first steps toward a resumption of general civilized advance from where the Romans had left off, it ceased to meet the organizational demands of western Europe and had to be abandoned. Some new political system able to encompass the region's revitalized economy, new technology, and burgeoning popular aspirations—a political framework of wider scope and greater flexibility—was required; and from the beginnings that papal officials and a few ambitious, clever feudal lords had already made toward creating new, centralized, judicially oriented regimes, it was shortly devised. It was the prenational, early modern state, the dynastic state.

The Rise of the Dynastic State

These dynastic regimes, which resulted from the destruc-

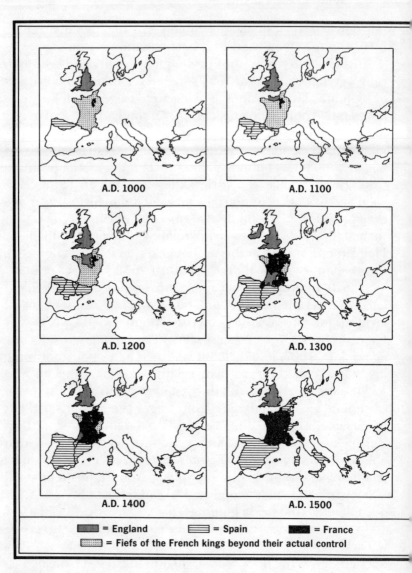

A.D. 1000

A.D. 1100

A.D. 1200

A.D. 1300

A.D. 1400

A.D. 1500

▦ = England ⬚ = Spain ▬ = France
▒ = Fiefs of the French kings beyond their actual control

Map 12. The Rise of the Dynastic States

tion of the feudal order in western Europe and which were harbingers of the modern era, proved to be at once more effective, more popular, and more extensive than the governments they superseded. Dependent for their function chiefly upon the exchange of money, the transmittal of written orders, and the movements of paid armies rather than the personal honoring of feudal commitments, they were able to defend frontiers, enforce laws, maintain domestic peace, and promote economic well-being throughout whole regions rather than in single localities; and with their advent, political organization on a scale and of an effectiveness approaching that of Rome once again became a reality in western Europe.

The original model for the growth and development of the dynastic state was the Papacy, the first and foremost of medieval western Europe's suprafeudal governments. Almost from the outset of the era, the papal regime pioneered in the development of dynastic institutions and methods of rule. From the tenth century onward, its central objective was to make good the pretense of papal supremacy by enforcing the Pope's will uniformly throughout Christendom; and in order to implement that policy, papal officials gradually had to make of the Papacy a dynastic regime—the first of its kind, and therefore the pattern for all the rest to follow.

In doing so, they drew heavily upon the precedents of both manorial feudalism and the despotism of the later Roman Empire (insofar as it could be remembered). What resulted was a highly centralized, highly juridical government focused upon a single man, the Pope. Administratively, he headed a bureaucracy that was an extension of his own and other clergymen's households. Judicially, he presided over a series of courts similarly made up of his own and other clergymen's advisory councils. And symbolically, he fulfilled the role of God's vicar on earth—a supreme, divinely appointed, incontestable authority.

Not unexpectedly, the political regime that gave this symbolism a degree of substance soon attracted imitators among the more astute feudal lords. Eager not only to enhance their personal power but also to find some remedy for the increasingly apparent disintegration of the feudal order, such men perceived in the Papacy a pattern that might make it possible to fulfill both these objectives. Furthermore, it was a pattern that dovetailed nicely with steps they had already taken to concentrate the remnants of the crumbling manorial system about its still-viable judicial machinery and about themselves as the chief manorial judicial officers. Consequently, papal government became the model for secular dynastic development; and numerous western European rulers undertook to reconstruct their regimes along similar lines.

Such imitation produced dynastic monarchies and duchies throughout England, the Low Countries, France, and Spain, which, like the Papacy, were typified by centralization and legalism. They were also focused upon the ruler by means of the same devices of pretense, the household, and the advisory council; and they likewise were directed through such agencies in accord with a uniform legal code and a fixed administrative procedure. Even the mode of taxation they adopted, based on comprehensive annual levies on land or agriculture, was patterned upon the papal tithe.

Nevertheless, there were differences, too. For example, the focus of the secular dynasts' claim to authority fell upon the claimant rather than the position he occupied; and this rendered the succession familial rather than official, giving rise to regular hereditary dynasties rather than elective ones like the Papacy. Similarly, the secular rulers were concerned with centralization in both a territorial and an administrative sense, not merely the latter. Nor did their new legal codes hew too closely to the model of canon law, since they were based not only upon it but also upon feudal custom and surviving Roman law. Likewise, secular pretensions to power, although theoretically quite as absolute as the Pope's, were tempered in practice by the strong counterclaims of the traditional elite —and, to a degree, even by incipient popular rights.

Consequently, as the western European dynastic regimes evolved, they proved to be far less despotic than they might have been: less systems of comprehensive arbitrary rule than arbitrary central authorities contending with provincial and local remnants of the feudal system. Generally speaking, they emerged as prenational governments pitting an ambitious king or duke and his relatively reformed, progressive, efficient administration against the declining feudal elite and its traditional, increasingly ineffective government of custom and contract, in a contest for comprehensive political supremacy.

In other words, the secular dynastic state as it acquired definitive shape in the late medieval era was a combination of feudal remnants and Roman revivals. It was at once the initial stage in the resumption of Western Civilization's political development along Roman lines of unity, efficiency, justice, and public service, and the continuation of western Europe's political development along Germanic lines of martial prowess, individual leadership, personal loyalty, and native custom. It was, in sum, an attempt to surmount the stagnancy and regression of medieval feudalism by adopting in its stead an amalgam of the most effective known political methods —ancient and medieval, civil and clerical alike.

The Leading Dynastic Regimes

The foremost dynastic states arose along the Atlantic littoral of western Europe, in the region where the interaction of the Roman and Germanic traditions was most pronounced, and where the degeneration of the medieval order first noted in Italy initially became acute. Between 1450 and 1550, the governments of England, Spain, and France were all transformed from weak, fragmented medieval monarchies into strong, unitary dynastic regimes (see map 12). That transformation restored state power to nearly Roman levels within their bounds, as well as establishing a pattern for the subsequent development of other Western governments, and thereby determined the character of the political order throughout virtually the entire West for the duration of the early modern era.

The first tentative steps toward secular definition of the dynastic state and political order were taken in England midway through the medieval era. In 1066, the Normans, inhabitants of a large duchy in northern France, invaded and conquered the country, then immediately set about overhauling its entire political system. During the next two centuries, a series of able Norman kings centralized England's administration, levied a general land tax, imposed a uniform legal code (the common law), and otherwise laid the foundations for a strong dynastic regime in the course of solidifying their hold upon the island.

Unfortunately, the promise of this brilliant beginning was not soon realized. The later, less able Norman monarchs, dazzled by their predecessors' successes, began to dream dreams of empire; ere long they undertook their fulfillment, embarking on an orgy of overseas expansion in both their ancestral homeland of France and Ireland. Eventually, they were defeated and all but driven out of both countries, a reversal that brought down the Norman regime, plunged England into a half century of tumult during the mid-1400s, and stultified the development of the dynastic state within its bounds.

Not until a new ruling house, the Tudors, firmly established themselves in power toward the end of the fifteenth century did such development resume and shortly proceed to fruition. Under their direction, the thwarted political promise of Norman times was at last fulfilled. During their more than century-long reign, a vigorous, efficient dynastic state was re-created to rule England—a state seemingly dominated by the monarch, but in fact run by him and his central administration only with the consent and cooperation of the feudal elite and the populace as a whole, as manifested through Parliament (a national legislative assembly of feudal origin), the provincial judicial system, and the local administrations.

Under this so-called mixed government, England rapidly reached a new pitch of dynastic political development, preparing the way for the onset of the modern national state there during the seventeenth century. Furthermore, thanks to such development, the Tudors were able to keep the peace, revive prosperity, and nurture a budding sense of national unity, thereby restoring England's much depleted strength and rendering it once more a leading western European country. However, because the Tudor regime concentrated its attention on domestic affairs to achieve these ends, it failed to exercise much influence on the overall development of the dynastic state in western Europe as a whole.

The more powerful Spanish dynastic regime had an equally negligible influence on such development, this in spite of an entirely different history. That history began when northern Iberia successfully withstood the Moslem invasion of the peninsula in the eighth century. As conditions stabilized, the medieval kingdoms of Spain—Asturias, Aragon, Castile, Navarre, and León—arose there; and by the end of the fifteenth century, after generations of war, intrigue, and political maneuver, they had been combined to form a single Spanish dynastic state.

These kingdoms were brought together not by the efforts of a single one of their number but rather by a common determination to defeat the Moslems and oust them from Spain. This determination gave rise to numerous alliances by marriage among the several ruling houses; and in the late 1400s, the union of Ferdinand of Aragon and Isabella of Castile culminated the process by bringing all of Christian Spain under a single government, a government that quickly defeated and conquered the Moslems still in Iberia.

The new regime then swiftly began to transform itself into a full-fledged dynastic state; and under its auspices, Spain embarked upon a half century of explosive development. As government was centralized, uniform law imposed, and all the other aspects of dynastic reform carried out, the economy boomed; expeditions were launched to the New World; brilliant marriage alliances were made with a host of Europe's ruling houses; and Spain's armed forces were made the most powerful in the West.

The interaction of all these forces abruptly turned Spain into a huge, polyglot dynastic empire dominating the entire West (including most of the just-discovered Americas) during the sixteenth century. Under Charles V, the grandson of Isabella and Ferdinand, and later his son, Philip II, Spanish gold made and unmade Popes; Spanish troops terrorized Protestants, Catholics, Moslems, and American natives alike; and Spanish kings attempted to alter the course of Western history singlehanded. No more powerful regime had been seen in western Europe since Roman times, no more pervasive influence felt since the medieval heyday of the Papacy.

But the hastily formed dynastic state at the foundation of it all was rife with defects as well as strengths; and it remained a power to be reckoned with only so long as wealth continued to pour into its treasury from the New World, so long as its armies and fleets remained victorious, and so long as its possessions in Europe remained prosperous and obedient. When privateers and the exhaustion of the American mines cut the flow of precious metals, when northern European innovations in warfare both on land and sea swept away its military supremacy, and when its lands in Italy sank into depression and those in the Netherlands revolted, the Spanish dynastic regime precipitately tumbled from its predominant position, stagnated in its development, and shortly permitted itself to become a puppet of its far more successful French counterpart, having made little or no lasting impression on the character of the general western European political revival.

That role was left to France, whose political development from 1450 to 1550 provided the norm that neither England's nor Spain's did. That development really commenced in the fourteenth century when the English imperial thrust into

France was checked and the English conquests there were retaken and annexed by the French Capetian dynasty. Once the Capetians had defeated the English, inflating their prestige and securing at least a semblance of control over the provinces that nominally owed them allegiance, the dynastic state began to flower in France.

Yet it did not come into full bloom until a new ruling house had supplanted the Capetians. This family, the Valois, quickly began to exploit their predecessors' hard-won prestige and territorial-administrative base to create a strong and extensive central administration, organize a standing royal army, conquer France with that army, and thereby establish sufficient control over the whole of it to levy a national tax on land. Since local and feudal influences remained quite powerful, however, and were not harnessed to the dynastic state either by means of representative agencies (such as England's Parliament) or national sentiment, they continued to disrupt life in the countryside and to hinder the nationwide imposition of uniform law and royal justice.

By 1450, the Valois dynasty had sufficiently centralized French government and unified the rich territory it ruled to make France the most powerful country in western Europe—which, except when briefly outdone by Spain, it would remain for the next three centuries—and to render the Valois regime the archetype of the dynastic state throughout the entire region.

It was a form of government notable for its despotism but not for its omnipotence, for its centralization but not for its efficiency, for its pretensions but not for its accomplishments, for its judiciary but not for its justice—in short, a modern, postfeudal regime at the royal center dwindling away to archaic, still-feudal governments at the provincial and local periphery. Viewed another way, the dynastic state was an attempt to Romanize western European government, which instead papalized it; an effort to remedy the shortcomings of feudalism by broadening the basis of political participation to a national scale, which instead polarized political power about a single man. To be sure, it revived effective, region-wide government in western Europe, but only by minimizing the role of the formerly dominant warrior-priest elite and leaving the masses still largely excluded from political life, thereby planting the seeds of eventual antidynastic revolution.

On the Threshold of a New Era

Nonetheless, in the short term, the rise of the dynastic state served to rescue wallowing western European politics from the morass of decaying feudalism; and in doing so, it initiated modern Western political development, set the course of that development in the nationalistic direction that would subsequently characterize it throughout the modern era, and closed the door firmly on the medieval era.

The age of recovery from Rome's collapse had at last come to a close. The feudal, manorial, Christian order that had prevailed for a millennium was disintegrating and being replaced by a dynastic, prenational, secular order. Western Civilization's center of gravity was manifesting itself anew and shifting northward from where the Romans had dropped their burdens toward Paris and London, toward a chilly, maritime world of ingenuity, efficiency, and prosperity—a world devoted to material enterprise rather than spiritual salvation. As governments of Roman effectiveness began to emerge once again in western Europe, the entire West stood poised on the brink of a new age of further civilized advance, on the threshold of a new era.

It had reached that threshold almost ten centuries later than it might have, because of the Germanic invasion and destruction of an already moribund Roman Empire. For to rise from the gloom and barbaric pandemonium into which the collapse of Rome and of ancient civilization had thrust it, the West required nearly a millennium. To struggle back upward to the light of further civilized advance, it needed virtually the entire medieval era, rendering the history of that era a tale of Western Civilization's survival and resurgence rather than of its progress.

The initial chapters of that history spanned the fragmentation of the Roman Empire, the eastern half transmuting itself into the still highly civilized domains of Byzantium and Islam, and the western half declining into a congeries of Germanic kingdoms in which civilization barely survived under the protection of the Frankish Empire and the Latin branch of the Christian church. The ultimate recovery of the West was at the same time being assured, by making good the fatal economic deficiency of the classical period via an agricultural revolution in western Europe comparable in scope and results to that effected by the Mesopotamians at the very outset of the civilized epoch.

Unfortunately, the economic potential of this second agricultural revolution was not to be fully exploited for centuries to come. Meanwhile, the Papacy undertook to reunify the West religiously—by fulfilling the Christian mission, as it were. When, in due time, the effort foundered, discrediting the church and signaling the onset of disintegration throughout the medieval order, the scholars of western Europe turned back to the classical heritage in search of new direction. The success of their quest consummated the medieval recovery of Western Civilization to Roman levels in western Europe by initiating the intellectual and artistic Renaissance. Hard on its heels, the restoration of regional political power via the development of the dynastic state heralded the onset of a new, modern era of renewed civilized advance.

Thus, just as the medieval era had been initiated by the failure of the West's classical economy, the destruction of its Roman system of government, and the subsequent collapse of ancient civilization within its bounds, so was that same era brought to a close by the revolutionary reconstruction of western Europe's economy and by the creation of new modes of government there, within whose bounds civilization could be revived to Roman levels and then advanced further. In other words, Western Civilization, at the stage to which the Romans had developed it, depended first and foremost upon a framework of order and well-being that only political organization and economic development equal to or better than that achieved by the Romans could provide; and so the recovery of civilization after Rome's fall depended primarily upon the restoration of such political organization and the generation of such economic development.

The task took the entire medieval era and in effect defined it, economic development dominating the first half of the period and political reorganization the second half. In short, the medieval era acquired its historical significance initially from the spontaneous agricultural revolution that occurred in western Europe and finally from the calculated political recovery that the revolution enabled. Thus, it was essentially an interlude between the ancient and modern phases of Western Civilization required to make good the West's fundamental defect of economic weakness and to repair the damage the Germans had done to its political structure. It was at bottom an era devoted to the search for a substitute for the Roman Empire, which material insufficiency and barbarian invasion had destroyed, an attempt to recover Rome that brought forth instead the modern world.

Part III

The Triumphant or Modern Phase

CHAPTER 10

The Religious Fragmentation, A.D. 1550-1650

The Medieval Religious Legacy

The principal fruits of the medieval era in western Europe were the material achievements in economics and politics, upon which the revival of Western Civilization there was based. They were brought forth in an atmosphere of spirituality rather than materialism, however—in an intellectual environment focused upon religion rather than economics or politics; and in spite of the Renaissance, that environment still persisted to a considerable degree in 1500, forming a basic obstacle to western Europe's civilized advance in the new, modern era. Consequently, the first major task the region faced in the new era was the nullification of the medieval religious legacy; and that task was carried out in large part from about 1550 to 1650, the period generally known as the Reformation.

To be sure, the triumph of Humanism during the Renaissance had in large measure already stifled traditional spirituality within western Europe's cultural elite; but the lingering obsession with religion among the population at large still remained a formidable roadblock athwart the route to modernity. In order to utilize fully the post-Roman achievements in agricultural production and political reorganization so as to advance the whole of Western Civilization beyond the level previously attained by the Romans, it was necessary somehow to gain acceptance of the new, pseudoclassical ideology of the Renaissance—or some other, equally materialistic ideology—on a sweeping, comprehensive scale rather than merely among intellectuals and artists. Further material progress required the widespread adoption of a kindred mode of thought; and before that could be achieved, the widespread abandonment of medieval spirituality, of traditional Latin Christianity, had to be secured.

The Prelude of the Reformation

The first overt signs that such an abandonment might be effected appeared during the fourteenth century, when a series of events suddenly accelerated the disintegration of the medieval order so much as to make it manifest to western Europeans in every walk of life. The cumulative impact of the Black Death (a devastating epidemic of bubonic plague in 1348-1349), the Great Schism (the division of the Latin church's hierarchy into two rival Papacies from 1378 to 1417), and the Hundred Years' War (the long struggle for dominance in France between the native Capetian dynasty and the Norman dynasty of England from 1339 to 1453) shook medieval society in western Europe to its roots, cracking its foundations and challenging its most fundamental premises, especially those of a religious nature. In the wake of these shocks, although economic recovery and sociopolitical reorganization were relatively swift, the damage done to religious belief proved irreparable.

The decline in spirituality had probably begun unnoticed even earlier, namely during the forepart of the thirteenth century, when at the height of its predominance the Latin church failed to make any significant innovations to strengthen its hold upon the mass of the people or to reform itself. Instead, at this best of times for Christianity in western Europe, it made only haphazard efforts to preserve and promote the faith among the region's inhabitants, generally leaving such work to monks and parish priests, who too often were either indifferent to it or ill-prepared to carry it out. In short, even when at the peak of its power and influence, the medieval Latin church simply neglected to attend to the spiritual welfare of the western European masses; and that neglect doubtless permitted the first traces of spiritual decline to set in among them.

The subsequent spread of corruption and worldliness among the clergy and within the church contributed markedly to the continuance of spiritual decline among the people, undermining the prestige not only of the religious authorities but also that of the sacraments they administered and the beliefs they proclaimed. The gradual spread of agricultural and commercial improvements produced a similar effect, since it made the testimonies of faith seem increasingly unimpressive in contrast to those of everyday life. Likewise, the failure of papal efforts to unify Latin Christendom by force plunged the agents and institutions of religion in western Europe still further into disrepute. Finally, the gradual emergence of materialism (via the triumph of Humanism) and of nationalism (via the rise of the dynastic state) as possible alternatives to spirituality and Christian commonwealth culminated the process. Indeed, so far had the erosion of established religion's foundations in the Latin West progressed by 1500 that the final nullification of the region's lingering medieval religious legacy and the wholesale commencement of its modernization awaited only the further implementation of nationalism and materialism on a more widespread, popular scale. This was the task of the Reformation.

The Protestant Revolt

The execution of that task began in roundabout fashion early in the sixteenth century when a German clergyman named Martin Luther openly challenged the beliefs and the authority of the Latin church in the name of religious reform. Luther's program, based on the agitations of a few independent-minded Bohemian and English clerics during the late medieval era, protested the many shortcomings of the disintegrating western European Christian order and proposed their correction through the simplification of traditional ritual and the curtailment of the higher clergy's authority. It quickly attracted adherents among German churchmen by the force of its arguments; and quite as quickly, it won the support of several petty dynasts of the Holy Roman Empire, who saw in it a pretext for breaking free from both papal and imperial authority and for seizing valuable church offices and property within their own borders. The net result was the so-called Protestant movement.

Resistance to the movement—in effect, the response of the faithful to Luther's heresies—was not long in materializing. Led by the Hapsburg monarchs (the kings of Spain and their relatives in Germany) and the Papacy, it sought to maintain already tattered medieval religious and political tradition and thereby to preserve outmoded spirituality and Christian unity as the cornerstones of western European life. And, like Protestantism, it was initially focused in Germany, where medieval tradition remained strongest, where the medieval spiritual legacy was most pronounced, and where the political interests of both the Papacy and the Hapsburgs were concentrated in support of the rickety feudal structure of the Holy Roman Empire.

Consequently, it was in Germany, that perennial seedbed of difficulty for Western Civilization, that the struggle to reform the Latin church—the Protestant Revolt—began. Initially, it consisted solely of a war of words, an extended series of disputations pitting reformist theologians of Luther's stripe against kindred defenders of the established faith. But when words failed and these preliminary jousts proved indecisive, both sides hastened to take up arms, thereby loosing a holocaust on Germany and western Europe that was to last for over a century.

The military conflict began in 1546 when the first of many armies raised by the Hapsburgs marched forth with the Papacy's support and blessing to snuff out Protestantism; and it did not end until 1648, when the last of these belated crusades (see map 11) had been decisively checked well short of its objective by a combination of Swedish, English, and French counterthrusts—Sweden and England having meantime emerged as the principal Protestant powers, and the still largely Catholic French having elected to oppose their coreligionists on grounds of dynastic and national self-interest.

In the course of the fighting, which reached its pitch during the Thirty Years' War from 1620 to 1648, little was achieved save the devastation of Germany and the modernization of western European military practices, neither of which redounded decisively to either side's advantage. Thus, while the burgeoning scale of battle and the widespread adoption of guns forced abandonment of the irregular host in favor of the professional army, displacing the swarms of bowmen and pikemen who had defeated the feudal knights with well-disciplined, Roman-like units equipped with firearms and supported by artillery, the change had no discernible influence upon the balance of military power. Nor did the repeated, earth-scorching campaigns both sides waged up and down the length of Germany, using the new methods of warfare.

The end result of the wars of the Reformation was therefore military stalemate and Protestant survival. Catholic

might succeeded in halting the further spread of Protestantism but not in uprooting it where it had already become
established prior to 1546. Physically unable to reconquer
these regions, the champions of the Latin church were equally
unable to restore them to its spiritual domain. As a result,
when the fighting at last ended, almost the whole of northern
Europe from Sweden to England—virtually all of onetime
Latin Christendom beyond the easy reach of Hapsburg
power—remained committed to its newfound faith even after
a century-long effort to restore it forcefully to the old.

The survival of Protestantism and of the several dynastic
states that had embraced it—and the corollary destruction of
any further prospect for western Europe's political reunification along Roman lines—were thus the most immediately
apparent consequences of the Reformation. Nationalism had
won out over the expiring dream of Christian union, the
rising dynastic states over the fading Papacy and its secular
cohorts. In lieu of the objective of a peaceful European commonwealth, the religious wars had substituted the reality of
hostile national states, inclined to settle their differences by
force and associated only by the tenuous international con-
ventions developed in conjunction with such antagonism. In
short, the Protestant Revolt established the modern system of
international relations, and did so along fundamentally Germanic rather than Roman lines, thereby confining the effective development of political power in the Western world
within national bounds for centuries to come.

Even more important, it made final the disestablishment of
spirituality as western Europe's prevalent mental attitude,
thereby freeing the development of intellectual inquiry in the
West from the last stifling limitations of the medieval religious
legacy. By lifting that heavy cowl from men's minds, by dealing that legacy a deathblow, the Reformation opened the way
for the continued elaboration and refinement of Renaissance
Humanism into modern science, and for science's eventual
adoption as the primary mode of Western thought. In other

words, however inadvertently, however unintentionally, the strife Luther initiated cleared a path for the adoption of a predominantly materialistic outlook in western Europe during the seventeenth century, an outlook that all but assured the further material advance of Western Civilization in the modern era.

What had begun as a monks' quarrel in Germany therefore eventuated not only in the terminal fragmentation of Latin Christendom and the elevation of political nationalism in its place, but also in the widespread abandonment of religion as a dominant cast of mind in western Europe and the adoption of materialism in its place. Luther's revolt had precipitated not the reform and reaffirmation of Christianity he sought, but rather its further disintegration and ultimate discard in favor of modernity. In waging religious war against one another, Catholics and Protestants alike had unwittingly helped free western Europe once and for all from the medieval religious legacy, thereby finalizing the destruction of the medieval world and the advent of its modern successor.

CHAPTER 11

The Western European Ascendancy, A.D. 1650-1750

The Unfolding of the Modern Era

The liberation of western European thought during the Reformation from the shackles placed upon it by medieval Latin Christianity set the stage for the transformation of Western Civilization during the next three centuries—a transformation symbolized by the emergence of modern western Europe and its swift ascent to a position of predominance throughout the West. For whereas the Western world on the eve of the Reformation had been divided into Latin, Orthodox, and Moslem spheres of roughly equal power and degree of civilization (see map 9), in its wake the Latin West abruptly began to outstrip both its rivals to the east. Taking a commanding lead in civilized development by the mid-seventeenth century, it rose to dominate the remainder of the Continent and the West as a whole and to dictate the course of

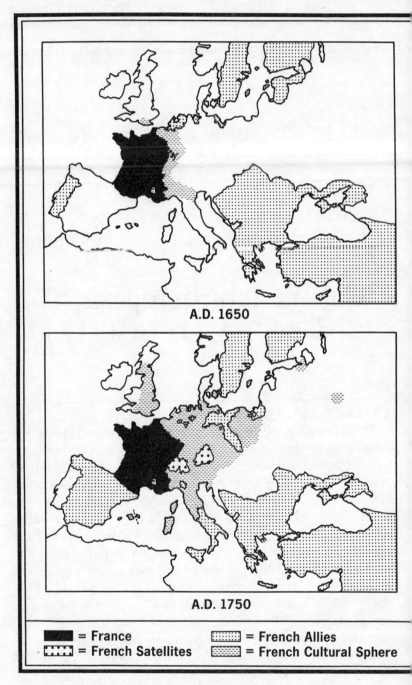

A.D. 1650

A.D. 1750

■ = France ▦ = French Allies
▦ = French Satellites ▦ = French Cultural Sphere

Map 13. Europe Under French Domination

Western Civilization's advance for the next 250 years, the duration of the modern era.

During the first, century-long phase of this ascendancy from 1650 to 1750, France rose to a similar position of dominance within western Europe, the first of several national states to achieve a singular if temporary mastery of Western development during the modern and contemporary eras. The most populous, wealthy, and cultured nation in all of seventeenth-century Europe, the French led the way in the revival of Western Civilization and the corollary emergence of modern western Europe along nationalist and materialist lines. Devoting themselves to the encouragement of science, the popularization of the arts, the promotion of economic prosperity, the spread of their influence abroad, and the further refinement of their dynastic regime at home, they hewed and fit together the foundation stones upon which western European predominance during the modern era would rest.

The French undertook these tasks and established their domination during a civilized interlude in which western Europe rested and recovered from the trauma and devastation of the Reformation. The character of this interlude was therefore quite conservative, in spite of the revitalization of Western Civilization effected in the course of it. The route of recovery having already been fixed by the struggles of the preceding century, it remained only to follow it: to transform the ideals upon which the modern era had been founded into the practical accomplishments upon which western European (and French) predominance during the era would be founded. Consequently, this transformation of settled objectives into tangible realities became the primary concern of western Europeans, especially Frenchmen, from 1650 to 1750.

The century of plodding, pragmatic reconstruction that resulted from this concern was perhaps most aptly characterized by the label "Augustan" tardily applied to it in England. On the surface, at any rate, it bore a surprising resemblance to the reign of the first Roman emperor. The initial order of business was recovery from decades of upheaval and the resumption of civilized advance; the organizational framework erected to facilitate such recovery was legal and political and was based on the principles of natural law and centralized absolutism; and the spirit of the times was phlegmatic, secular, staid. Likewise, the age's culture was largely derivative and increasingly popularized; and the main thrust of day-to-day activity was focused on efforts to create and maintain material prosperity via the development of commerce. Yet, like its Roman counterpart, the period proved most notable in the end not for its own practical, material accomplishments but rather for the ideological groundwork it laid for the succeeding era: namely for the development of the concept of scientific progress (akin to the first Augustan age's development of the concept of progress itself).

But because of the difference between these two concepts—scientific progress in contrast to progress per se —the post-Reformation era was not, in spite of all its similarities to the Roman past, simply a Roman revival. Thanks to the advent of science during the preceding sixteenth century and the further remarkable scientific advances made during the period itself, it witnessed a new forward thrust of Western Civilization rather than a mere continuance of the long-ago interrupted Roman advance. It was a civilized interlude, to be sure, but not a stagnant one; a second Augustan age perhaps, but one much improved over the first by the development and application of science.

The Advent of Science

The basis for scientific advance during the hundred years or so after the Reformation was laid during the Reformation itself. The discoveries made during that turbulent period created modern science by defining its fundamental principle—the mathematical regularity of nature—and by elaborating the methods by which it could be demonstrated both theoretically and practically. In the century to follow, it remained only to systematize and apply what had been discovered in order to render scientific progress the preeminent Western civilized ideal and reality.

Scientific thought began to emerge during the Reformation principally in connection with the study of natural phenomena rather than history or art (which had been the focuses of intellectual interest during the Renaissance). Scholars seeking a more correct understanding of nature initiated its development by making certain observations in astronomy, which, when interpreted critically in the Humanistic manner, enabled them accurately to describe the solar system in mathematical terms, terms that revealed the mass and motion of the planets to be completely regular in character.

This amazing discovery of demonstrable uniformity in the heavens predictably intensified the study of nature as a whole, accelerating the early development of science. By suggesting that all natural phenomena might be mathematically regular, the revelations of the astronomers spurred the creation of both the new mathematics required to confirm or deny the proposition theoretically and the new methodology of logical induction and experimentation required to prove or disprove it physically.

Hastening to apply both, scholars quickly began to demonstrate the general validity of scientific thought and technique. On the one hand, they showed that a good many basic, natural phenomena, such as the motion of objects and the behavior of gases, were indeed mathematically regular; on the other, they shed new light upon the understanding of more complex natural processes, such as the circulation of the blood. And by doing so, they offered irrefutable proof that scientific thought was a more accurate mode of understanding than any previously known to Western mankind, prompting its rapid adoption by learned men throughout western Europe in the course of the Reformation.

The next stage in the development of science was the initial systematization of scientific knowledge; and it was carried forward rapidly after 1650 by a host of scholars. Mathematicians, philosophers, collectors, experimenters, and cataloguers all over western Europe unearthed, sifted, sorted, related, and tested the rapidly growing body of scientific evidence in a comprehensive, international first effort to organize it and thereby make it an integral and useful part of Western Civilization. In the course of their work, they also sought to perceive the preordained or natural ways in which such organization should be carried out; to discover the natural laws that the evidence followed and systematize it accordingly, thereby making Western man's understanding of nature as objective as possible.

The single most important contribution to such an understanding, made in the course of the post-Reformation effort to systematize scientific knowledge, was Isaac Newton's double-edged theoretical discovery of the basic laws governing the motion of all physical objects and the constant force of gravity interrelating those laws. Perhaps the greatest mathematical thinker the world has ever known, Newton, an Englishman who reached his prime in the latter part of the seventeenth century, achieved what he did by collating a great deal of scientific evidence, inventing a new form of mathematical notation (differential calculus) with which to manipulate and consolidate it, and then making a series of spectacular inductions on the basis of this refined and partially ordered information. His was the supreme accomplishment of the post-Reformation systematizers; and it provided the capstone to the solid foundation they had constructed by their labors for the further rapid advance of all scientific thought during the next two centuries.

Applied science was not blessed with a Newton in the period from 1650 to 1750 or during the preceding century, but it nonetheless fared sufficiently well at the hands of a great many lesser men to lay an equally sturdy if far less extensive foundation for later development. In its most apparent form, that of the development of precision instruments and measrement, the effort to employ scientific thought to solve practical problems was closely related to abstract scientific study. For in the pursuit of their inquiries scientific pioneers often called on mariners, cartographers, and instrumentmakers for assistance; and in the course of rendering it, such men often became sufficiently familiar with science to begin borrowing its methods and discoveries to improve their own work. Just as the scientists sought their help in attempting to comprehend and define the theoretical regularities of heaven and earth, so did they in turn begin seeking the scientists' help in attempting to measure and chart the practical regularities of the world around them. As a result, they were soon able to make significant improvements in mapping, navigation, timekeeping, and measurement generally; in the techniques of precision manufacture required to make the new instruments of measurement; and in the maritime activities of shipping and exploration, in which such methods and instruments alike found their chief practical application.

The connection between scientific theory and common practice so evident in these same spheres was also established at the same time in the fields of mining, metallurgy, and machinery manufacture. To be sure, the inquiries being conducted during the period into these processes and the materials they employed were usually not scientific, but their results were often scientifically worthwhile and were just as often put to sound practical use. Thus, from the inspired dabbling of alchemists, the careful observations of the miner and the smith, and the purposeful puttering of mechanics all over western Europe during the sixteenth and seventeenth centuries, new and more scientific methods were discovered with which to mine, smelt, and fabricate metals. And as these methods were widely adopted, they pointed the way not only to ever more extensive exploitation of the earth's mineral resources, but also to the accelerated construction and application of cheap, durable machinery—some of it driven by artificial power sources—to facilitate such exploitation.

In other words, even without a Newton, applied science did quite as well during its first two formative centuries as did theoretical science; and it played an equally important part in the overall impact of scientific development on early modern western Europe. Through the advances it made possible in measurement, metallurgy, and a number of affiliated fields, it established the physical basis for the kind of overseas expansion, technical improvement, industrial growth, and material prosperity that would typify Western Civilization for the duration of the modern era.

Thus, in both its theoretical and applied aspects, science had established and proven itself by the mid-eighteenth century; and the notion that further civilized progress depended on further scientific progress became one of the paramount orthodoxies of Western Civilization. By that same juncture, the laws of nature had been sufficiently well-observed to allay nearly all rational doubts concerning the validity and efficacy of science. Having dispensed with their traditional religious mode of belief, the inhabitants of western Europe began to attempt to understand nature objectively rather than mystically. They began to free themselves mentally from its tyranny, as by the prior development of civilization their predecessors had long endeavored to free themselves physically. By organizing their views of nature rationally, they started to civilize their thinking about it, to adopt the scientific outlook. Thenceforth, that outlook was increasingly accepted as the prevalent mode of thought throughout the West; and the direction it indicated—toward greater conformity with natural law—was increasingly accepted as the proper direction of Western Civilization's further development.

The Modernization of Culture

As science and the scientific outlook were thus embraced, western European culture imperceptibly began to sink into eclipse, deteriorating from the traditional elite enterprise of creativity and appreciation climaxed by the Renaissance into the modern bourgeois pastime of imitation and possession, which would reach its apogee in the Victorian period of the nineteenth century.

This decline started, like so much else in the modernization process, when the religious struggles of the sixteenth and seventeenth centuries finalized the destruction of the Latin church's unity and culminated the erosion of its authority. Western European culture, long a creature of the church, was gravely affected by these blows; and in their wake it gradually lapsed into a period of uncertain purpose and diminished accomplishment. Deprived of religious patronage and an overriding sense of direction, artists and intellectuals alike (excepting scientists) sought refuge in diversification on the one hand and in continued, closer imitation of the ancient past on the other. But diversification, while it expanded culture's range and appeal, also compounded its confusion and blurred its standards. And neoclassicism, while it continued and elaborated the traditions of the Renaissance, also hardened them into canons and stifled creativity.

Therefore, the principal result of this casting about for new cultural moorings was the unwitting debasement of aesthetic and nonscientific intellectual endeavor—particularly the former—throughout western Europe. Almost unnoticed, the Renaissance splendor and certainty of the fifteenth century gave way to the baroque gaudiness and pretense of the sixteenth and seventeenth; and by 1650 it had begun to succumb to the rococo triviality and confusion of the eighteenth. Only in the sphere of letters did genuine cultural achievement persist; and as scientific thought developed, overshadowing its humanistic counterpart, it started to ebb even there.

At this juncture, France's cultural influence became predominant and stabilized the situation. Recognizing that cultural decline could not be halted by longing to restore the past, the French instead looked to their own time for the means to do so. To give western European culture a new focus, they sought to reorient it about the rising forces of nationalism and materialism. To overcome its increasing lack of substance, they sought to stress its still-improving artisanship and techniques. And to bolster its fading support, they sought to expand its audience. In short, they accepted the existing level of mediocrity as the new cultural norm and sought to prevent further decline by making culture patriotic, profitable, and popular, by linking it with the rising forces of the state, the economy, and the people.

This modernization established the character of post-Reformation western European culture, and French predominance over it, for the duration of the modern era; and in doing so, it transformed such endeavor from a predominantly intellectual mode of artistic expression and critical appreciation into a predominantly technical means of ethnic representation, commercial stimulation, and personal gratification. Under the impact of modernization, the region's culture became, and for the most part thereafter remained, a matter of form rather than substance, of the possession of skillfully made imitations rather than of creativity and appreciation; and France became and for some time thereafter remained the chief producer of those imitations as well as the arbiter of what they would imitate. French luxury wares became Europe's most sought-after commodities, French fashion Europe's mode, French artistry Europe's aesthetic ideal, French literature its reading matter, and the French language its universal tongue (displacing Latin). In a word, culture became French, not only in western Europe but throughout the Western world. And because the French were at the time Europe's most populous, materialistic, and nationalistic people, it also became popular, material, and national. Culture as significant aesthetic and nonscientific intellectual endeavor had been modernized out of existence, destroyed by the advent of nationalism, materialism, populism, and scientific progress; and it had been replaced by culture as trivial imitation and material accumulation.

The Economic Plateau

Meanwhile, in the midst of such refined adjustments to the outcome of the Reformation and the advent of modernity, economic life went on much as before. Throughout western Europe, agriculture remained the principal means of production and its practices remained essentially medieval. To be sure, there was considerable further technological development—most of it pragmatic but some of a semiscientific nature—in farming during the initial centuries of the new era; but its cumulative effect was not noteworthy prior to 1750. Only in commerce and industry did modern influences begin to prove significant in the post-Reformation period; and even there they did not become predominant. On the whole, therefore, western Europe's economy remained agrarian, traditional, and unscientific (see fig. 10).

Nonetheless, it performed well enough to keep pace with the region's rapid population growth from 1650 to 1750 and to maintain living standards there at a level higher than any previously achieved, with the result that the inhabitants of western Europe found themselves on what appeared to be a new plateau of prosperity in the period (see fig. 11).

This happy situation was largely due to the onset after 1500 of the long-delayed realization of medieval agriculture's potential (see fig. 8), thanks to favorable political change, rapid population growth, and the rise of modern finance. Politically, the development of the dynastic state and the parallel decay of feudalism had stabilized local conditions in western

Europe sufficiently to make possible the cultivation of lands beyond the pale of manorial protection, bringing large amounts of new acreage into production. Demographically, a swift increase in the number of people in the region had created new markets for foodstuffs, particularly grain, inducing farmers to make more extensive use of already available but little-employed techniques for increasing its output. And financially, the invention of new means for the organization, transfer, and profitable employment of wealth had made available the capital required to finance such expanded agricultural production.

These latter advances in the pecuniary arts, crucial not only to the development of agriculture but also commerce and industry in the post-Reformation period, reflected the beginning of general economic development along modern lines and constituted the origins of the modern financial system, capitalism. Initiated by the advent of a money or fluid-wealth economy as the manorial system of self-sufficiency and barter finally disappeared in the fourteenth century, and then fostered by the sudden increase in western Europe's supply of money, which progress in the mining of precious metals made possible in the fifteenth, this new system was refined and solidified into the precursor of the modern economy in the sixteenth century by the connection established between wealth and maritime enterprise.

That connection's first link was forged, rather surprisingly, by the scientific improvement of navigation and its aids; for as this made oceanic commerce and exploration more and more feasible, it simultaneously increased the need for maritime investment and the likelihood of profiting therefrom. Longer, riskier voyages with bigger and better ships, such as improved navigation made possible, meant higher costs but also promised to return higher earnings, prompting the rich to invest in maritime activity on an unprecedented scale during and just after the Reformation. Their increased investments in turn necessitated the invention or refinement of means to organize and utilize the extraordinary amounts of money thus made available—in other words, stock companies, banks, insurance, credit, etc.

The success of these new financial devices was so swift and sweeping that maritime enterprise grew at a far more rapid pace than any other branch of economic endeavor in the period, yielding large profits all the while—particularly in the form of huge quantities of gold and silver brought back from the New World. Indeed, so dazzling were these results that the financial practices that had enabled them were soon adopted in industry and even agriculture to finance a general economic advance, which made it possible for western Europe to keep pace with its population growth and stabilize living standards atop a new plateau of prosperity. Consequently, by 1750, capitalism had become the established mode for the organization of fluid wealth throughout the region, the first truly modern aspect of Western economic endeavor.

The adoption of capitalism also seemed to produce drastic if not revolutionary changes in other aspects of western Europe's economy, since the value of production in the region shot up as it was effected, raising nominal per capita income there to nearly three times its former peak under the Roman Empire. But behind this apparent boom lay not real increases in output or living standards but rather drastic inflation (by then-current standards), its magnitude indicated by the threefold increase in western European prices from 1500 to 1750—inflation induced principally by the flood of precious metals from the New World. In short, due to an extraordinary increase in the supply of money, the value of goods spiraled upward as capitalism was being adopted, but the quantity of them being produced per capita remained almost constant once the post-Reformation plateau of prosperity was reached.

Thus, in spite of the advent of capitalism, the West's economy during the post-Reformation period remained essentially unchanged in character, although considerably enlarged in scope, from what the medieval agricultural revolu-

tion had made of it. The modernization of finance had initiated a fuller realization of the established production
system's potential, creating a modicum of prosperity for a
great many people, but nothing more: the comprehensive-
transformation of Western Civilization's economy from a
medieval to a modern basis would not be effected until midway through the nineteenth century.

Europe's Overseas Expansion

The groundwork for such a change was already being laid
in western Europe from 1650 to 1750, notably in maritime
enterprise, the most advanced branch of the early modern
economy. It manifested itself not only in the extensive, already discussed development of capitalism, the vanguard of
the modern economy, in this quarter, but also in the parallel
establishment of a comprehensive system of government regulation to oversee and exploit not only conventional shipping
upon the West's home waters but also exploration, conquest,
settlement, and commerce across more distant seas. Together, the two tendencies comprised a form of economic
endeavor known at the outset as mercantilism.

Mercantilism established most of the precedents for the
subsequent development of the entire Western economy
along modern lines of private finance and control, subject to
state regulation and encouragement. It was initially employed
most prominently to supervise and stimulate western
Europe's overseas expansion during the sixteenth and seventeenth centuries. Almost every European country bordering
on the Atlantic Ocean took part in this movement and did so
in the mercantilist manner, launching privately financed,
company-run, state-supervised expeditions toward Asia, Africa, and the Americas in search of profits for the stockhold-
ers, new domains for the monarch, and advantage for the
nation.

The methods employed were essentially piratical; and,
thanks to the advantages modernization had begun to give

western Europe in naval and military affairs, they achieved startling success. Western spheres, generally only economic in the already civilized and well-populated Orient but all-encompassing in the more backward and sparsely populated New World and Africa, were created by force of arms everywhere Europeans ventured, disrupting the native political structures, destroying the more backward native societies, subverting vast non-European populations to European rule for centuries to come, and in some cases rendering their territories permanent European domains. In the name of private profit and national power, the countries of western Europe during the single century from 1650 to 1750 abruptly

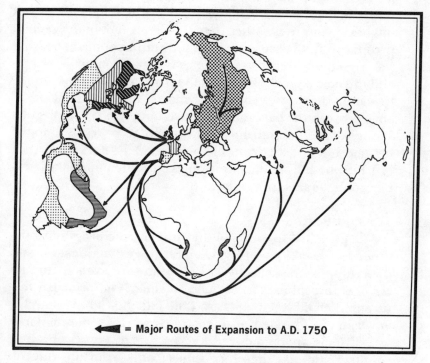

◄■■ = Major Routes of Expansion to A.D. 1750

Map 14. The Initial Overseas Expansion of the West

established an economic and political hegemony over the rest of the world, one that would grow still stronger in the course of the next 150 years and would persist until the mid-twentieth century.

Having fostered this sudden extension of Western Civilization's dominion, mercantilism—or imperialism, as it would come to be called in its later stages of development—naturally became the favored mode both of Western economic organization beyond the realm of productivity and of Western political organization beyond the bounds of Europe for the duration of the modern era. Both were to be developed along predatory and ethnocentric lines (after the German fashion) rather than along cooperative and cosmopolitan ones (after the Roman fashion). Both were to be devoted to the maximization of private profit and national power in favor of western Europe's wealthiest individuals and mightiest countries rather than to the promotion of general prosperity and peace in favor of the entire population. Using the precedent of successful overseas expansion, the new rich and the new monarchs would modernize the West's economy to benefit themselves and their cohorts. The perennial imbalance between the haves and the have-nots, which had plagued Western Civilization from birth, was not to be resolved in the new age but instead drastically accentuated—not within western Europe but, thanks to its mercantilistic-imperialistic expansion overseas, throughout the world.

The Old Regime

The principal sponsors of this unfortunate program at the time of its inception were western Europe's dynastic states and their supporters, collectively known in the seventeenth and eighteenth centuries as the Old Regime. The principal feature of the Old Regime was so-called divine-right monarchy, government founded on the proposition that the monarch was divinely appointed to rule (as a sort of Pope in his own country) and was therefore subject only to divine control.

Appropriately derived from papal precedents, this concept had been given sufficient justification by Renaissance students of political science and sufficient religious sanction during the Reformation to make it the prevalent principle of western European government during the post-Reformation era. And as such, it manifested itself chiefly in efforts to maximize the tendencies already incorporated in the dynastic state, particularly the centralization of political power in royal hands via the development of a more comprehensive, more efficient national administration.

Generally speaking, the power thus accumulated was arbitrarily employed to enhance the monarch's supremacy and glory by waging war, promoting economic development, and stimulating culture. The only effective checks upon its exercise were the passive ones of popular inertia, traditional rights, and the inherent difficulties of governing in the age. And the only beneficiaries of that exercise were the monarch and his favorites. To be sure, benefits could and occasionally did accrue to all the ruler's subjects, but for the most part they did so only by accident or insofar as the royal will happened to coincide with the popular will. In and of itself, the divine-right monarchy took no account of the whole population: rather, it was a political system for the arbitrary imposition of a single man's will—an anachronistic amalgam of late Roman, feudal, and papal tendencies toward absolutism that had managed to evolve into western Europe's predominant form of government during the confusion of the medieval era's collapse and then survive in the early modern era by harnessing all the major elements of budding modernity in its service.

Consequently, the Old Regime in western Europe, being composed of such governments and their partisans, was typified by the increasing exploitation of nationalism, materialism, and science on behalf of a handful of men. In order to serve the selfish interests of the rich and the powerful few, especially the monarchs and the nobles of their entourage, the most significant achievements of the emerging modern era were being shackled more and more completely to some of the worst surviving tendencies of the past by an increasingly perverse, backward-looking, nugatory political system; and the bond threatened to stifle the new era's promise before it had begun to unfold.

Conditions in France under Louis XIV (1643-1715) vividly exemplified the threat posed by divine-right monarchy to the further advance of Western Civilization, graphically illustrating all the shortcomings that riddled and undermined the Old Regime throughout western Europe. Internally, the nation was harried by religious oppression, arbitrary government, and self-defeating economic regulation, the welfare of its people having been sacrificed to the king's biases on behalf of religious unity, administrative centralism, and mercantilist control. Externally, the country was perpetually at war, draining the treasury, weakening the armed forces, and risking defeat, the security of its people having been sacrificed to the king's hunger for greater glory and more territory. And all to no purpose, save the satisfaction of the monarch's whim, since the oppression was mindless, the arbitrariness and regulation ineffective, and the wars inconclusive except for the damage they wrought on the home front.

As a result, France, which had been western Europe's most cohesive, populous, and prosperous nation when Louis XIV ascended the throne, found itself at his death torn by internal dissension and surrounded by foreign enemies, its wealth and resources severely depleted, its willpower sapped, and its further predominance in Europe unnecessarily jeopardized. The archetype of the divine-right monarch, Louis had made France the model and cornerstone of the Old Regime; but in doing so, he had so undermined its power and sway as to render its position in Europe thereafter seemingly dependent on that flawed order's survival, which was to be short-lived after 1750.

Long prior to that juncture, even before Louis's death, the forces of modernity had begun to set the stage for a general

attack upon the Old Regime. Seeking to resist further en-
thrallment by the worst vestiges of the past, leading political
thinkers of the new era throughout western Europe began to
devise the necessary ways and means to precipitate the eventual overthrow of political reaction and its agents. Well before
1700, they were elaborating new theories to counter the
claims of divine-right monarchy and devising new systems to
replace the arbitrary, centralized, largely administrative
machinery of the royal dynastic state. Because of the nonpolit-
ical character of the post-Reformation period, however, and
the reactionary political example set by France, the predominant power in that period, only one actual attempt to effect
such a new disposition had been made—in England. Elsewhere, the Old Regime status quo prevailed. The civilized
interlude from the mid-seventeenth to the mid-eighteenth
century had consummated the revival of Western Civilization
by the consolidation of scientific achievement, the modernization of culture, the limited realization of the promise of
economic prosperity, and the expansion of Western influence
overseas rather than by the promotion of domestic political
progress.

Consequently, by 1750 western Europe, its emergence to a
position of Western-wide predominance complete, faced an
impending political crisis within its own borders. Having recovered from the Reformation, stabilized itself, and carried
forward the process of modernization, but having simultaneously permitted the rise of reactionary divine-right monarchy
to a position as its prevalent form of government, the region
was confronted with the necessity of abruptly replacing that
system with some more modern alternative if revived civilized
advance was not to be halted again. Drastic governmental
reorganization, already too long postponed, had to be undertaken very soon if the West's just-recovered momentum was to
be maintained or increased. The stage was set for political
revolution.

CHAPTER 12

The Democratic Revolution, A.D. 1750-1815

The Renewed Quest for Ancient Ideals

The political crisis the West faced at the close of the post-Reformation period culminated about 1750 to 1815 in the latter phases of the Democratic or Rational Political Revolution. Precipitated by the unwarranted continuance in being of the Old Regime, this upheaval belatedly initiated the modernization of Western government and politics along lines of greater democracy, more representative institutions, more rational exercise of state power, and greater administrative decentralization. By doing so, it destroyed the Old Regime in parts of western Europe, challenged it throughout the remainder of the Continent, and initiated a long-term struggle between rationalism and reaction to fix the further direction of Western political development.

Physically, the Democratic Revolution had three centers,

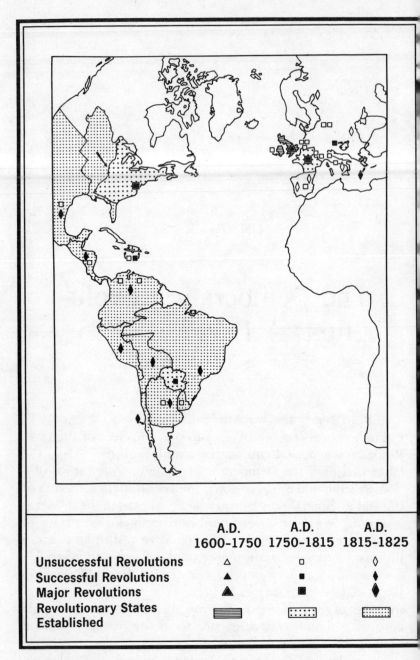

Map 15. Rationalistic Revolutions in the Western World

one in England, the pioneer of political modernization; another along the Atlantic coast of North America, probably the most important single portion of England's overseas empire; and the third in France, the bastion of the Old Regime in western Europe. But ideologically the entire movement derived from the same common source: the West's Greco-Roman heritage, the same influence that by 1750 had already transformed or helped transform so many aspects of life in the Western world.

From the beginning of their attack upon it, critics of the Old Regime turned almost uniformly to the ancients, especially the Romans, or to their medieval imitators for instruction. In searching for the means to overthrow the established political order and to construct a system with which to replace it, they relied almost without fail upon classical precedents or classically derived medieval precedents for their strongest arguments.

Thus, in accordance with the Greco-Roman concept of natural law, the Roman tendency to regard most law as contractual, and related feudal agreements such as England's Magna Carta, they contended that the proper constitutional foundation of the modern state was not one of divine appointment to rule but of political contract between ruler and subjects. Furthermore, they proposed that the powers and functions of government ought not to be placed in the hands of a single man and his agents but instead should be proportionally divided among the parties to the political contract or among bodies representing them, citing as precedents Greek and Roman advisory or legislative popular assemblies, medieval councils and parliaments, and the participation of such institutions' appointed delegates in the administration of the state.

In short, the critics of the Old Regime sought its discard and replacement by a more democratic and decentralized political system. That is, they concluded that in order to remedy the evils of divine-right monarchy, Western political development had to be turned in a more rational direction, toward popular or at least representative government. Such was the ideological result of the renewed quest for ancient ideals. The practical result was the Democratic Revolution, which endeavored to make the theoretical turn toward political rationalism a reality. It began in early seventeenth-century England, when the first concrete steps were taken to supersede the Old Regime with a more broadly representative form of government.

The English Revolution

These steps were taken at several intervals from about 1620 to 1700, and they revolutionized England's political life, transforming its government from one of Europe's foremost examples of dynastic absolutism into the Western world's first quasimodern regime, from a citadel of divine-right monarchy into a seedbed of increasingly rational, increasingly representative, increasingly popular government.

The pragmatic origins of the upheaval that produced these changes, as opposed to the ideological ones, were to be found chiefly in the compromise and delay that characterized the English Reformation. The Tudor dynastic state resorted to such tactics in order to keep England stable, prosperous, and contented during the tumultuous sixteenth century; but by doing so, it created a legacy of unresolved political and religious issues, which were to plague the nation throughout the seventeenth century.

This legacy first became troublesome just after 1600, when the Tudors, uniformly adept at the kind of manipulation and conciliation required to preserve their own Reformation settlement, died out and were succeeded by the far less capable Stuarts. Inept and pretentious, the new dynasty soon so alienated both Parliament, the country's national assembly, and the dissenting Protestant religious minorities (collectively known as the Puritans), that they allied themselves against it and began pressing for a more rational disposition of political and religious power.

At length, their efforts—and the Stuarts' continued bungling—led to an open challenge of royal authority; and when the king took up arms to reassert it, England was plunged into eight years of intermittent revolutionary civil war (1642-50). In the course of that struggle, the religious and political problems deferred under the Tudors were settled once and for all by force, rounding out the English Reformation and ushering the country irrevocably into the modern era. When the war ended, the monarchy had been defeated, swept away, and replaced by a military dictatorship, the Commonwealth, with a puritanical-parliamentary bias and a republican form. In politics and religion alike, the lingering medieval order of things had been permanently destroyed, and a radically modern alternative elevated in its place.

But the Commonwealth soon proved too radical for most Englishmen's taste and ignominiously collapsed the moment its leader Oliver Cromwell died, barely ten years after establishment. Thereupon the Stuart dynasty was restored by general consent, albeit with certain limitations upon royal power; and the country settled down to digest the consequences of the civil war.

When the Stuarts, having rendered the restoration of the monarchy successful and permanent, threatened to disrupt this process by reverting to their prewar behavior, they were unceremoniously but peacefully ousted a second time in 1689 and replaced by the stolid Orange dynasty from the Netherlands. At the same time, religious toleration was legally guaranteed; further curbs were put on the royal power in favor of Parliament and the people; and the central administration was modernized, particularly its financial machinery, thereby institutionalizing the fundamental settlement imposed by the civil war and climaxing the English Revolution.

The radical, violent, mid-seventeenth-century effort to dispose of England's lingering Reformation legacy and its vexatious divine-right monarchy had been completed by a second, moderate, peaceful follow-up effort. By 1700, the religious issue had been settled by the institution of legal tolerance; the menace of dynastic absolutism had been checked by creating a postdynastic monarchy of limited power; and the need for modern government had been met by guaranteeing certain fundamental political rights to individuals, by strengthening the role of the most broadly representative legislative branch of the regime, and by streamlining the machinery of administration, most notably the fiscal administration. Reluctantly but steadfastly, England had begun to make over its ruling order in accord with the new rational political ideology derived from the ancients. Even before the Old Regime was challenged on the Continent, the island kingdom had transformed itself into the prototype of the modern, progressive, enlightened national state.

The American Revolution

The next phase in the West's rational political development occurred, not altogether unexpectedly, where the English system of government had the maximum opportunity for further evolution—in England's North American colonies. It culminated in the American Revolution from about 1770 to 1790, when thirteen of those colonies forcibly broke away from the mother country and united to form a new federal republic, the United States of America, the first avowedly rational modern government.

The genesis of this new model of the modern national state began with England's colonization of the middle zone of North America's Atlantic seaboard during the mid-seventeenth century, just when the English Revolution had entered its most radical phase. Predictably, therefore, the colonial order established in the region was from its inception more rational and more modern, if also more rough and rude, than its parent order back in Europe. Even before 1700, religious toleration was prevalent, representative institutions were commonplace, administrative decentralization was widespread, democratic sentiment strong, and royal influence weak within England's North American sphere. In effect, due to their remoteness from the mother country and the indifference of the central government, the region's colonies had independently evolved into isolated vanguards of Western Civilization's rational political development.

Friction with England first began to develop when, in the wake of the English Revolution, the regime in London undertook to reshape the colonial governments to suit, not realizing that in most respects they had already outdistanced the home country in the pursuit of political modernity. The colonists, suddenly faced with what amounted to an attempt to curb or perhaps even stifle their well-advanced political development and curtail their established semiindependence, quickly aroused themselves to protest and resist the proposed changes, largely on rational ideological grounds.

Throughout the first half of the eighteenth century, they protested and resisted with ever increasing vigor until by 1765 colonial spokesmen were arguing that Great Britain —formed in 1707 by the union of England and Scotland —had no right either to tax its American dominions without first granting them representation in Parliament (according to English precedent), or to interfere in their internal affairs save within strictly prescribed limits (according to classical precedents). Meanwhile, British officials likewise persisted in their efforts to assert their political authority in North America by seeking to uphold and exercise those same disputed rights to tax and to interfere, spurred on not only by the resistance they had encountered but also by the mercantilistic notion that colonies should benefit the mother country. By the early 1770s, they had become determined to prevail, if need be by armed force, the only apparent means left to them.

Given that British determination and the colonists' equally firm resolve not to yield, open warfare became all but unavoidable and erupted in America in the spring of 1775. The ensuing struggle lasted eight years, during which time the British enjoyed military superiority for the most part but could not decisively defeat the ragged colonial forces opposing them. Nor could they prevent a tentative union of all the warring colonies to form a new nation, the United States of America, or that nation's negotiation of an alliance with France, the most powerful nation in Europe. This master stroke by the colonists and the subsequent military victories, made possible by the combination of their own forces with those of France, in the end decided the war against Britain and won the United States its complete independence in 1783.

It then remained only to recast the new nation's government in permanent form to complete the American Revolution; and this was done during the late 1780s and early 1790s under the leadership of a remarkable group of men: George Washington, Thomas Jefferson, Benjamin Franklin, Alexander Hamilton, John Adams, and James Madison, among others. Drafting a written constitution, they outlined a political system based on the radical premise of popular sovereignty and designed to balance the major governmental functions of legislation, execution, and adjudication against one another. Then after submitting their handiwork to the people's representatives in the several ex-colonies' legislatures, they secured their approval and proceeded to create just such a government as they had proposed—a government that rationalized the political process, through democracy and decentralization, more fully than any Western regime ever had.

This achievement, together with the preceding war of independence, comprised a feat without parallel in the history of Western Civilization: for the first time, a people had deliberately and formally reorganized their political affairs on the basis of their avowed ideals, thereby establishing a regime devoted to securing human rights, promoting the general welfare, and nurturing popular participation in government rather than to buttressing privilege. A sweeping demonstration of political rationality had been given, which could not be ignored. Combining the best from both the English and the classical political heritages, the democratic federal republic that the Americans created to govern the United States after their separation from Britain set an example for the entire Western world, establishing a new and enduring model for the modern national state, and pointing the way politically into the modern era. To enter that era, the countries of western Europe had only to follow the American lead.

The French Revolution

France, ally of the United States and bastion of the Old Regime, headed western Europe's effort to emulate the Americans by modernizing politically. It did so during the last decade of the eighteenth century by seeking to overthrow its own well-entrenched divine-right political order on the one hand and on the other to frame a rational political order to replace it. The resulting French Revolution constituted the third and climactic phase in the West's Democratic Revolution.

Based on essentially the same ideological foundations as was the American Revolution (if perhaps placing more stress on the classical heritage in preference to the English), the French upheaval nonetheless was not too similar in character, nor did it enjoy the same degree of success. For while it gave voice to a similar set of concerns for more rational and democratic government and expressed its related reforms in similarly formal terms of a written constitution and a supplemental bill of individual rights, it also served as an outlet for long pent-up fears and hatreds of the Old Regime and manifested the consequences of their release in terrible episodes of civil strife, mass hysteria, and destruction, for which the American experience offered little or no precedent.

As a result of these latter influences and other complications, the French Revolution in the end fell somewhat short of its professed objectives, failing either to destroy the Old Regime completely or to replace every portion of it that was destroyed with more rational and progressive or simply more satisfactory alternatives. In fact, the net result of France's political trial by fire was not enduring political reform but rather perpetual political instability. The overthrow of the old order there did not result in the permanent establishment of either a limited monarchy as in England or of a democratic republic as in America. Instead, it plunged France into a condition of unending revolutionary political transformation for the duration of the modern era, a condition that would keep French government oscillating in its outward form between the English and American prototypes of modern government throughout the nineteenth century.

The train of events that led to this somewhat less than rational outcome of the Rational Political Revolution on the Continent began with the already described ensconcement of the Old Regime in France under Louis XIV—and with the parallel birth of criticism directed toward its overthrow. By the mid-eighteenth century, the two movements faced each other across a void of hostility, open conflict between them impending.

They clashed head-on in 1789 in the midst of a national financial crisis brought on by decades of the Old Regime's restrictive economic regulations and fiscal irresponsibility. The French townsmen or bourgeoisie initiated the collision. Denied political influence under the Old Regime, even though they had grown numerous enough and wealthy enough to comprise a so-called middle class in society, they had long since become the chief critics of the political status quo. Consequently, when the king convoked the States General, a dormant national assembly roughly akin to England's Parliament, to deal with the financial crisis, they were prepared to seize the opportunity to bid for power.

The bourgeois delegates to the States General did just that, capturing control of the gathering at its formative sessions, hastily reorganizing it as the National Assembly, and proclaiming that assembly to be the supreme governing body of France. At the same time, the populace spontaneously rose up to take over the government of several major cities —including Paris, the national capital—and to destroy the last vestiges of feudalism in the countryside, thereby allying themselves with the bourgeoisie.

Once having seized the initiative, this revolutionary coalition retained it by hurriedly completing the overthrow of the bankrupt old order and creating a nominally solvent and rational new government to replace it. A constitutionally defined, limited monarchy with a democratically representative legislature and a decentralized, reformed administration and judiciary, the revolutionary regime was to have been financed by confiscated church lands. Before this or any other aspect of the new government could be matured, however, unexpected events overwhelmed it.

The monarchy and the aristocracy, initially stunned by the revolutionary onslaught, began to recover their composure and rally to the defense of the Old Regime. The aristocracy, although previously divided in its support, linked hands with the king because it had begun to fear execution at the hands of the revolutionaries; and together they secretly planned a counterrevolution. It was launched in June 1791, when the king tried unsuccessfully to flee the country; and almost simultaneously the Old Regime governments of Austria and Prussia launched an invasion of France with the object of destroying the revolutionary regime.

In response, a new wave of popular radicalism swept the country, overthrowing the constitutional monarchy in favor of a more democratic republic, rallying the nation to repel the invaders, and initiating the previously feared extermination of France's former ruling elite (including the royal family). Thereupon, Britain, Spain, and the Netherlands also joined in the war against France; and political strife tantamount to civil war broke out within its borders, as the increasingly divergent revolutionary factions fought both the adherents of the Old Regime and each other for supreme authority.

In the ensuing melee, the French political order was radicalized once again, producing a government based on the collective dictatorship of a few committees of the new republic's Convention or national assembly—the so-called Reign of Terror. Though short-lived, the Terror nonetheless proved remarkable, both for its successes in defending France against a host of adversaries abroad and for its excesses—40,000 executions, strict economic regulation, attacks on religion, etc.—in carrying forward the revolution at home. But once having blunted the threat of foreign invasion and discredited if not exhausted revolutionary fervor within France by these excesses, it gave way to yet another but far more conservative regime, the sham republic of the Directory (1795-1799). And it in turn presided over the expiration of the revolution within France, consolidating the improvements wrought there since 1789 and redirecting the nation's energies abroad, toward the defeat and conquest of its foreign enemies.

By 1800, therefore, the French Revolution was over, having destroyed the Old Regime in France and replaced it with an uncertain bourgeois radicalism. But the Democratic Revolution had not yet fully run its course. Continuing to spread eastward into Europe from France and westward overseas into Central and South America, via both armed force and the contagion of ideology, it would go on harrying the forces of conservatism and reaction more and more throughout the next decade, driving them to build wall after wall of resistance until at last they raised up one sufficiently strong to withstand the shock of the revolutionary floodtide and finally halt its onrush.

War and Counterrevolution

Ironically, the foundations of that barrier were laid in France itself, beginning with the rise to power of Napoleon

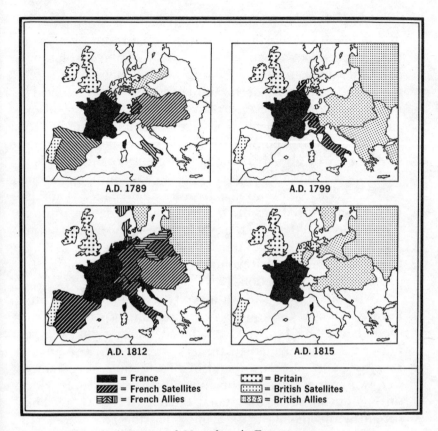

A.D. 1789

A.D. 1799

A.D. 1812

A.D. 1815

■ = France   = Britain
▨ = French Satellites   = British Satellites
▧ = French Allies   = British Allies

Map 16. Revolutionary and Napoleonic Europe

Bonaparte, a Corsican general in the French revolutionary army. Exceedingly ambitious, exceedingly clever, and exceedingly able in both war and politics, he successfully conspired to overthrow the Directory in 1799 and to replace it with another sham republic, the Consulate, in which he soon came to exercise dictatorial powers. Then, in less than five years, he transformed the Consulate into a Napoleonic Empire (1804-1814) under his absolute sway, thereby effecting a restoration of divine-right monarchy in France (in streamlined form) with himself as monarch.

Napoleon reversed rather than advanced Western political development by carrying out this imperial restoration, even though he took care to preserve many of the revolution's practical achievements. To be sure, he undoubtedly consummated the political modernization of France (in a technical if not an ideological sense), by turning the struggling, disorganized bogus republic he had taken over into the most efficient and powerful empire Europe had seen since Rome. But in doing so, he also created a government not only efficient and cohesive but also oppressive and chauvinistic, a regime not only less decentralized and democratic than its revolutionary predecessors but even more absolute and authoritarian than the monarchy before them had been, a political order derived quite as much from the Old Regime as from the Rational Political Revolution and no more typified by progress than by reaction.

In spite of this kinship with the Old Regime, Napoleonic France, almost continuously throughout its fifteen-year lifetime, remained at war with the coalition of Old Regime powers initially formed to combat the French Revolution. Likewise, until almost the end of that lifetime, it remained victorious, too, enabling Napoleon to extend his sway throughout most of continental Europe (see map 16). Possessed of the mobile mass armies that the revolution had created from the revived legionary forces of the Old Regime (via drastic expansion, better supply, and improved leadership) and supported by the efficient regime that he himself had brought to its pitch, Bonaparte fought all the other Western powers, together and separately, from before 1800 to 1812, readily defeating every one of them within easy reach —Austria, Prussia, and Spain—and occupying or making allies of them. But try as he might he failed to subdue the countries remote from France or protected from it by the sea, namely Russia, Sweden, and Britain. And after 1812, they were finally able to turn the tables, defeat France decisively, and overthrow both Napoleon and his empire.

This triumph of Old Regime counterrevolution over Bonapartism—itself merely counterrevolution modernized—was produced by fear of France, not only as a revolutionary breeding ground of the Old Regime's destruction but also as a nation simply grown too powerful to trust. The countries that fought Napoleon and finally defeated him did so because they felt threatened, not only by the Corsican and the French Revolution, but also by the concerted power of the French nation itself. A group of competing but relatively equally matched national monarchies, they saw in the Napoleonic Empire not the modernized quintessence of national monarchy it was, but rather an overpowering force bent on either destroying or subduing them; and they felt compelled to resist it by any and all possible means—even mutual cooperation among themselves.

Consequently, in the first major instance of its kind, the nations of Europe allied to resist the most formidable and threatening of their own number in order to preserve the political status quo established by the Reformation—to maintain the balance of power, as the tactic came to be called. Confronted with the menace of France, the French Revolution, and Napoleon, they combined to wage war not only to uphold the existing political order and prevent the spread of a new political ideology, but also to block the creation of a new trans-European imperium and thereby ensure their own survival as independent nations. They united in opposition to Napoleon so as to preserve the Germanic elitism, diversity, and backwardness of the European political order: to maintain the Reformation politial settlement by rebuffing the more Roman, more modern alternative posed by the Democratic Revolution on the Continent and its Napoleonic denouement. And together they prevailed.

The Compromise Peace

The extent of the national monarchies' success against the forces of political modernization was delimited by the peace settlement concluded with France in 1814-1815 at Vienna, the terms of which regulated the course of political development in the West for the next hundred years. In spite of the monarchies' victory on the battlefield, the peace represented a compromise between the Old Regime and the Rational Political Revolution, more or less restoring the international order established by the Reformation but permitting the survival of regimes in France and certain of its former satellites that were far advanced (along the lines of limited constitutional monarchy) over their prerevolutionary counterparts.

Some concession of this sort was inevitable, since the victorious countries had been able to defeat Napoleon only by imitating him, which meant transforming their own regimes along revolutionary lines—albeit for reactionary purposes —resulting in a measure of rationalization and democratization of government virtually throughout Europe from 1805 to 1815. Beyond that, the victors realized full well that the clock could not be turned back, and so they contented themselves with restoring what they could and for the rest trying to effect stabilizing compromises. Having achieved their principal objective, survival, they were prepared in 1815 to recess the struggle for political predominance and grant Europe the quietude and stability it wanted and needed more than anything else. And such sensible moderation combined with the exhaustion induced by the preceding quarter century of revolution and war to win acceptance for the Vienna settlement.

The meaning of that acceptance was that the Democratic Revolution had ended in stalemate, leaving the future direction of the West's political development still undetermined. For the moment, the expectation of completely modernizing Western politics had to be abandoned; and the survival of the Old Regime, in many respects strengthened by technical modernization, had to be admitted. Indeed, the Vienna settlement in effect constituted a proclamation of the national monarchies' continuance in being, their principles scarcely altered, their powers scarcely abated. They had endured a wholesale onslaught against them and emerged almost as strong as ever at the end of it everywhere except in France and along the French border. To be sure, they had been unable to prevent the further deflection of Western Civilization's political development in the direction of more democratic government, more representative institutions, more rational exercise of state power, and greater administrative decentralization; but they had managed to frustrate or distort in their own favor much of the effort to give practical realization to such ideals, particularly within their own domains. Everywhere east of the Rhine, therefore, the forces of political modernization had been defeated and those of political medievalism preserved. The Democratic Revolution had triumphed on the periphery of the Western world in North America and to a lesser extent in Britain; but on the Continent, it had succeeded only in part and only in the French sphere of western Europe, forcing political rationalism to accept, as per the terms imposed at Vienna, a tenuous armistice with political obscurantism, still entrenched in central and eastern Europe. Therefore, in the wake of France's defeat, the further rationalization of Western civilized development would soon come to depend on economic rather than political innovations. The Democratic Revolution having ended in stalemate, the coming Industrial Revolution would prove the pacesetter of modernization during the remainder of the modern era.

CHAPTER 13

The Industrial Revolution, A.D. 1815-1890

The Foundations

The Industrial or Rational Economic Revolution began in Britain in the mid-eighteenth century and then proceeded to revolutionize the economy of the entire West during the following century, enriching the region beyond its inhabitants' wildest dreams and rendering it predominant not only in the world economy but in world affairs as a whole for a hundred years after 1850. The key development of that revolution was the transformation of Western Civilization's primary mode of production from an agricultural to an industrial basis, from the passive harvest of the earth's bounty by hand to the active exploitation of all its combined resources by machine. In short, by shifting the focus of Western economic activity from the traditional, muscle-powered, naturally regulated enterprise of growing food for subsistence to the new, machine-

179

powered, technologically regulated enterprise of making goods for consumption, the architects of the modern economy finally ushered in the age of prosperity, which had long been one of civilized Western man's fundamental goals and which enabled the West to establish its hegemony over the rest of the world during the nineteenth and twentieth centuries.

The industrial transformation that made this prosperity and hegemony possible was prefigured by and founded on prior achievements in agriculture, trade, and science—to wit, the increasing realization of the medieval agricultural revolution's promise in the fifteenth and sixteenth centuries, the commercial boom of the sixteenth and seventeenth centuries, and the scientific advances made in the techniques of production and transportation throughout the early modern era.

The first of these achievements, the gradual development of medieval western European agriculture's largely unfulfilled potential, was wrought in the period from the end of the Black Death to the end of the Thirty Years' War, or roughly 1350 to 1650. It resulted in an annual supply of farm products sufficient not only to meet even a much-expanded population's subsistence needs but also to pay for the purchase of nonessential goods by increasing numbers of people, thereby creating an unprecedented demand for such goods (see figs. 8, 10, 11, & 12).

Commerce, domestic and foreign alike, accordingly expanded rapidly after 1500 to meet a portion of that demand. In addition, such expansion made available the commodities and capital with which to supply the remainder via domestic production. Furthermore, it also provided the necessary incentive to stimulate such increased production by demonstrating that large profits could be made by trafficking in popular nonessentials, no matter whether they were obtained through trade or manufacture (see figs. 10 & 11).

Moreover, science, from the very outset of its development,

gradually revealed the technical means by which commerce and production of this sort could be engaged in, showing artisans and entrepreneurs how they could make, move, and sell a maximum of commodities—in particular, native western European manufactures such as woolens and ironware—so as to satisfy a maximum of demand over and above subsistence needs and produce a maximum of profit.

It was in mid-eighteenth-century Britain, by then leading the West in agricultural prosperity, commercial activity, and scientific development, that such scientific know-how first combined with commercial and agricultural growth on a sufficiently large scale to set the stage for an industrial transformation. Once this combination had occurred, it remained only to introduce the right catalyst to precipitate an economic revolution more far-reaching than Western Civilization had previously witnessed.

The Beginning

What that catalyst might be was of little concern to mid-eighteenth-century Britons. Indeed, the likelihood of an economic upheaval occurring, however induced, in the near future in their country probably seemed nonexistent to most of them. For while the conditions for industrial revolution had already been established there, so had those for agricultural stagnation; and prior to 1750 the latter appeared destined to become the permanent order of things in Britain.

At any rate, the evidence of a stability verging on stagnation was everywhere to be seen. In the economy, a modicum of prosperity had been assured more or less perpetually by the already mentioned realization of a larger share of the potential of medieval agricultural innovations. In politics, the strife of the seventeenth century had been ended by the establishment and widespread acceptance of a semirational, partially representative constitutional monarchy. In religion, the conflict of the sects had been composed by the institution of toleration. In society, class antagonism and friction had been reduced by the adoption of a hierarchical but nonfeudal social order that permitted some upward mobility. In public life, the martial spirit and other disruptive influences of the kind had been profitably diverted from the domestic scene into overseas imperialism. In short, an Augustan spirit of conservative contentment had become prevalent. As the eighteenth century moved into its middle decades, satisfaction with the status quo seemed the dominant mood throughout most of British life, giving apparent affirmation to that life's stability, permanence, and torpor. With or without the necessary catalyst, an industrial revolution appeared to be a remote prospect at best.

Then around 1750 Britain's population, after decades of stagnation, suddenly began to grow very rapidly. The causes of this unexpected proliferation of numbers have never adequately been explained, but the principal one was probably a succession of inordinately bountiful harvests during the preceding two decades. For since every extra worker—even a child—was likely during good times to increase net income by contributing to more intensive cultivation and therefore higher yields, this series of good harvests may very well have prompted Britain's rural lower class—by far the majority of the nation's population—to begin having larger families in the belief that they could both readily support and profit by them. Whatever the reason, Britain's population abruptly shot up midway through the eighteenth century; and in doing so it provided the necessary catalyst to precipitate the Industrial Revolution in that country.

It did so primarily by increasing the demand for basic commodities and the supply of labor beyond the British economy's immediate capacity to satisfy the former or utilize the latter, thereby threatening widespread destitution and famine and forcing an expansion of both production and employment in order to avoid them. Fortunately, since the full potential of medieval agriculture still had not been entirely realized in Britain, the existing economy was capable of such expansion: all that was required to exploit it was better organization and utilization of extant methods and resources for production.

This rationalization, or taking up of slack, in Britain's early modern economy generally took the form of concentration —in terms of ownership, control, and operation of productive enterprise of every kind, whether agricultural, industrial, or commercial. Contrary to what might be supposed, there was little new capital investment made to finance increased productivity at the outset of the Industrial Revolution: it simply was not required (and probably was not available, in any case). Rather, the transformation of economic life was made possible by the more efficient utilization of the existing stock of capital, by the intensification of the very processes in agriculture, commerce, and industry that had built up that stock since the dawn of the modern era. In short, the initial effort required to activate the Industrial Revolution, once the extraordinary population growth had precipitated it, was primarily a mental rather than a material one, a rationalization of economic life rather than a reconstruction of it, an extension of the principles of science and pseudo-Roman thinking into the most fundamental process of civilized life —an economic parallel to the ideological Enlightenment that prepared the way for the Rational Political Revolution.

The Industrial Revolution in Britain

Material consequences rapidly followed in the wake of rationalization of the economy in Britain and soon became the most prominent feature of the Industrial Revolution, both there and elsewhere. As existing farm practices were intensified, and as existing methods of manufacture and distribution were made more efficient, Britain's economy began to produce additional commodities and to employ additional workers, to a degree that in the short term not only matched but exceeded the new demand for the former and the new supply of the latter, induced by population growth. By working the acreage already in use more thoroughly, by bringing the common fields and wastelands of the three-field system into cultivation (the process of so-called enclosure), by equipping workers with better tools, by specializing production processes, by centralizing the management of such processes, and by improving both transportation (with more and better roads, canals, and ships) and finance (with better accounting, banking, and currency), unprecedented increases in both production and employment were soon realized in every phase of economic endeavor.

This, in turn, sufficiently lowered prices, increased buying power, and otherwise encouraged the purchase of goods to induce the rapid sale of all that had been produced in excess of current demand and to stimulate the production of still more. It also sufficiently raised wages, created labor shortages, or otherwise fostered the popular sense of well-being to assure continued population growth, even after the series of good harvests had come to an end. That proliferation stimulated further rationalization of the economy, further expansion of production, and so on, setting in motion for the first time the onrunning process of interdependent population and production growth that typified the Industrial Revolution wherever it occurred.

The firm establishment of this process was completed in Britain by about 1815, a date that therefore marks the end of the first phase in that country's pioneering economic metamorphosis—namely, the rationalization of the early modern economy and the maximization of its productive potential—and the beginning of the second and perhaps more familiar phase of industrialization per se—in which the rationalized economy and national life as a whole were transformed from an agricultural-commercial to an industrial-commercial basis.

This transformation, which for all practical purposes was accomplished in Britain in only three decades (1815-1845), was necessitated by the continuing growth of population beyond the fully developed agricultural-commercial economy's ability to supply it. That is, the steady increase in the number of people, made possible by the rationalization of the traditional system of production, rapidly outstripped that same system's limited capacity for further output, thereby resurrecting the specter of widespread destitution and requiring some further rationalization of the economy to assure a continued growth of output sufficient to meet popular needs. This was done by invoking and applying scientifically derived technology with ever greater frequency, together with an increasing share of the available fluid resources of production, to industry and commerce (both more amenable to innovation than agriculture), a two-pronged thrust that not only expanded output to the degree required but also fundamentally and permanently altered the British economy's character by industrializing it.

The most salient characteristic of such industrialization, as of the earlier taking up of slack, was concentration. In an age deficient in subtle manipulative skills, it was only by means of concentration—of talent, wealth, manpower, and raw materials—that the kind of changes in the economy that science suggested could be implemented. In order to render the productive and distributive processes more efficient and more bountiful, it was necessary to regularize further both their means and their manner: to apply scientific technology and then to submit to its dictates. Every aspect of nonagrarian economic life, from the assembly of labor forces to the disbursement of capital earnings, had to be recast along more systematic lines. All productive and distributive enterprise had to be brought more nearly into conformity with the mathematical regularities of nature as science revealed them, if the application of scientific technology to the economy was to succeed. And since the only readily apparent way of achieving such conformity in the early nineteenth century was through concentration, the initial and primary task in industrializing Britain's economy was largely an organizational one, just as had been the case in rationalizing it.

That task was carried out from 1815 to 1845 by means of various devices, chief among them the power-driven machine and the state-chartered company. The powered machine was the foremost contrivance employed to concentrate the actual means of production and distribution. In order to accelerate and enlarge the making and moving processes of the economy simultaneously, a host of new mechanisms —instruments to measure, tools to fashion, implements to fabricate, engines to drive, and vehicles to transport—were devised and adopted. These highly successful contrivances in a few decades transformed the physical aspects of British industry and commerce, drastically increasing both the capacity and the efficiency of production and distribution. Hence, the machine became prime agent and appropriate symbol of physical industrialization.

Its less familiar counterpart, the public company, played a similar role in regard to the more intangible aspects of industrialization. In its two most common forms, the multiple partnership (for smaller enterprises) and the joint-stock corporation (for larger ones), the chartered company served as the principal vehicle for concentrating the control and funding—that is, the manner—of production and distribution in early nineteenth-century Britain. It did so by providing means through which increasing amounts of capital could be raised from increasing numbers of people for use by increasingly centralized management. For without unduly involving the rights or endangering the entire wealth of participating individuals, enterprises so constituted could still promise sizable financial returns. For this reason, they were an attractive focus for investment and therefore an apt means of concentrating wealth and all the other resources wealth could command. Furthermore, because managerial concentration enabled them to function in a centralized, tight-knit manner, they could put that wealth and those resources to the kind of efficient, profitable use dictated by science. In other words, the multiple partnership and the joint-stock corporation provided the less personal, more mathematical mode of financial-managerial organization best suited to carry out the industrial economic transformation—the same transformation being effected at a more mundane level by the machine.

Consequently, as the public company and the power machine were widely adopted in Britain from 1815 to 1845, phenomenal economic development ensued. A national railway network was built; heavy industry was converted to steam power; the population was urbanized; and national output was roughly doubled. The intensified organization of the nonagrarian sectors of the economy to facilitate their reconstruction along more scientific lines reshaped the entire economy in less than a generation, deluging Britain's markets both at home and abroad with cheap manufactured staples, making everyone associated with industry or commerce, from millhand to factory owner, more prosperous and rendering industry the predominant economic force in the country's national life thereafter.

At that point, the industrialization of Britain had been effected, and the Industrial Revolution had reached its initial climax there. Having evolved from the mere development of an already extant productive potential into a burgeoning, incessant, self-sustaining, interdependent growth of both population and production; and having simultaneously rendered Britain unquestionably the most prosperous, powerful, and therefore potentially influential country the West—or the world—had ever seen, the Rational Economic Revolution had completed its two pioneering British phases of rationalization and industrialization: the next in its development would be one of diffusing the results of the British experience abroad.

The Industrial Revolution in Europe and America

The spread of the Industrial Revolution beyond Britain probably began almost as soon as did the revolution itself, but it did not become a really significant phenomenon until about

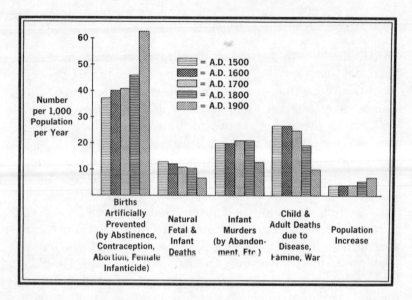

Fig. 13. The Demography of the Modern West

1820. From that time, however, the most prosperous and scientifically advanced regions in the West outside Britain —namely, northwestern Europe and northeastern North America—began to undergo economic and demographic changes very much like those that had occurred in Britain during the course of the preceding century.

To a degree these changes were of indigenous origin, as they had been in Britain, but to an even greater extent they were born of imitating the British example. Such imitation was in large part prompted by sheer proximity, trade, or long-established association. Britain's closest neighbors, best customers, and former American colonies were the first to emulate its new organizational and production methods and to recast their economies along similar lines. Furthermore, they obtained much of the know-how, money, and equipment to do so from Britain itself via the emigration of its engineers, the loan of its capital, and the sale of its machinery to them. In

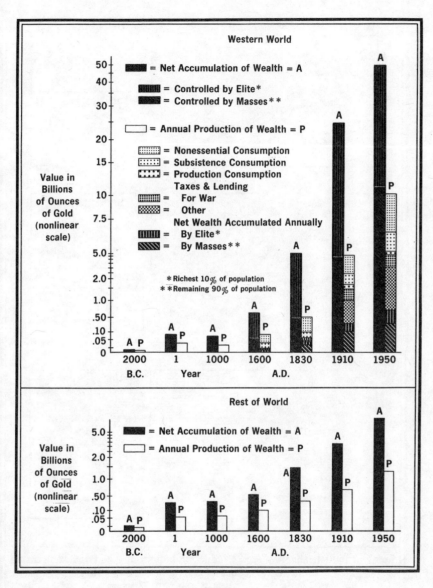

Fig. 18. The Production and Accumulation of Wealth

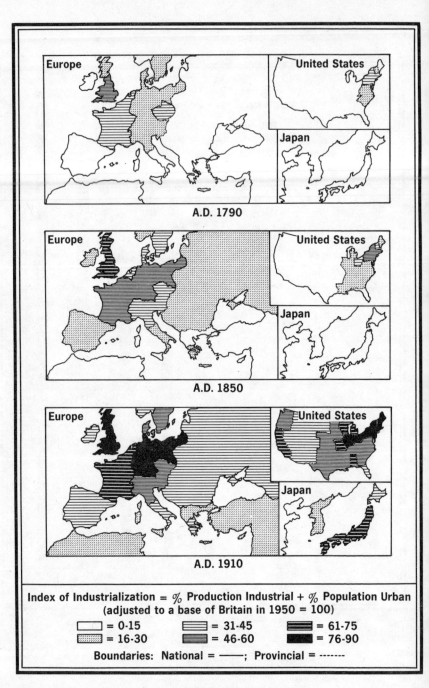

Index of Industrialization = % Production Industrial + % Population Urban
(adjusted to a base of Britain in 1950 = 100)

☐ = 0-15   ☐ = 31-45   ☐ = 61-75

☐ = 16-30   ☐ = 46-60   ☐ = 76-90

Boundaries: National = ———; Provincial = -------

Map 17. The Diffusion of the Industrial Revolution

short, as the Industrial Revolution transformed the British economy, it became part and parcel of it and was exported for profit right along with Britain's other staple products, carried away duty-free in the heads and hands of emigrants, and sloughed off by the friction of ordinary contact with nearby countries.

Consequently, as the weight of Britain's influence abroad increased in proportion to its economic growth, so did the rate at which the ingredients of that growth were spread abroad. Similarly, the impact of Britain's swelling economic strength rendered the countries most subject to it ever more prepared to emulate the British example in the hope of thereby combatting British influence more effectively. Finally, the same countries were neither immune to the attractions of material progress nor impervious to the demands of sudden population growth.

The combined effect of all these factors prompted the rapid transformation of the economies of France, Germany, and the United States from an agricultural to an industrial basis in the half century after 1850. Led by France, then Germany, and finally the United States, all three countries rapidly rationalized their existing agrarian economies and then set about industrializing them in great flurries of mechanization and corporate organization (increasingly favored over the multiple partnership) during the latter decades of the nineteenth century. Indeed, so rapidly and aptly did they carry out this imitation of Britain that two of the three —Germany and the United States—overtook and passed their mentor in both population and production prior to the end of the century, a sure sign that the diffusion of the Industrial Revolution had become a major factor in its onrunning development.

In the wake of such diffusion, mass prosperity ensued. By emulating the British example to the point of outdoing it, Germany and the United States led the West out of the grip of economic scarcity that had held it fast since the dawn of civilization and into a new era of plenty. Population grew at an unprecedented rate, but productivity grew far more swiftly, increasing the quantity—and, since prices remained relatively constant, the value—of manufacturing and commercial output more than tenfold from 1850 to 1900 and of agricultural output more than twofold (see figs. 14, 15, & 16). As production spiraled upward, so did income, increasing so much that, in spite of the perpetuation of major inequalities in its distribution, the masses became more prosperous right along with the elite (see fig. 17). Indeed, such was the sheer volume of mechanized, incorporated industry's bounty that they even began to accumulate wealth on a significant scale for the first time in civilized history, increasing the lower 90 percent of the population's share of that wealth from one-tenth of the whole to two-tenths before the nineteenth century had run its course (see fig. 18). In short, as the Industrial Revolution enriched the West far beyond the rest of the world, so did it enrich the mass of the people there far beyond their predecessors, improving their lot—in spite of their greatly increased numbers—relatively more than it improved that of the privileged few.

The principal manifestations of this preeminently rational result of science's application to production were to be seen in shorter working hours, better nutrition, improved sanitation, greater literacy, better health, more leisure, increased nonessential consumption, and longer life for the population at large. On the other hand, the housing, the working conditions, and the aesthetic tenor of the common people's lives certainly were not improved by industrialization, since it forced more and more of them to take up residence in congested, noisy, dirty, unsafe, impersonal cities and to seek employment in very similar factories in order to participate in the new prosperity. Nor did the ideological aspirations, cultural sensitivities, or moral character of the working class show much sign of improvement under the impact of that prosperity. Rather, the common tendency was to spend what-

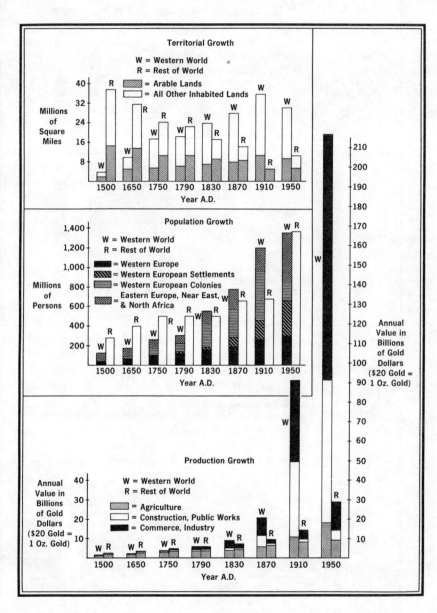

Fig. 14. Indexes of Development in the Modern World

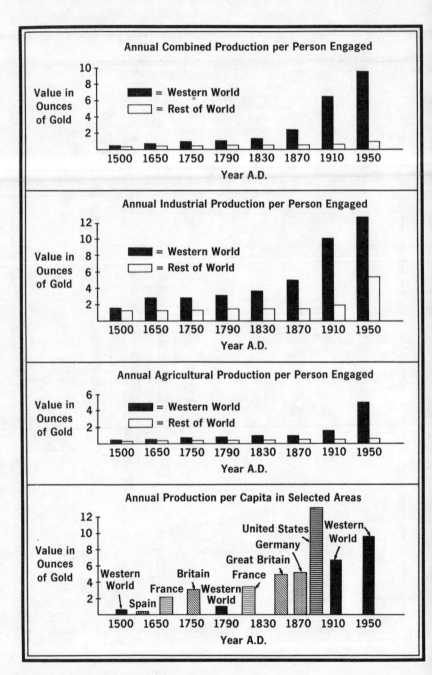

Fig. 15. Productivity in the Modern World

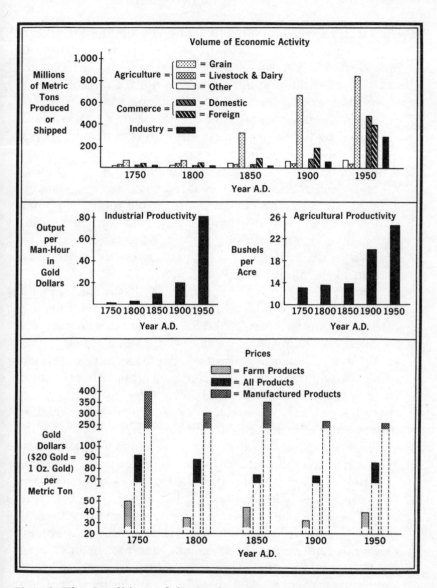

Fig. 16. The Conditions of the Modern Western Economy

ever was gained on individual improvements of a strictly material kind, to transform the working man's life from an episode that was "nasty, brutish, and short" into an existence that was at least physically tolerable, if not abstractly notable.

In other words, the initial fruits of mass prosperity harvested in the latter decades of the nineteenth century were employed by the beneficiaries chiefly to improve the fundamental material conditions of their lives—that is, to create a decent general standard of living—and the popular pursuit of more exalted and intangible civilized goals was left to future generations. Suddenly enriched, the people applied their new wealth to meet their most immediate needs, rationally using rationality's most significant contribution to Western Civilization up to that time and appropriately consummating the Industrial Revolution's popular impact.

In spite of its broad scope, however, that impact and the long-awaited achievement of modest mass prosperity that caused it by no means reflected the fundamental character of the West's economic transformation during the latter half of the nineteenth century. Instead, continued organizational concentration did reflect that character, remaining the dominant feature of the Industrial Revolution even after it had spread from Britain to northeastern North America and northwestern Europe. Still the primary precondition for the successful application of science to economic life, it was also required to cope with new conditions created by the spread of industrialism. For not only had the manufacturing and marketing of staples been dramatically expanded by the introduction of new techniques of mass production and mass distribution, but entirely new industries, such as those producing chemicals and electrical equipment, had also been created. Even agriculture had been transformed into a semi-mechanized process. And in order to direct these new and changed enterprises, together with the old ones, in a more efficient, more effective manner, Britain's successors resorted to further concentration, chiefly in the form of gigantic corporate agglomerates, such as cartels, monopolies, trusts, and holding companies (see fig. 17).

Such firms, which became numerous in Germany and the United States by 1890 (and which have typified the Western economy ever since), generally were designed to gather control of several or sometimes all phases of a particular process—from the procurement of raw materials through each of the stages of manufacture and marketing to final delivery for consumption—into the hands of a single small group of professional managers. For example, in the manufacture of ferrous metals, such a group might well direct not only the furnaces and mills where iron or steel were actually made, but also the coal and iron mines supplying the necessary raw materials and the factories turning the metals into rails, machinery, or other finished commodities. Indeed, the new corporate behemoths often owned or otherwise controlled even the railways and shipping companies that moved their goods, the banks that financed their operation, the insurance companies that protected their property, and the communities that housed their factories and employees. So formidable, in fact, did some of these firms become that they began to dominate the provincial or state governments within whose jurisdiction their operations were centered, and to exercise a major influence even on national regimes, particularly in shaping economic policy.

In the hands of such multi-corporations, the Western economy was becoming so highly organized, centralized, and mechanized by 1890 as to render it sufficiently powerful to rival government itself, long Western Civilization's preeminent mode of organization, centralization, and exercise of power. Likewise, within the population at large, the impact of economic organization and industrialization had also begun to surpass politics as the predominant influence on men's lives. Once further political development along rational, modern· lines had been drastically curtailed by the Old Regime's military defeat of France, at the beginning of the

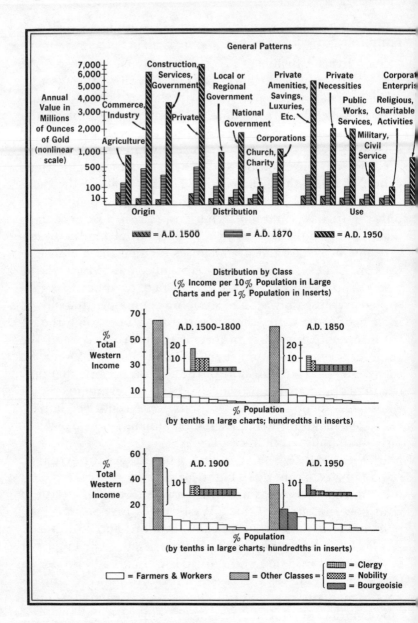

Fig. 17. Income in the Modern West

nineteenth century, the rational consolidation and accelera-
tion of economic activity along scientific lines gradually became the main force behind the continuing modernization of
Western Civilization throughout the whole of Western society. Indeed, by the last decade of the nineteenth century, this
same Rational Economic Revolution, having transformed
economic life, seemed on the verge of nullifying politics altogether and ushering the Western world into a new golden
age of universal prosperity, peace, and contentment, based
entirely on the material fruits of triumphant rationalism.

Unfortunately, this benign prospect took no account of the
dour, nonrational political developments that had followed in
the wake of the Democratic Revolution's frustration. By 1890,
at the culmination of the Industrial Revolution, these developments had all but broken down the Vienna settlement,
reviving the rationalist-reactionary political struggle to determine the further course of Western advance as the
foremost problem of Western Civilization. Furthermore, during the next twenty years, they would complete the job, plunging the West into a maelstrom of political strife that would
overshadow economic development, destroy many of its
benefits, and blunt its great promise throughout the first
half of the twentieth century.

CHAPTER 14

The Modern Culmination, A.D. 1890-1910

The Legacy of Rational Revolution

The modern era came to an end during the latter half of the nineteenth century in the midst of climactic industrial triumph and resurgent political strife, both the result of rational revolutions begun a century earlier. Once begun, the drastic rational transformation of Western economic and political life proved to be a continuing process. Indeed, in economics it soon developed an inexorable momentum all its own (as was seen in the preceding chapter). In politics, however, the pace of rationalism's development was more erratic, initially due to its advocates' military defeat at the beginning of the nineteenth century, and then to their ill success in carrying on by peaceful means thereafter. At the same time, a countereffort to halt and reverse such development was also begun. Consequently, the modern era—the era in which the

rational advance of Western Civilization was fully renewed
—ended not on an appropriate note of sweeping rational
triumph but rather on an incongruous one of renewed political crisis.

The Obscurantist Reaction

The crisis was brought on principally by the Old Regime's
continuing campaign after 1815 to stifle the militarily defeated Democratic Revolution entirely. Originating as an attempt to solidify the Vienna settlement, the effort was soon
reduced to a search for an antidote to the gospel of revolutionary rationalism. And ere long it produced a palliative of the
kind hereinafter called obscurantism, a doctrine and practice
calculated to conserve and reinvigorate the dynastic national
monarchies and the entrenched ruling elites that composed
the Old Regime.

Ideologically, obscurantism was based on the contention
that reason simply was not a trustworthy mode of thought.
Ergo, it followed that men ought to reject it and fall back upon
emotion and intuition as a basis for judgment. Exalting impulse over calculation, the advocates of obscurantism argued
that life ought to be lived by trusting the heart and not the
head, by heeding inspirations rather than ideas, by following
instincts rather than precepts, by doing rather than thinking.
In short, they repudiated all the postulates and premises upon
which rationalism and the whole meaningful ideological history of Western Civilization were based; and as an alternative,
they proposed the renewed embrace of intellectual
barbarism—of a cult of irrationality.

On a somewhat less abstract plane, they likewise proposed
the complementary embrace of the historical myth that the
medieval era had been not a backward age to be transcended
but a memorable one deserving of emulation if not revival. In
the context of this myth, the postclassical period was supposed
to have been a time in which life was noble, romantic, and
adventurous—an era when heroes prospered, virtue was

honored, and living was experienced to the full; when mystery and feeling and genius were the ruling tenets of existence, debarring grim practicality and dangerous reason from exerting any significant influence. Such being the case (according to the myth), it was apparent (according to the myth's purveyors) that Western Civilization owed the best of what it possessed to this same medieval era, or at least to the era's surviving remnants and devotees.

The ideologues of obscurantism also endeavored to make the case that the nation and the national monarchy—the two foremost modern political instrumentalities derived from medieval times—were necessarily imbued with merit. They argued that the predatory, ethnocentric, national mode of politics established by the rise of the dynasties, entrenched during the Reformation, and institutionalized in the Old Regime was an ideal political system for the Western world, since it was aptly contrived to serve the conflicting self-interests of the region's many separate peoples and their ruling elites. Furthermore, they insisted that the monarchies that formed the hub of this system were the best possible governments—at once divinely inspired, infallible, permanent, benevolent, protective, and efficient. That is, the obscurantists portrayed the nation and the dynastic state as the truest political manifestations of a specific people's character and will, thus endeavoring to make obedience and devotion to both (particularly the latter) seem supreme acts of patriotism, enlightened self-interest, and political good sense.

The practical efforts made during the forepart of the nineteenth century to persuade the multitude to give such obedience and devotion took two general forms. On the one hand, government was simply made more efficient and far-reaching (as in the case of the pre-1815 wartime reforms undertaken to defeat France), thereby enhancing the national monarchies' reputation and appeal as powerful and effective agencies. And on the other, the various agencies of bourgeois culture were widely invoked to spread the cult of irrationality, foster the medieval myth, and promote nationalism among the people, all with the intent of inducing them to accept the nation as a new nexus of community and a new fountainhead of identity. In other words, by extending the range of governmental and cultural influence to reach the mass of the people and then trying both to impress and to entice them, the obscurantists sought to enlist popular support for their program.

To a considerable extent they succeeded, albeit at the expense of fostering the mushroom growth of extant administrations and finalizing the decay of traditional culture. Thus, as revolutionary enthusiasm was displaced by the rituals of nationalism throughout much of Europe, governments ballooned into monstrosities of structuralized executive procedure, consuming more and more political energy in red tape and giving rise to the so-called bureaucratic regime of modern times (typified by Prussia). Similarly, as more and more aesthetic expression was popularized and devoted to such themes as barbarism, nationalism, the national monarchy, and the medieval past, the surviving remnants of culture were reduced to a mere adjunct of obscurantism, giving rise to the misnamed Romantic cultural movement (typified by the masterworks—and the imitators—of men like Scott and Hugo in letters, Wagner and Chopin in music, and Delacroix and Géricault in painting).

In this way, through the cultural and administrative nurturing of nationalism and its established political forms, mass support for the old order was covertly solidified during the forepart of the nineteenth century, enabling its adherents to begin the overt pursuit of power by more familiar means during the latter half of the century. Through the aegis of ideological inversion, historical distortion, cultural debasement, and bureaucratic function, the fruits of the Old Regime's military victory over the Democratic Revolution were so well conserved and exploited during the ensuing peace that by 1850 the national monarchies had fully recovered their nerve and strength. And, once recovered, they were prepared to take the offensive and resume the unresolved struggle for political preeminence in the West.

The Persistence of Reason

The success of the obscurantist reaction, however, before mid-century was limited; and rationalism's influence upon modern Western Civilization continued to grow, albeit in ever more nonrevolutionary form. To be sure, the rise of obscurantism curtailed that influence somewhat in politics; but even as it did, the accelerating development of industry and science continued to expand the overall sway of reason. In fact, rationalism did not actually surrender much ground to obscurantism even in politics. Rather, it only forsook the tactics of revolution for those of reform, a necessity virtually imposed upon it, in any case, by military defeat prior to 1815. Consequently, reason persisted as the single most important influence upon Western development throughout the nineteenth century, notwithstanding the obscurantist reaction.

Such persistence was in good part a product of the unprecedented industrial advance already discussed in the preceding chapter. For not only did the Industrial Revolution rationalize the economy insofar as company-enabled and machine-enabled concentration could, but it also rationalized men's everyday lives insofar as a modicum of prosperity could. Likewise, it fostered the continued development of applied science via the design and construction of machines and the elaboration of new industrial processes. Indeed, so pronounced was the combined weight of these influences on behalf of reason that the steam engine, preeminent symbol of industrial advance, also became a prominent symbol of rational advance in general.

Outside the economic sphere, reason's influence was greatly expanded down to about 1850 by the continued development of theoretical science and the spread of its new discoveries. Some of the foremost of these were made in chemistry, physics, and electromagnetism, much improving Western man's basic understanding of energy and matter and thereby rounding out the Newtonian achievement. Others, based less on mathematics, logic, and experimentation than on observation, collection, classification, and chronological analysis, gave rise to a whole new branch of scientific inquiry, the so-called natural sciences. As a whole, theoretical scientific advance served to extend the range of rational inquiry (and rational influence) in every direction—from the present into the past, from the visible toward the invisible, and from the inanimate to the animate.

A direct consequence of this scientifically induced spread of rational influence was the rise of a number of pseudosciences, such as sociology and economics, and pseudoscientific political movements, such as socialism and liberalism, after 1815. These offshoots of scientific rationalism were at once a manifestation of the continuing rationalistic effort to subsume mankind beneath the fundamental natural law of mathematical regularity, as well as the vanguard of a conscious rationalistic effort to counteract the obscurantist upsurge. In particular, the pseudoscientific political movements that emerged in western Europe in the wake of the Democratic Revolution were intended to serve as a barrier against and an alternative to obscurantism—as both the shield and the lance of political rationalism.

Socialism, which formed the left side of that array, was the popular branch of post-1815 political rationalism. Broadly speaking, it comprised an amalgam of humanitarian, cooperative, unionist, radical, collective, and revolutionary movements, all of which sought the reconstruction of either government or society (or both) along more scientifically rational lines for the material and moral benefit of the multitude. The basic aims of such reconstruction were the guarantee of human economic and political rights, the establishment of more democratic government, and the general resolution of mankind's other major problems; and the majority of socialist programs called for achievement of these aims by means of the more equitable redistribution or complete elimination of property and/or wealth, either peaceably or forcibly. Early socialism was, in short, a many-faceted, economically predicated, popularly oriented rational impulse toward fulfillment of the West's primary civilized goals of material prosperity and sociopolitical equality; and as such, it served during the forepart of the nineteenth century as a relatively effective counterpoise to obscurantism among the mass of the people—this in spite of its lack of success in actually transforming either Western governments or Western society.

Liberalism, which formed the right side of rationalism's political front against obscurantism in the wake of the Vienna settlement, was by contrast more successful in reshaping government and society than in preserving popular allegiance to the rational cause. Essentially the political philosophy and program of triumphant bourgeois radicalism, it found expression in the credos of the governments in Britain, France, and the United States throughout the nineteenth century. It stressed constitutional government, minimal state power (especially over the economy), and the guarantee of human rights (insofar as they did not jeopardize bourgeois predominance). The primary aim of liberalism was the culmination of the stalemated Rational Political Revolution, via its fusion with the accelerating Rational Economic Revolution, to create a reasonable bourgeois order of peace and prosperity throughout the West. Its principal method was gradual reform via political maneuver and compromise, reform chiefly of the fundamental institutions of government and society, leaving those of the economy free to evolve independently. Liberalism's impact, although unequal to that of obscurantism, was nonetheless sizable, giving rise to the rationalistic technique of government by political party and the compromise of special interests, which, in one variant or another, eventually became predominant throughout the Western world.

Pending that eventuality, liberalism, together with industrial advance, abstract scientific development, the pseudosciences, and socialism in all its variants, managed not only to preserve rationalism in the face of the obscurantist reaction but to preserve rationalism's hegemony over Western development as well. Thus diversified, the thrust of rationality, although blunted by defeat in war and thereby prevented from fully revolutionizing the West's politics, nonetheless persisted as the vanguard of modernity. That is, in spite of the Old Regime's armed triumph and subsequent ideological, bureaucratic, and cultural machinations, reason, by relying more and more heavily on economic and scientific advance for additional strength and by developing moderate political means to conserve its extant strength, remained the foremost influence upon the further advance of Western Civilization from 1815 to 1850.

The Renewed Struggle for Political Supremacy

By 1850, however, the impact of the obscurantist onslaught had sufficiently narrowed the gap between rationalism and obscurantism to encourage the latter's adherents to redouble their efforts in the hope of eventually achieving predominance. As a result, during the latter half of the nineteenth century, the struggle for political supremacy in Europe stilled by the Vienna settlement was gradually renewed by the reactionary powers, casting a shadow over the last decades of the modern era, minimizing continued rational achievement, and bringing Western Civilization once again to the brink of political crisis on the eve of the contemporary era.

In its domestic aspect, this renewed struggle was initially typified by what first occurred in Britain, the pioneer modern country, from about 1850 to 1875 and soon thereafter in all the other major industrial countries. That is, it took the form of an electoral contest for government control between

rationalist and obscurantist political parties organized to so-
licit popular support. The rational party was liberal in character; and it sought to establish a more reasonable government,
a more just social order, and a more prosperous economy via
programs of gradual institutional reform, administrative improvement, mass education and enfranchisement, and unrestrained economic development. The obscurantists, for their
part, were gathered together in a party bearing the label
conservative; and they endeavored to preserve the status quo
by opposing the rationalists with obstructionist tactics, propaganda, and thunder-stealing programs of economic restraint
and minimal reform. The contest between the two parties
resulted in their alteration in power, the piecemeal implementation of the liberal program outside the economic sphere,
and the gradual deceleration of economic growth rates under
conservative auspices. In short, on the domestic scene, the
renewed rational-irrational political struggle produced a
peaceful compromise slightly favorable to the rationalists.

The outcome on the international scene was quite otherwise. There the rational-irrational contest was perhaps best
characterized by the resurgence of Germany. This resurgence
was begun about 1850 under the obscurantist auspices of the
northern German kingdom of Prussia. A citadel of political
reaction but a pioneer of economic, administrative, and military modernization east of the Rhine, Prussia initiated
Germany's revival by breaking with Austria and Russia, its
allies under the Vienna settlement. This done, it embarked
upon a unilateral policy of nationalistic self-aggrandizement,
or *Realpolitik*, calculated to establish German hegemony
—under Prussian leadership—throughout the West. The first
fifteen years in pursuit of this objective were spent eliminating
Austria as a rival influence in Germany, initially via diplomacy
and finally by armed force. The next five years were used to
unify most of the petty German states about Prussia in an
interim confederation. Finally, by way of climax, Prussia led
Germany to victory in war with France in 1870-1871 and, in

celebration, fused all the lesser German states unto itself to form a militaristic, chauvinistic, authoritarian German Empire. Thus, by steadfast resort to *Realpolitik*, Germany was transformed in scarcely two decades from a collection of political nonentities into the most powerful and least reasonable nation in Europe, revealing a pattern of obscurantist triumph that increasingly typified international relations throughout the West after 1850.

Indeed, even before the German Empire had been solidified, a number of kindred efforts at national unification or consolidation were made. Modern Italy was created (1859-1860), Russia was reformed (1855-1863), Austria was reconstituted (1866-1867), and eight wars were precipitated by the application of *Realpolitik* throughout the West prior to the culmination of the Prussian tour de force. Consequently, the formation of the German Empire signaled not only the resurgence of Germany as a major Western power but also the victory of obscurantism over rationalism on the international scene throughout the Western world.

During the next two decades, the obscurantists labored to make the most of that victory, principally by seeking to entangle domestic politics with international affairs so as to make their triumph all-encompassing. Nor did they toil in vain. For, hardly had it been implemented when the rationalistic method of political compromise, evolved to cope with the renewed rational-irrational struggle on the domestic scene, began to break down. Increasingly unable to relieve the mounting strains generated in Western society by onrunning industrial development and population growth, Western politicians began to find the technique of party compromise lacking before it had even been adopted, and to search farther afield—in the non-Western realm overseas—for remedies to the West's burgeoning domestic problems. As a result, the adherents of obscurantism were everywhere encouraged and commenced to press forward with increasing vigor toward their objective of eventual political predominance, producing a second phase in their challenge of rationalism, from about 1890 to 1910, that was at once a domestic and an international phenomenon—a diplomatic tussle, a propaganda contest, a class struggle, an economic competition, a territorial rush, and an arms race all rolled into one.

Imperialism

This brief, imperialist period in Western history had roots in the distant past, for there had been economic as well as political strife of all kinds evident, both within and among the nations of western Europe, since the Reformation. In fact, its foundations were laid with the advent of the dynastic monarchies and their common adoption of a domestic political outlook based on factional conflict, an international outlook based on national antagonism, and an affiliated overall economic policy of mercantilism. Yet, for want of major strains at home and major strength to deploy abroad, rational-irrational friction in the preindustrial age never even began to blend into a single amalgam, let alone to become the West's predominant problem.

But after 1800, once the simultaneous onset of the Democratic Revolution and the Industrial Revolution had suddenly rendered rationalism predominant and spurred its enemies into vigorous opposition, the struggle between reason and reaction became both more widespread and acute. As the nineteenth century wore on, these traits were steadily magnified; and by 1890, the rational-irrational contest for political supremacy had evolved into a single nexus of class strife at home and national rivalry abroad—into the all-encompassing phenomenon of imperialism that increasingly dictated the course of Western and world development during the last two decades of the modern era.

On the domestic scene, the advent of imperialism was most closely associated with growing unrest among the ever-expanding industrial labor force. Such unrest began to develop as workers started seeking a larger share of the new wealth being produced and some amelioration of their still dismal living conditions. Their efforts took the form of strikes, riots, the organization of unions, and, most of all, a determined quest for popular political rights. Unfortunately, even as that quest started to succeed and the workers of the Western world began to win the right to affiliate, vote, and hold office, the rational value of the victory was being neutralized by the growing impact of obscurantism within their ranks. For as more and more of them were impressed by reactionary successes on the international scene and began to succumb to its domestic propaganda and concessions, they likewise began to believe elitist claims that mass and elite interests were identical and to exercise their newly won political power accordingly, in support of the old order. Such misplaced allegiance predictably curtailed the advance of working-class interests and helped keep its members materially poor, politically impotent, and seething with resentment of both conditions. Consequently, from 1890 to 1910, popular unrest became steadfastly more self-perpetuating and self-defeating, increasingly bolstering obscurantism rather than reason.

The same was true of the intensifying international struggle for supremacy after 1890, a struggle that growing mass support of obscurantism, particularly in foreign affairs, did much to sustain. At the outset, such rivalry arose principally in connection with the newly consolidated, newly industrialized countries' search for elbow room and markets outside the constricted, tariff-ridden bounds of Europe. But as politicians began to regard foreign adventures as a safety valve for domestic pressures, and as markets were increasingly sought after simply by overwhelming the native regimes controlling them, the international rivalry became increasingly an irrational exercise in *Realpolitik* on a global scale. Ere long, it developed into a pell-mell race among nearly all the industrial nations of the West to extend their spheres—economic, military, political, cutural, and territorial—to the ends of the earth by any means required and for every conceivable purpose, from economic necessity to racial superiority.

Such latter-day mercantilism run amok shortly transformed the international political situation, albeit at a spiraling cost in wealth, good will, and reason. It did so outside the West proper by effecting the territorial partition of Africa into Western colonies, the political or economic partition of most of the rest of the non-Western world into Western spheres of influence, and the combination of these spheres and colonies into polyglot Western empires of global proportion. Within the West's own bounds, imperialism had an equally telling impact, for it prompted the participating countries to align themselves, along roughly rationalistic and obscurantist lines, into two opposing camps and then to begin making hectic preparations for a gigantic clash of arms to determine Western Civilization's further political direction once and for all.

That preparation, confirming the resurgence of politics as the West's foremost problem, also confirmed the breakdown of the Vienna settlement and of the political stalemate, both domestic and international, that it had formalized. To be sure, the continuing development of science and industry after 1850 had prevented the eclipse of rationalism as the overall guiding force of Western Civilization; but in politics such forces had little positive impact. There the failure of liberalism—of the attempt to consummate the Democratic Revolution through reform, pseudoscience, and compromise—and the parallel upsurge first of *Realpolitik* and then of imperialism had precipitated a renewed struggle for political supremacy, a contest that by 1910 produced an armed confrontation between rationalism and obscurantism throughout most of the Western world.

The Retreat from Reason

The onset of this crisis in the political arena signaled the approaching end of the modern era; but the less evident,

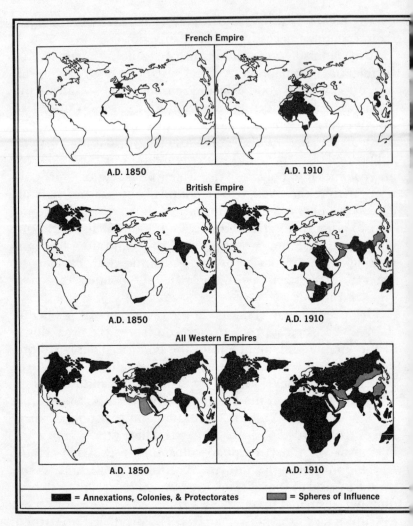

Map 18. The Terminal Overseas Expansion of the West

simultaneous onset of similar crises in the realms of Western consciousness and Western society were what truly terminated the era. They did so by eroding men's belief in the preeminent value of reason as a guide to civilized development, by undermining the notion that man was capable of reasonable thought and reasonable behavior, by displacing certainty with doubt as the cornerstone of Western man's estimate of his own potential for self-improvement.

The intellectual component of this erosion of faith in reason was chiefly a product not of the nineteenth century's virulent obscurantist propaganda but rather of the widespread misinterpretation of scientific development after 1850. Such misinterpretation originated at mid-century when Charles Darwin, an English naturalist, proposed his theory of evolution. Darwin's hypothesis was that the random selection of traits that promote the survival of species tends to determine the character of all living things across time; and in advancing it he suggested a fundamental new law of nature—a law so wide-ranging in scope and so well-supported by available evidence that it was shortly adopted as a framework for the systematization of the natural sciences. Indeed, so impressive was Darwin's theory of evolution that, outside scientific circles, it soon became regarded as *the* fundamental law of nature, a grave misconception that in turn gave rise to the grotesque notion that men, like all animate things, were mere pawns of nature's random processes; that they were, according to science, guided not by reason but rather by such nonrational impulses as the survival of the fittest and the primacy of force.

The pseudoscientific discreditation of rationality thus set in motion was climaxed half a century later by the similarly erroneous interpretation of yet another major scientific refinement of fundamental natural law: the theory of relativity. First advanced by Albert Einstein, a German mathematician, and others, it hypothesized that all of nature was governed by random occurrences, most of them taking place at speeds and magnitudes beyond the range of ordinary human perception. As this proposition was elaborated, it became apparent that the abstruse phenomena it treated could best be described mathematically in relation to their particular frame of reference rather than in terms of traditional, sensibly absolute Newtonian expressions. Once adopted, this descriptive relativism was widely but mistakenly interpreted by nonscientists as scientific proof of the relativity of all natural law; and from that grossly false premise, the further, equally erroneous conclusion was drawn that all thought processes and human values must also be relative—and therefore hardly susceptible to reason, given the irrational evolutionary state of nature.

The general interpretation placed upon the discoveries of Einstein and his colleagues only appeared to confirm what the earlier Darwinian discoveries had wrongly been taken to mean: that rationality had little to do with the scientifically revealed natural order of things. Thus, as a result of placing bogus constructions upon the foremost theoretical advances in science during the latter half of the nineteenth century, rationalism was thoroughly discredited within the population at large as a worthwhile mode of thought.

Likewise, reason was also undermined as an effective material instrumentality by wholesale misinterpretation of the unimpressive practical results of attempts to organize industrial Western society more rationally from 1850 to 1910. The majority of these efforts originated as part of the widespread movement to improve the material circumstances and the political status of the masses urbanized by the onset of industrialization. Initially, they took the form of crude unions and political associations characterized by incoherence, confusion, and ineptitude; but with the passage of time these pioneer agencies were refined into cooperatives, trade unions, and socialist parties with much broader appeal and much better organization. Unfortunately, their effectiveness in achieving popular objectives did not show commensurate improvement, due in part to the countervailing influence of obscurantism, in part to the political and organizational inexperience of the industrial labor force, and in part to the enormity of the problems at issue. Whatever the causes, the result was that by 1910 a great many workers throughout the West still felt powerless and nurtured the dim conviction that reasonable methods had somehow failed them. That attitude in turn served to discredit reason as a means of material (especially social) improvement quite as thoroughly as the misinterpretation of science had discredited it as a means of thought. Its hard-won reputation thus clouded, rationalism's further preeminence was placed in doubt not only in Western politics but also in Western consciousness and Western society. And at that juncture the modern era was over.

The End of the Modern Era

Begun in the forepart of the sixteenth century with the violent fragmentation of Latin Christendom and the abandonment of Christianity as the guiding spirit of Western Civilization, the modern era ended in the first decade of the twentieth century with the West still fragmented and still quarreling over the sort of new values and directions with which to replace Christianity. But in the interim the character of Western Civilization had been fundamentally altered. From a spiritually oriented, feudally organized, economically and intellectually stagnant agrarian society, it had been transformed into a materially oriented, nationally organized, burgeoning industrial society of great prosperity and advanced scientific achievement. In short, from a rationalistic viewpoint, the modern era was a triumphant phase in the history of Western Civilization.

The basis of that triumph was laid at the very outset of the period when, in the course of the Reformation, the ideological focus of Western life was shifted from religion to materialism and nationalism, and the geographical focus of Western society was shifted from the poor and backward Mediterranean region where the Romans had left it to northwestern Europe, a far richer and more progressive region. This reorientation served to initiate further civilized advance during the seventeenth and eighteenth centuries along the rational lines first sketched by the Romans. Under the leadership of the French, Europe's most populous, prosperous, and cultured nation, the consolidation of scientific achievement, the modernization of culture, the limited realization of economic prosperity, and the expansion of the West overseas were rapidly carried forward in this period. But in politics the perpetuation and elaboration of divine-right monarchy—particularly in France—prevented the simultaneous creation of a modern political system.

The Democratic or Rational Political Revolution therefore erupted in the wake of the first surge of renewed civilized advance. It sought to modernize Western politics along classical lines of greater democracy, increased popular representation, more reasonable exercise of power, and greater administrative decentralization. The upheaval began in seventeenth-century England, then spread to North America and finally to France toward the end of the eighteenth century. After achieving a measure of success everywhere it occurred, it was finally defeated militarily on the Continent in 1815 by the allied national monarchies of the Old Regime, thereby perpetuating the struggle to modernize the West politically for at least another hundred years.

Meanwhile, the Industrial or Rational Economic Revolution, beginning in Britain, started to transform material life in the West via an onrunning process of interdependent growth of both population and scientifically enabled production. As it developed and spread after 1815, it so suddenly and drastically enriched and strengthened the West that it abruptly rendered nonagrarian economic activity the dominant force in Western Civilization and thereby assured continuation of the West's overall development along rationalist lines.

But at the same time the political struggle stalemated by the defeat of the Democratic Revolution remained unresolved;

and the forces of both obscurantism and rationalism soon busied themselves trying to effect such a resolution within the limits set by the Vienna settlement. The rationalists, buoyed up by continuing economic and scientific growth, for their part resorted to gradual reform (liberalism) and mass organization (socialism), but without marked success. Their obscurantist rivals, on the other hand, invoked ideological propaganda and national self-aggrandizement (*Realpolitik*); and during the latter half of the nineteenth century, they were able to garner sufficient strength to break down the Vienna settlement and make a bid for Western-wide political predominance, confronting the West with a renewed political crisis at the end of the modern era.

In sum, that era witnessed the triumphant rationalization and revitalization of virtually every aspect of Western Civilization but the one that preoccupied Westerners most throughout its entire duration—politics. The development and application of science had transformed the economy, enriched the West's inhabitants beyond their fondest expectations, and elevated progress in place of Christianity as the preeminent mode of Western belief. But the principles of rationality upon which these intellectual and material achievements were based proved for the most part inapplicable to aesthetic and associative endeavor, with the result that, during the modern era, culture everywhere became stagnant and degenerated into a mere adjunct of politics, and politics in much of the West remained hopelessly backward. In other words, while scientific rationality drastically improved Western man's understanding and utilization of his material environment, nonscientific rationality failed to make a corresponding improvement in his organization and direction of either his artistic expression or his collective behavior. The triumph of the modern era was the achievement of long-sought rational control over nature: the principal task still facing Western Civilization at the end of it was the achievement of equally long-sought rational control over human nature.

Part IV

The Uncertain or
Contemporary Phase

CHAPTER 15

The Second Germanic Regression, A.D. 1910-1945

The Dawn of the Contemporary Era

Western Civilization during its first three thousand years was primarily a struggle to organize human life more effectively. The Romans brought this undertaking to its initial climax by demonstrating that rational modes of organization were most effective. During the Christian millennium that followed their demise, civilized endeavor in the West became primarily an effort to preserve and revive the Roman organizational tradition in spite of the onslaught of Germanic barbarism. That objective was partially fulfilled in the succeeding modern era by Western man's achievement, through science, of an unprecedented degree of rational control over nature; but at the same time the persistence of the Germanic tradition in politics prevented the achievement of a similar degree of rational control over men. Consequently, the latest, contem-

porary era came to be dominated by a political struggle between advocates of the civilized, rational, Roman tradition of
organization and those of the barbaric, irrational, Germanic
countertradition to establish control over Western mankind
and thereby achieve complete mastery of further Western
development.

In 1910, at the outset of the contemporary era, the order of
battle for that impending struggle had already been determined. By then the steady intensification of political rivalry
between rationalism and obscurantism during the last several
decades had divided the West into two opposing camps and
produced an armed confrontation between them. On the
rational side, Britain and France formed the front rank,
tacitly supported by the United States and reluctantly allied
with Russia, a citadel of reaction; on the obscurantist side,
their principal opponents were Germany and Austria-
Hungary, uncertainly associated with Italy and the Ottoman
Empire.

The initiative lay with the Germanic camp, as it had for the
most part since its political reorganization and consolidation
during the 1860s and early 1870s. The nationalist monarchies
that composed that camp, having survived and recovered
from the rational upsurge at the end of the eighteenth century only after a hundred years of strenuous effort, were in
1910 determined to press ahead with a bid for total predominance, to challenge the liberal democracies (and monarchist
Russia) for the right to dictate the future direction of Western
Civilization.

In the event of their triumph, the Roman heritage was to be
cast aside and replaced by the Germanic; and a new set of
fundamental propositions were to be adopted in place of
those established by rationalism. Nature was to be manipu-
lated rather than comprehended; force rather than justice
was to prevail; and the few rather than the many were to be
served. In other words, the total reconstruction of Western
Civilization—its government, its economy, its society, even its

consciousness—was to be undertaken along unreasonable lines.

This was to be done via *Realpolitik*, applied on a grand scale. Tested in unifying Germany and proved in the West's imperialistic conquest of the non-Western world, the policy of ruthless nationalist self-aggrandizement was now to be invoked on behalf of an entire ethnic group or "race" and the way of life it championed. The politics of hegemony were to be simultaneously mythicized and globalized, and the rational advance of Western Civilization thereby halted in favor of a relapse to pseudobarbarism. A second Germanic regression was in the offing.

Indeed, by 1910 it had become all but a certainty. For by that time, so powerful had the impetus of the obscurantist impulse grown that probably nothing short of the impending, Western-wide armed conflict could have stopped it. The control of events had simply begun to slip from the grasp of reasonable men, too long reluctant to act decisively on behalf of reason. By default, the course of Western history had started to become less a function of the hard-won, difficult-to-revive tenets of rationalism than of contrary obscurantist urgings, less a flow of clear waters into a sea of promise than a spilling of molten lava out of a volcano of menace, a volcano that threatened to erupt momentarily and either destroy or turn to dross all that Western mankind had wrought to lift itself up from primordial barbarism.

In the year 1914, just as the contemporary era was getting well under way, just such an eruption occurred, exploding into the cataclysm of total war—the First World War, the initial phase of a second Germanic regression in the forward progress of Western Civilization.

World War I

The outbreak of war in 1914 engaged all the major Western powers and their allies in what soon became an unlimited, devastating, insane, catastrophic conflict that caused enor-

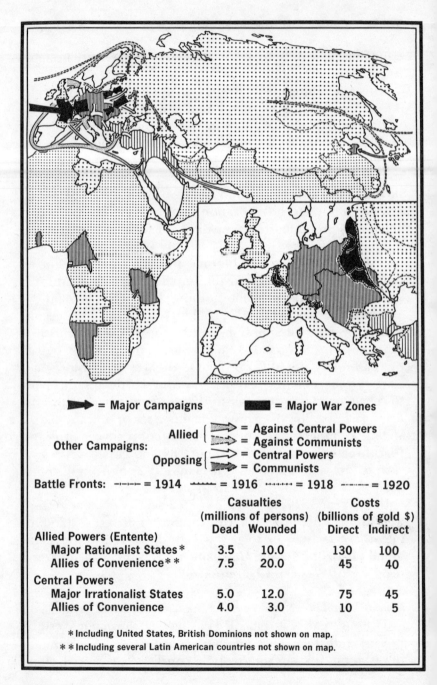

= Major Campaigns   **= Major War Zones**

Other Campaigns:
   Allied { = Against Central Powers
           = Against Communists
   Opposing { = Central Powers
           = Communists

Battle Fronts: —·—·— = 1914   —·—·— = 1916   ·········· = 1918   ------- = 1920

	Casualties (millions of persons)		Costs (billions of gold $)	
	Dead	Wounded	Direct	Indirect
Allied Powers (Entente)				
Major Rationalist States*	3.5	10.0	130	100
Allies of Convenience**	7.5	20.0	45	40
Central Powers				
Major Irrationalist States	5.0	12.0	75	45
Allies of Convenience	4.0	3.0	10	5

*Including United States, British Dominions not shown on map.

**Including several Latin American countries not shown on map.

Map 19. The First World War and Its Aftermath

mous casualties and destruction of property among nearly all the participants. Still worse, it resulted neither in the establishment of Germanic hegemony in the West nor in the decisive frustration of such ambitions. Instead, it culminated in military victory for the rationalists in western Europe and in social revolution everywhere east of the Rhine, a combination of circumstances that engendered an uncertain peace in the West; widespread civil war, chaos, and famine throughout much of central and eastern Europe; and a postwar era of continued political instability and stagnated civilized development everywhere in the Western world except in America. Indeed, the one definitive and positive result of the war and its revolutionary aftermath was the permanent destruction or nullification of all the national monarchies in Europe, the self-same regimes that initiated the conflict to further their own special interests.

That suicidal act was perpetrated in August 1914, on the pretext of avenging the assassination of the heir to Austria's throne. Seizing the opportunity thus presented them, Germany and Austria-Hungary hurled their armies against the potentially far more powerful Anglo-French-Russian alliance in the hope of quickly defeating it with a single stroke of overwhelming force.

The plan, devised years in advance, narrowly failed for want of steadfast execution and sufficient manpower; and by the end of 1914, after six months of heavy fighting, the Germanic onslaught had everywhere been stemmed. To be sure, the attackers remained in possession of large areas of France, Belgium, Russia, and the Balkans; and they had brought the Ottoman Empire into the war on their side (whereas Italy joined their enemies in 1915); but the conflict had been reduced to a stalemate, and this condition would ultimately prove fatal to the Germanic cause.

For the next three years, that stalemate persisted, on land in a bloody slaughter between huge entrenched armies, at sea in a blockade of central Europe countered by German submarine attacks on Anglo-French shipping, and in the home countries in an ever-widening struggle to mobilize all available resources in support of the armed conflict. During this harrowing period, the war degenerated into a contest of attrition and manufacture, each side seeking to wear the other down to defeat not by generalship or innovation but rather by maximizing the destruction of enemy resources and the utilization of friendly ones, by exhausting and outproducing the other side in lieu of being able to rout or to outmaneuver it.

This belated modernization of Western warfare was, of course, born of the prior modernization of Western Civilization. For example, the industrialization of the economy prompted the technical improvement and mass production of weapons; the reorientation of society on a popular basis led to the replacement of professional armies and navies by those based on popular levies; and the barbarization of politics made military practices increasingly ruthless. A multitude of such changes had been wrought during the nineteenth century, and their combined effects transformed the West's armed forces from the gun-armed Roman revivals of the Napoleonic wars into huge behemoths that were of such size, determination, and firepower by the turn of the century that they could scarcely be maintained, directed, or defeated.

Consequently, when in 1914 they were finally pitted against one another in earnest, the resultant struggle soon degenerated into a defensive war of position and attrition, into a contest not to capture territory or win victories as of old but rather to erode and grind down the opposing hosts by maximizing (or altogether avoiding) battlefield destruction and then achieving eventual preponderance via the more rapid replacement of casualties and materiel—a contest of prowess not in the use of arms but in the mobilization and disposition of manpower, productivity, and resources.

The cost of such a contest was enormous: nearly twenty million dead (including civilians), over forty million wounded, and almost $400 billion worth of goods and services con-

sumed, chiefly by useless destruction (see map 19). Furthermore, it was a cost well in excess of the West's ability to pay it
from current revenues, resulting in a severe (if temporary)
check to the region's population growth, substantial inroads
upon its extant accumulation of wealth, and heavy borrowing
against its future income. And in addition to these material
losses, incalculable damage was done intangibly to the fabric
of Western Civilization. Indeed, so gigantic were the war's
costs that only the fundamental nature of the real issue at
stake—the direction of further Western development—kept
the participants fighting once the true extent of those costs
began to be felt.

The weaker countries began to falter in 1916, and by early
the next year even the strongest had become uncertain of
their ability to continue the struggle much longer, their productive resources already strained to the limit and the morale
of their decimated armies about to fail. In France mutiny, in
Italy rout, in Austria desertion, and in Germany hunger, all
signaled imminent exhaustion. Only Britain, with its vast imperial resources, still remained reasonably strong. Then, almost simultaneously, Russia collapsed into social revolution,
quitting the anti-German coalition (in which, as a reactionary
regime of the worst kind, it had never really belonged any-
how); and the United States, aroused by the Germans' renewed submarine campaign and increasingly apparent overall intentions, stepped forward to join that same coalition in
Russia's place.

This abrupt substitution of the world's most advanced and
powerful democracy for its most backward and impotent autocracy in the ranks of the rational cause decided who would
win the war and fixed the character of its conclusion. For
although Russia's disintegration rendered the Germans temporarily victorious in eastern Europe, the enormous resources of the United States soon tipped the overall balance
against them in western Europe. Thus, the major fighting
ended late in 1918, once a sufficient weight of American

manpower and materiel had been brought to bear to enable the anti-German forces to mount an overpowering offensive on the western front.

But while this cessation brought the rationalists military victory, it did not bring the West peace. Throughout much of Europe, social revolution, often compounded by civil war and nationalistic schism, erupted in the wake of the armistice just as it had in Russia the year before. Efforts to contain or stifle it—including limited military intervention by the rationalist victors and the defeated Germans alike—were for the most part ineffective; and almost everywhere east of the Rhine, the old order of things was abruptly and finally destroyed during the strife-ridden months of 1919 and 1920. Once that had been accomplished, once the last of the national monarchies that had precipitated the cataclysm of world war had been destroyed, then peace was finally restored throughout the Western world.

The Russian Revolution

This destruction of the old order throughout eastern Europe was initiated and paced throughout by the violent revolution that racked Russia from 1917 to 1921. The same upheaval also breathed life into communism, the political-ideological movement that replaced dynastic monarchy in the east, immediately in Russia and eventually elsewhere in the region. In addition, it began the transformation of Russia into one of the most powerful nations in the contemporary era and started to entangle it, as the champion of communism, in the still unresolved struggle for mastery of the West's further development. Yet extensive and far-reaching as it proved, the Russian Revolution was born of the confluence around 1900 of two then relatively unimportant historical currents —Russian history and Marxism.

The former first became significant in relation to Western history as a whole when Russia emerged as a nation in the area between the Baltic Sea and the Ural Mountains at the beginning of the modern era. It was formed by the princes of Moscow's territorial-political consolidation of the region's many petty districts into a rude and ruthless dynastic state. In order to facilitate that consolidation and press ahead with the acquisition of territory until readily defensible natural frontiers were reached, these princes, who soon styled themselves tsar (from Caesar), shortly became absolute despots and subjugated all the inhabitants of their domain to perpetual state service, the masses by binding them to the land as serfs and the elite by making their station in life utterly dependent on the tsar's favor.

Russia remained in this condition of total enslavement and total autocracy almost to the end of the modern era. Meanwhile, it expanded to approximately its present size and developed into a major Western power, as a result not only of that expansion but also of rapid population growth and strenuous efforts to modernize its still medieval government and armed forces. Consequently, the tsarist autocracy was able to exert an increasingly decisive influence in Western affairs, never more so than during the period of the Democratic Revolution, when it played a leading role first in containing the revolution itself, then in defeating Napoleon, and finally in reviving the national monarchies and fostering obscurantism.

By the mid-nineteenth century, however, the Russian autocratic system began to break down, cracking under the strains imposed by quasi-modernization in some quarters, persisting backwardness in others (particularly agriculture), and too ambitious foreign policy. Shaken by military defeat at the hands of Britain and France in the Crimean War of the early 1850s, the tsarist regime reluctantly freed the serfs and initiated other sweeping reforms during the next decade in order to forestall its demise. The ploy succeeded; but from that point onward, revolutionary activity became increasingly endemic in Russia, a symptom of the autocracy's continuing disintegration. And half a century later, in 1917, that process reached its terminal climax when, strained beyond the breaking point by World War I, the tsarist government collapsed.

This debacle quickly resulted in Russia's total military defeat by the Germans, widespread cessation of economic activity, vehement popular demands for drastic reform, and hectic political activity on all sides. An ad hoc emergency government of liberals and socialists was set up in an attempt to apply rationalistic remedies that might save the situation; but after six turbulent months in office it had made little headway, leaving Russia still in dire straits, desperately in need of a new political order. The stage was set for the communists to make their entry and initiate the transformation of Russia and, eventually, eastern Europe as a whole.

The development of Russian communism, which, like that of Russian history, prefaced this transformation, began midway through the nineteenth century, when Karl Marx, the German founder of Marxism, first defined his doctrine. On the basis of his analysis of the early Industrial Revolution in western Europe, Marx contended that Western society was, and since the onset of civilization had been, organized fundamentally in terms of property ownership, giving those who owned the most property control of human affairs. They supposedly used such control to enrich themselves further by exploiting the multitude whose labor actually generated most wealth. The multitude in turn sought to prevent this, the effort resulting in perennial friction or class struggle between them and the property owners. And that struggle, Marx argued, would, in keeping with predetermined patterns of historical development, eventuate in the multitude's revolutionary upsurge and triumph, the subsequent abolition of property ownership, and the ensuing reconstruction of society along classless, utopian lines.

How all this was to be done Marx did not say; but, even without realistic tactics, his pseudorational gospel of inevitable popular ascendancy through victorious revolution exerted a considerable appeal. Cloaked in the guise of a historically revealed natural law of human development, it proved especially attractive to Russian conspirators because it promised to lend an air of certainty and reason to their desperate schemes to overthrow the tsarist autocracy. Consequently, during the last decades of the nineteenth century, after unsuccessful experimentation with native alternatives, many Russian revolutionaries embraced Marxism.

Having done so, they were then compelled to reinterpret the doctrine, based as it was on conditions in largely industrial western Europe, to suit conditions in largely agricultural Russia. The undertaking abruptly splintered the fledgling Russian Marxist movement into several factions, one of which—V. I. Lenin's Bolsheviks—eventually became the Russian communist party. The Bolshevik program was based on Lenin's argument that the advent of Western imperialism was what required a revised interpretation of Marxism to fit Russia. It did so, he contended, because, by giving the property owners of the industrial nations effective control of the more backward countries, like Russia, imperialism had so intensified the exploitation of the backward peoples as to shift the focus of the class struggle from western Europe to these same countries. This being the case, Russia became one of the most likely and proper places to begin the Marxist revolution; and the best way to do so, lacking guidance from Marx, was the way best suited to extant conditions in Russia. Consequently, Lenin felt that the formation of a conspiratorial Marxist faction, in keeping with Russia's tradition of revolutionary conspiracy, was the proper way to initiate such an upheaval; and it was therefore along these lines that he molded the Bolshevik splinter and developed it into the communist party—as a select, secret instrument for the seizure of power.

As a result, the Bolsheviks were one of the few political groups in Russia in 1917 prepared to vie for political predominance with determination and calculation. So when the provisional government had proven ineffective and began to totter, they exploited that advantage by seizing the shredded reigns of government and proclaiming a communist revolution in Russia.

Once at the helm, Lenin and his followers immediately set about mobilizing all available resources to cope with the diverse problems of German invasion, economic stagnation, social tumult, and political anarchy to which they had made themselves heir. Since this undertaking entailed simultaneously rebuilding Russia's armed forces, reviving its economy, quieting its popular unrest, and instituting a stable political order, they soon felt compelled to adopt ruthless and expedient measures in attempting to carry it out.

Institutionally, this resulted in the creation of a new communist regime in Russia very similar to the old tsarist autocracy, since the communists, lacking precise plans of their own, had little choice but to follow precedent and pattern the structure of their new order upon the old. And, however reluctantly, they did just that, establishing a political system in which the communist party had simply replaced the monarchy, leaving everything else relatively unchanged.

Likewise, lacking prior experience in government, they were forced to invoke the only tactics they knew—those of revolutionary conspiracy and stern party discipline—to run their administration. This resulted not in effective domestic government or foreign policy but rather in a reign of terror at home and a campaign of international revolution abroad, abruptly surrounding the communist regime with a miasma of authoritarian brutality and rapacious expansionism quite as bad as that which had clung to the tsarist autocracy.

Notwithstanding the desperate measures that produced that aura and gave their regime an autocratic structure and an incendiary reputation, the communists failed abysmally in their initial efforts to restore and reshape Russia along Marxist lines or to spread their revolution abroad. In spite of making mass arrests, wholesale imprisonment, and summary execution the order of the day at home; and in spite of making incessant propaganda, aid to foreign insurrectionaries, and implacable hostility to established governments abroad (whether obscurantist or rationalist) the order of the day in foreign relations, Lenin and his colleagues achieved almost none of their avowed objectives during their first months in power. A year after their takeover, they had succeeded only in completing the utter ruin of the Russian economy, in driving their domestic opponents into armed resistance, in losing control of all Russia save for the immediate environs of a few major cities, and in turning most Westerners, and most Russians, irrevocably against communism. As a result of their hopelessly inept misgovernment, Russia in the fall of 1918 lay torn by civil war, verging on the brink of famine, and threatening to disintegrate altogether as a nation.

Then World War I unexpectedly ended, transforming the situation. Victorious in western Europe, the rationalistic powers suddenly freed Russia of the Germans by compelling them to withdraw the bulk of their forces to their own borders; and in doing so, they saved the communists from a ruination of their own making. Overawed and distracted by a cohesive, million-man German-Austrian army occupying western Russia in mid-1918, Lenin's government by year's end confronted only a fragmented, largely irregular, counterrevolutionary force less than half that size—a decisively favorable shift in the balance of arms (courtesy of the exertions of Britain, France, and the United States) that gave the desperate communist regime just the degree of military advantage and freedom of action it required to save itself.

Quick to take advantage of this windfall, the communists exploited it sufficiently well during the next eighteen months to win the civil war within Russia and secure the nation's much-reduced borders against foreign invaders. This armed triumph, together with the corollary reenforcement of the administrative reign of terror initiated in 1917, also finally made good the communist regime's authority throughout

Russia, thereby assuring its survival in spite of its dismal failure to initiate domestic recovery or to provoke further upheaval abroad.

Once the communist revolution had thus been made viable, steps were taken to make it permanent and effective as well. The political situation, already stabilized by stringent terrorism, was ossified into a monolithic, one-party, Marxist-Leninist state, nominally based on rationalism and popular sovereignty but actually based on the ruthlessness and repression of a pseudorational authoritarian elite. The government likewise was solidified in the institutional image of tsarist autocracy as the Union of Soviet Socialist Republics or Soviet Union. The ruined economy, on the other hand, was revived and widespread famine ended by the drastic backward step of reestablishing private property and private enterprise (except in heavy industry). Likewise, Russia's restoration to the community of Western nations was secured by abandoning armed confrontation and stilling the call for communist revolution the world over. In short, the communists consolidated their narrow victory in Russia by consolidating their enforced hold on power and by reverting in virtually every other way to prerevolutionary modes of organization and behavior—by, in effect, substituting one-party Marxist-Leninist autocracy for one-man monarchist autocracy.

This substitution had been completed by 1923, signaling the end of the Russian Revolution. Having begun as an effort to destroy the old order and replace it with a communist utopia, and then having run its course by devastating Russia, that upheaval ended by institutionalizing one-party political absolutism there. Revolution against monarchist autocracy had succeeded only in transforming it into communist autocracy—in updating eastern European political-ideological irrationality so that, ere long, it would once again become a major participant in the onrunning struggle for control of Western Civilization's further development.

The Uncertain Peace

Meanwhile, for at least a decade after World War I, communism did not play a major role in Western history, pending Russia's full recovery. Instead, the victorious rationalistic powers of Britain, France, and the United States held the center of the stage. Preoccupied with the multitude of problems created by the war, their initial concern was the conclusion of a peace settlement, one that would confirm and uphold the apparent victory of transatlantic rationality over Germanic obscurantism. Unfortunately, such were the difficulties facing the victors immediately in the wake of victory that they could not, for all their good intentions, deliberations, and stern resolves at Paris in 1919, do more than conclude a peace that was at best uncertain.

The consequences of the war were simply too overwhelming to be adequately dealt with by fiat or accord. After four years of armed conflict, Europe, if not the West as a whole, was mauled and exhausted, its wealth greatly depleted, the flower of its young manhood dead or crippled, civilian morale utterly shattered, and the normal processes of civilized life everywhere disrupted. Indeed, such was the extent of the destruction and disruption that, in many quarters, the development of Western Civilization itself had come to a virtual standstill. In short, the victory won by rationalism had been so costly in life, wealth, and the substance of civilization generally as to prove almost wholly military in its effects.

The most immediately apparent result of this was rationalism's inability to extend its sphere eastward across the Rhine after the fighting ended. In spite of their revolutionary origins, none of the postwar governments formed in that quarter were truly rational. Instead, they ranged in character from the ersatz liberal democracies created in Germany, Austria, and Czechoslovakia through the conservative military-aristocratic dictatorships of Hungary and Poland to the one-party communist autocracy established in Russia. And all together they summed up to a new political order in central and eastern Europe hardly less irrational than the old prewar one had been.

Nor was the new political order established in western Europe and overseas by the major liberal democracies much of an improvement over the status quo ante. Outlined by the formal peace treaties they dictated and imposed at Paris, that order sought to guarantee and make meaningful the rational victory by punishing the vanquished, strengthening the victors, and recasting the system of international relations on rational principles. But from the outset it proved deficient, not only due to its inherent self-contradictions but also for want of determined support and implementation.

Indeed, the pivotal plan to rationalize international relations by the establishment of an international peace-keeping organization or League of Nations, largely the handiwork of the United States' wartime president, Woodrow Wilson, was doomed to failure even before the League was formed, Wilson having already lost the domestic political support he required to involve the United States in the scheme and so give it some prospect of success.

The more conventional plans to keep the defeated countries down and prop the victorious ones up were little more successful. To be sure, Germany and its wartime allies were disarmed, deprived of their colonies, reduced in size, and subjected to heavy bills for war damage. But before long their conquerors reduced their own armaments, fell to quarreling over the colonial spoils, permitted (in the name of national self-determination) the rise of hopelessly weak and selfish petty states in the European territories taken from the defeated countries, and lent funds to, rather than collecting anything from, those same countries. In short, having devised plans for the preservation of rationalism's hardwon victory and then having declined to implement them, the victorious liberal democracies created a postwar political situation in their sphere nearly as irrational as the one revolution and exhaustion had established in central and eastern Europe. By doing so, they only compounded the uncertainty of the peace settlement, leaving the contest for control of Western Civilization's further development still unsettled, and raising the specter of irrational resurgence and renewed world war.

Economic Recovery and Depression

For a time, that specter went unnoticed, overlooked in the midst of general preoccupation with the economic problems created throughout the West by the war. The most immediate of these, of course, arose from the enormous destruction wrought in much of Europe. In addition, the economies of all the combatants had to be restored to a peacetime basis and reintegrated into the global nexus of production and trade. Finally, efforts had to be made to restore significant economic growth so as to satisfy popular expectations of a better standard of living, expectations too long frustrated by wartime austerity. Consequently, national leaders in nearly all the major Western countries, victorious and defeated alike, addressed their principal attentions during the first postwar decade to the restoration of prewar economic conditions of wealth, prosperity, and growth. As the downfall of Rome had shown, the first prerequisite of a civilization's survival was material well-being among its people; and it was to this problem rather than to political affairs that the West wisely devoted most of its attention in seeking to recover from the catastrophe that had befallen it in 1914.

Nor was it a problem easily solved, for the inroads of four years of total war and several more of revolutionary strife were too severe to overcome easily. The runaway destruction of wealth had produced a grave shortage of capital for reconstruction; readjustment to peacetime conditions proved everywhere difficult; finance was thrown into confusion by the tangle of wartime loans, reparations, and subsequent de-

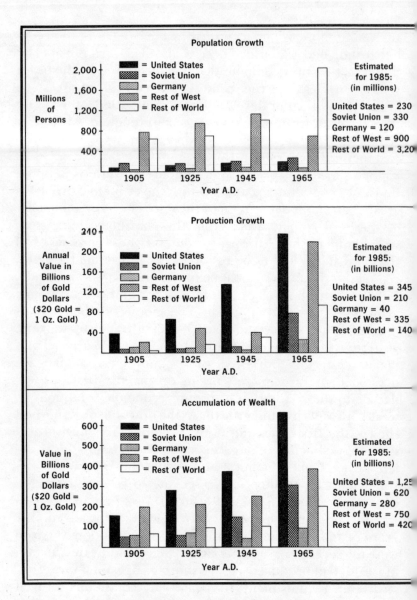

Fig. 19. Indexes of Development in the Contemporary World

faults on both; and a surprising dearth of further scientific and technical innovations hindered the further growth of industrial production.

Nonetheless, recovery of a sort was soon achieved simply on the basis of an almost automatic impetus toward recovery. By substituting credit for capital, by advertising heavily to stimulate demand and thereby revive production, by maintaining primary features of the wartime economy, such as standardization and assembly-line mass production, and by papering over financial chaos with new loans, currency adjustments, stock issues, and manipulations of every other sort, real economic activity was revived with surprising rapidity throughout the wartorn countries.

Once the destruction wrought during the war had been made good, the basis of such activity became the restoration and further elevation of popular living standards from depressed wartime levels. Combining prewar technology with postwar expediency, the Western economy proceeded to accomplish that restoration throughout the West in a few years' time, before the 1920s had run their course. Indeed, in the United States, living standards were advanced well beyond prewar levels, bringing electricity into the home, automobiles to the street, a varied diet to the table, popular entertainment to the senses, durable ready-made attire to the wardrobe, decent housing to the cities, and so on.

But such a promising preview of the future was only one more in the series of deceptions affiliated with economic recovery. For in spite of such promise and in spite of the lesser, more general gains actually made, the uncorrected difficulties left from the war began to make themselves felt before the end of the first postwar decade. On the one hand, production began to stagnate for lack of technological innovations and fresh markets; and on the other, the artificial supporting structure of ballyhoo and manipulation began to quake under the loads imposed by the slowdown. Consequently, by 1929 harsh remedies were in order if the still grossly maladjusted Western economy was to remain functional.

Such remedies were not forthcoming, chiefly because not enough people in positions of responsibility called for them; because not enough people wished to believe the economic recovery was in jeopardy; and because not enough people any longer possessed faith in man's ability to determine his own destiny. The profound psychological shock of the war persisted throughout the Western world, accelerating the prewar drift away from rationality and fostering an attitude of materialistic fatalism, ennui, and irresponsibility. Disillusioned with the very premises of civilization by the enormous, seemingly futile destruction of lives and property from 1914 to 1920, most Westerners a decade later still lingered in a shroud-like malaise that all but obscured the tenets of rationality from view and precluded sensible action to save the economic situation. Just beneath the surface of events a miasma of negativism and irrationality lurked, waiting for an opportunity to surface.

Consequently, in the fall of 1929, when the pace-setting American economic boom suddenly ran hard aground on the shoals of overproduction, overextension, and overspeculation, the entire Western economy (excepting its puny Russian branch) reacted by plunging headlong into psychologically induced economic depression, to depths never before plumbed. Following the American lead, Europe's financial exchanges experienced appalling reverses, factories closed, unemployment spiraled, production slowed, and living standards commenced to recede. By 1933 output in the West as a whole had declined to 80 percent of that in 1929; the postwar economic recovery's gains had been swept away; and the last bastion of rationalism—economic progress—had been thoroughly discredited. The way was open for an active resurgence of antirational forces; and, with the ruins of their efforts to stage a rational recovery by economic means spread before them, many Westerners took that way.

Totalitarianism

The abrupt, depression-induced revival of irrationality as a major force in Western life manifested itself principally in the guise of totalitarianism, the same system of absolute, terror-enabled, one-party political predominance that postwar revolutions against the old order had already established in Russia (under communism) and in Italy (under Fascism). Evidently, then, this new mode of irrational organization was at bottom not a revival of the obscurantist system developed within the national monarchies during the nineteenth century, but rather a revolutionary reformulation of the ingredients of modern barbarism to create a more effective contemporary successor to obscurantism—a reformulation calculated to supply irrational solutions to the same postwar problems, particularly economic ones, that rationalism had been unable to solve.

Hence, the advent of a whole range of totalitarian regimes during the 1920s and 1930s, varying in degree and kind from the United States' mild, liberal-democratic New Deal through Italy's *opéra bouffe*, neomonarchic Fascism to Germany's insane, racist-militarist Nazism and Russia's ruthless, communist Stalinism. Hence, too, the advent to power of all these regimes legally, without benefit of open revolution, the more benign governments preceding them (everywhere but in Russia) having failed to cope with postwar problems and therefore abdicating to extremism without a struggle.

Indeed, the principal trait that all the totalitarian regimes shared in common was their determination to resolve the problems exacerbated or created by World War I, which had undone their predecessors in office. This they proposed to do via the more total, more national, more mass-oriented, more intense organization of Western life. Under each of them,

nationalism was accentuated, and government was endowed
with far more comprehensive powers, especially economic
ones. Likewise, the economy was consolidated even further
(often via nationalization of key production facilities), rendered more self-sufficient, and revived, usually by fostering
intensified industrialization and initiating rearmament. And
the populace was subjected to a whole host of new regulations,
pressures, and manipulations. As a result, everywhere totalitarianism was adopted, fewer men came to exercise
greater—but not necessarily more expert—control over
human endeavor and human institutions; national self-
interest became increasingly predominant; and existence was
made more uniform for the mass of men than it had ever been
before. Such were the consequences of the extreme measures.
to which the various totalitarian regimes all resorted in seeking to dispose of World War I's heritage, the characteristics
they shared in common.

What distinguished them from one another was the degree
to which they manifested these same common characteristics;
this in turn largely depended on the manner in which their
creators interpreted the postwar dilemma. On the one hand,
the leaders of the American New Deal, accepting the situation
at face value as an economic crisis, regarded their task to be
that of overcoming economic depression without disrupting
the United States' traditional liberal-democratic institutions
and habits; and so they undertook to carry it out simply by
better organizing the economy under closer government
supervision. But on the opposite hand, both the Stalinists in
Russia and the Nazis in Germany, their perceptions blurred
by irrational ideology, imagined that postwar conditions provided them an opportunity, perhaps even a mandate, to undertake grandiose missions of comprehensive, radical change
in every sphere of human endeavor; and once in power they
immediately began to do so by means so drastic and bloody as
to be without precedent.

The Russians, under the dictatorship of Lenin's successor,

Joseph Stalin, long-time communist, onetime bank robber, and perennial archconspirator, had the less lunatic of the two major totalitarian programs of this sort. Its principal objectives were to secure communism in Russia and to secure Russia in the international arena by making the Soviet Union economically—and thereby militarily—self-sufficient on a contemporary industrial basis. These were by no means very limited aims, given the continental dimensions of Russia and the international revolutionary aspirations of communism, but they were nonetheless essentially defensive and essentially rational. What was irrational about the Russian program was the systematic, ruthless, wholesale reliance—much intensified after 1928 when Stalin came to power—upon political repression, police terror, and the extermination or enslavement of proscribed socioeconomic classes to put it into effect. Likewise, the resumption of forceful efforts to eliminate private property, create a classless society, enhance the predominance of the communist party, and foster international revolution contributed to the same grim coloration, rendering Russian Stalinism on balance even more irrational than either Leninism or tsarism had been.

Yet it was certainly less irrational than German Nazism, the other major form of extreme totalitarianism. The principal objective of Nazism was to assert Germanic supremacy in the West, not merely in terms of politics and ideology, but also in terms of race. Indeed, racism was the fundamental cornerstone of Nazism. One of nineteenth-century obscurantism's least noticed but most lunatic formulations, it was based on the atavistic notion that those directly descended from the barbarian Germans were inherently superior in all things to other men, particularly men of obviously non-Germanic origin (Negroes and Orientals) or culture (Jews and Slavs). And as such it provided Germans in the wake of World War I with an excuse to resume their just-defeated quest for predominance. It offered them bogus scientific proof that they ought to predominate (blood and soil—ancestry and place of origin

—having made them superior it was natural that they should); and by doing so, it also seemed to justify whatever measures they might have to take—even another great war—to establish such predominance. In short, racism provided the Germans with a perfect excuse for persisting in their irrational endeavor to seize control of the West; and the Nazis accordingly made it the basis of their totalitarian program for Germany.

Led by Adolph Hitler, a crazed, cunning, rabble-rousing megalomaniac, they preached racism, regimentation, and rearmament as the pathway to the assertion of Germanic supremacy in Europe and eventually throughout the world. More specifically, Hitler and his cohorts proposed to overthrow the peace settlement halfheartedly imposed by the rational countries and establish in its stead a new order based on Germanic predominance and rampant irrationality: an order to be created and maintained not only by the tactics of one-party rule, political repression, police terror, and the extermination or enslavement of proscribed groups already being used in Soviet Russia, but also by those of territorial conquest, general reversion to barbarism, and the untrammeled leadership of a self-anointed gutter elite.

Therefore, when in 1933 the Germans accepted Hitler as their chancellor and permitted him to begin establishing a new regime, ostensibly to overcome economic depression, they were in fact endorsing the creation of the Nazi new order. Given Hitler's often avowed intention of carrying out the Nazi program in the shortest possible time by whatever expedients he deemed necessary—whether political intrigue, diplomatic blackmail, or total war—the meaning of his election became evident. By allowing him to accede to power, the Germans were embarking on nothing less than a renewed effort akin to that which had failed in World War I, an effort to give Western Civilization an irrational direction. With the position of the victorious liberal democracies severely undercut by economic depression and moral lassitude, and with totalitarian methods of organization coming into increasingly widespread use, the Germans opted to try again to seize control of Western development by applying totalitarianism on behalf of irrational predominance. And by doing so, they made another world war—a second phase in the twentieth-century Germanic regression, likely to be even more terrible in its effects than the first—all but inevitable.

World War II

The global conflict precipitated by the Germans in their renewed attempt to assert their supremacy in the West began in 1939 and raged until 1945. It pitted the forces of fascism against those of liberal democracy and communism in a ruthless struggle to control the further direction of Western Civilization; and it was, even more than World War I, a total war for that ultimate objective. It resulted in the equally total frustration of fascist ambitions via the complete defeat and occupation of Germany and Italy by the armed forces of the Soviet Union, the British Empire, and the United States; and of Japan by the latter two powers and China. Like World War I, however, World War II did not eventuate in the clear-cut triumph of rationality and thereby settle the issue of Western mastery even temporarily. Instead, in the course of the conflict, the Soviet Union established a hegemony over most of the Eurasian land mass, and Anglo-America over most of the remainder of the globe, leaving the world still divided into two basically hostile political-ideological camps when the fighting ended in 1945. Thus, the net effect of the conflict (again like its predecessor) was not one of resolution but rather of destruction—not merely of fascism and would-be Germanic ascendancy but also of millions of lives, great wealth, and much of Western mankind's surviving faith in rationality as a successful mode of civilized endeavor.

The fighting that produced these results began in the fall of 1939 in Europe (in 1937 in China), when, after a year of diplomatic maneuvering and crisis, the Germans and Rus-

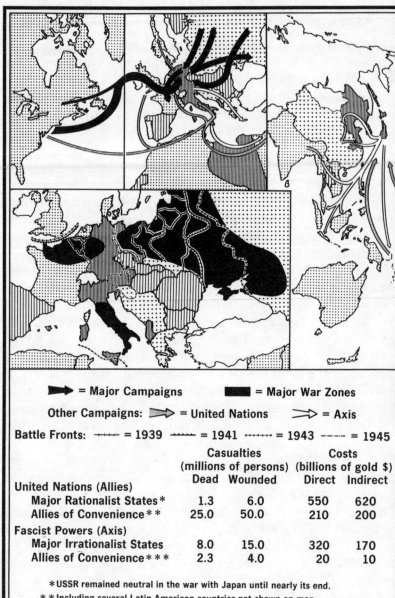

	Casualties (millions of persons)		Costs (billions of gold $)	
	Dead	**Wounded**	**Direct**	**Indirect**
United Nations (Allies)				
Major Rationalist States *	1.3	6.0	550	620
Allies of Convenience **	25.0	50.0	210	200
Fascist Powers (Axis)				
Major Irrationalist States	8.0	15.0	320	170
Allies of Convenience ***	2.3	4.0	20	10

*USSR remained neutral in the war with Japan until nearly its end.

**Including several Latin American countries not shown on map.

***Excluding Spain, a nonbelligerent, and Czechoslovakia, an unwilling satellite.

Map 20. The Second World War

sians concluded an alliance and consummated it by overrunning Poland. Britain and France declared war on Germany for this and contemplated war with Russia; but militarily they did almost nothing, hesitating to renew the holocaust of World War I. The resultant lull was abruptly ended the following spring by the lightning Nazi conquest of Denmark, Norway, Belgium, the Netherlands, and France. Its principal ally thus eliminated and the United States continuing to remain neutral, Britain, in its "finest hour," stood alone in defense of the flagging rational cause for the ensuing year.

Meanwhile, the Soviet Union persisted in its unsavory alliance with Germany. Then, in mid-1941, the Nazis, frustrated in the west by their inability to span the English Channel in the face of strong British naval and aerial resistance, turned to the east and hurled their forces against the Russians just as they had done in 1917, in an all-out effort to knock them out of the war. The stroke failed—like the German invasion of France in 1914—for want of sufficient manpower and determination of execution. But by bringing the bulk of the German and Russian armed forces into conflict, it escalated the conflict in Europe to a truly massive scale; and thereafter it assumed the ruthless, total character that had typified World War I almost from the outset, a tendency only reinforced by the United States' entry into the war at the end of 1941 under the spur of Japanese attacks on American, British, and Dutch colonial possessions in the Orient.

However, as it became total in mass and scope, World War II also became increasingly mobile—an ever more gigantic but also more mechanized, three-dimensional clash of armed vehicles on land, at sea, and in the air, which simply could not degenerate into a stalemate of attrition as had World War I. To be sure, as this new style of warfare between men encased in self-propelled weapons intensified, as the number of tanks, ships, and planes mounted into the tens of thousands, so did the resultant destruction of manpower, machinery, and materiel. Yet this destruction produced not only enormous demands upon the technological, manufacturing, and demographic resources of the combatant countries, but also decisive strategic results on the field of battle.

Consequently, the Germans and their allies, who were not long able to meet the demands generated by mechanized total war (in spite of having pioneered its successful application from 1939 to 1941), began failing to achieve their strategic objectives midway through the conflict. This first became apparent in the latter half of 1942, when the Russians stopped Hitler's armies short of the Caucasus oil fields, the British stopped a German-Italian force short of the Suez Canal, the Americans stopped the Japanese short of Australia, and the British and Chinese stopped them short of India.

Thereafter, the fascist armed forces were everywhere on the defensive, everywhere in retreat, everywhere less and less capable of waging a total war of both attrition and mobility. Their final defeat began in Europe during the latter half of 1944 and the first months of 1945, when simultaneous Anglo-American and Soviet offensives drove the German armies out of their conquests, encircled them in Germany, and then closed together to obliterate them and the Nazi regime they served. In Asia, while Anglo-American forces in Burma and Chinese forces in China were defeating the main strength of the Japanese army, an American amphibious drive was made across the Pacific to the threshold of Japan itself, destroying the Japanese navy and air force, bringing the nation itself under heavy aerial attack, and in mid-1945, when two atomic bombs were employed in that attack, producing a final surrender.

The Second World War was over, having caused the death of over 35 million people, the wounding of another 75 million, and the expenditure of over $2,000 billion (see map 20)—this havoc and waste wrought not only across the entire length of Europe but also in North Africa and much of East Asia, to say nothing of the oceans of the world. And, as in World War I, such costs far exceeded either the West's or the entire world's ability to pay them readily out of current fecundity or commodity production, once again resulting in retardation of population growth, erosion of accumulated wealth, and monumental expansion of indebtedness.

Because of the increase in population, production, and wealth between the wars, however, the burden of such costs was no more severe than it had been a quarter century earlier—perhaps even less so. The mechanization of warfare had increased its total but not its per capita costs. It may well have been on the verge of doing so during the last months of fighting, as frightful new weapons of mass destruction such as the German ballistic missile and the Anglo-American atomic bomb were brought into play, and as the Nazis frenetically endeavored to devastate the regions from which they were being expelled and to slaughter millions of the noncombatant residents thereof, but the end of the war fortunately came soon enough to prevent the further development of these dreadful new tendencies.

Unfortunately, aside from curtailing these hyperdestructive lunacies and obliterating the fascist regimes largely responsible for them and for the onset of the war itself, the conflict achieved very little. At the end of it, not only the West but the world as a whole remained divided into opposing political-ideological camps and plagued by difficulties of every sort. The forces of a battered but still formidable Soviet Union stood in control of Russia and eastern Europe; rival nationalist and communist factions vied for mastery in China; and the war-born Anglo-American alliance held sway in the rest of the world—a sphere beset in its war-torn European sector by desperate economic shortages and social disruptions (as was the battle-scarred portion of the Soviet sphere), and in its Afro-Asian sector by anti-Western, anticolonial, nationalist unrest tending toward revolution. Within their own borders, the victorious rational countries faced similar, only slightly less pressing problems of economic instability, democratic and equalitarian stagnation, and insidious totalitarianism. In short, having won through to military victory, the Anglo-American countries confronted not the vistas of peace but of continued struggle to cope with a host of monumental difficulties, some of them almost global in scale, others entirely domestic, difficulties that threatened to disrupt and destroy Western Civilization quite as thoroughly as had the twice-defeated irrational onslaughts of Germany.

Consequently, while the Germans had finally been rebuffed before the middle of the twentieth century in their bid to seize control of further Western development, the tendencies they had set in motion remained to be combatted and the damage they had done still awaited repair. They had done their work of disruption well; and after 1945, in the second postwar era of the century, the rational countries—especially the United States, by far the most powerful of their number—would be preoccupied with undoing it, with trying to remedy by rational means the gross, civilization-wide damage done to virtually every phase of Western life by the second, contemporary Germanic regression and the two world wars that began and ended it.

CHAPTER 16

The American Hegemony, A.D. 1945-1960

The Consequences of World War II

The conflict that raged from 1939 to 1945 was the second politically motivated, materially devastating, socially disruptive total war to beset the Western world in less than half a century; and it was therefore followed, almost of necessity, by a widespread search for political security, economic recovery, and social stability. That search, which dominated the first two postwar decades, grew out of the war aims of the rationalist powers and was conducted principally by the foremost of their number, the United States. It led to the restoration of an order of things in the West based largely on the material strength (rather than the ideological tenets) of the liberal democracies, to a latter-day version of the mid-nineteenth-century rationalistic status quo sometimes known as the Pax Britannica—a mid-twentieth-century Pax Americana.

The immediate origins of this postwar American order were to be found in the war itself, notably in the crisis that rationalism faced in the summer of 1940. At that juncture, France having just been defeated and overrun by the Nazis, Britain was left alone to cope with the onslaught of irrational totalitarianism in Europe. Bereft of its principal ally and most of its arms as well (lost in trying to defend that ally), the island kingdom's situation—and that of the rational cause it championed—was precarious, perhaps even desperate. Realizing this, Britain's leaders turned to the still neutral United States for material and moral support.

The United States responded positively to the British appeal, at first somewhat reluctantly but with steadily increasing vigor; and by doing so it committed itself to the destruction of latter-day irrationality and the restoration of rationality to a position of preeminence in the West. According to the terms of that commitment, as spelled out in the Atlantic Charter of 1941, this was to be accomplished principally by eliminating antagonism, discontent, and want, the supposed seedbeds of both fascism and communism, throughout not merely the West but the world as a whole, an extirpation to be effected largely by militarily obliterating fascism, politically reestablishing international peace, and economically restoring widespread material prosperity.

Collective action among as many nations as possible was regarded as the key to success in all these endeavors; and the means to facilitate such action—a unified rationalist military command, a political alliance of all the antifascist countries as the United Nations, and a program of mutual economic assistance or Lend-Lease among these same countries—were quickly developed under Anglo-American leadership to serve as cornerstones of the rationalist program. In this manner, the combined armed forces of the unconquered liberal democracies were soon concerted against those of fascism; the economic resources of all the antifascist countries, particularly those of the United States, were likewise swiftly brought to bear; and those same countries' political aims and actions were sufficiently harmonized to outline the terms of peace and sketch the character of the postwar world.

The United States, as the most powerful rationalist country, naturally played a major role in all of these undertakings, dictating basic rationalist military strategy, contributing most of the aid (about $45 billion worth) supplied under Lend-Lease, and wielding a predominant influence in forming the United Nations and defining its objectives. As the war ground toward its conclusion, devouring Europe's dwindling resources and devastating ever more of its territory, the American role became steadily more pronounced until in 1945, when the fighting finally ended, it had become virtually predominant in world affairs.

Indeed, of all the other major prewar powers only Britain, thanks to its insularity, and the Soviet Union, thanks to its size, remained viable national entities at war's end; and even they had to strain every available resource to do so, depriving them of any reserve strength with which to assist their less fortunate counterparts. The remainder of Europe lay prostrate, virtually the entire civilized structure its inhabitants had labored so long and arduously to raise up reduced to a shambles. Throughout large areas from eastern France to western Russia, government had simply ceased to exist and the industrial mainstay of economic life had languished (see fig. 19). In these regions, hordes of people found themselves unable to obtain the basic necessities of food and shelter; and in the struggle to do so they began to lapse into the throes of anarchy and barbarism, abandoning the fundamental tenets of Western Civilization in order to survive.

Given this desperate state of affairs and the impotence of the major European countries, the United States was all but compelled to persist in the extension of its power during the postwar era. In other words, the enormous damage wrought by World War II in Europe virtually necessitated its continuing to exercise, perhaps even expand, the predominance it

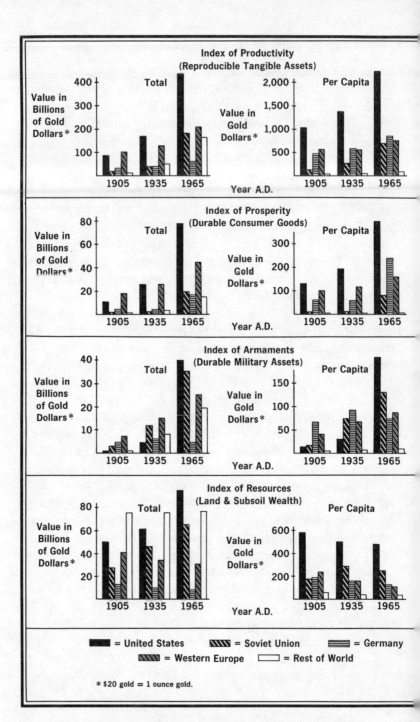

Fig. 20. American Hegemony in the Contemporary World

had established during the conflict. If the shredded fabric of Western Civilization was to be mended, the one country in 1945 still possessed of sufficient resources and willpower to cope with the war's dreadful consequences would have to undertake the task alone and unhindered.

Recognizing this fact, albeit imperfectly and somewhat belatedly, the Americans grudgingly accepted the responsibility thrust upon them by circumstances. Emerging from the war stronger than ever and brimming with confidence in themselves and their way of life, they agreed to continue making heavy economic, political, and military commitments abroad in order to fulfill the Anglo-American program settled upon back in 1940. By doing so, they not only undertook to effect the postwar recovery of the West but also rationalism's simultaneous revival—under American auspices—to a position of Western-wide hegemony.

European Economic Recovery and Political Decline

The initial thrust of this grandiose American effort was economic rather than political; and it took the form of an extensive foreign aid program akin to wartime Lend-Lease. In the first five years after the fighting stopped, the United States gave away more than $25 billion in this fashion, most of which went to sustain and rebuild western Europe. Similar assistance was offered to eastern Europe, but the countries in the area were prevented from accepting it by the Soviet Union, which feared the intrusion of American influence into its newly established sphere.

Where the aid was accepted, recovery to prewar levels was generally well under way by 1950; and during the next five years it was spurred to completion by the American-inspired rearmament and economic integration of western Europe. In eastern Europe, the onset of recovery was slower, for lack of Russian assistance similar to that proffered by America; but once begun, economic revival there was swifter and even more extensive relative to prewar conditions than in the west.

On the whole, material recovery from the ravages of the war was remarkable, if not phenomenal, throughout the Western world. By 1955, the devastated industrial heartland of Europe had been restored to full production and prosperity. As a result of the large-scale infusion of American aid, rearmament at American behest, and the energy of the Europeans themselves, the terrible material damage done to their homeland during World War II had been completely repaired in only a decade, ushering in a new era of mass material well-being in the West—all in all, a noteworthy demonstration of the industrial economic system's powers of recuperation (see figs. 14-19).

But no such demonstration was forthcoming in the postwar political realm. Surprisingly, the recovery of economic vitality was not paralleled by a like recovery of political influence. Instead, Europe's war-shattered international political power declined even further in the wake of the conflict. Exhausted by a generation of strife, the European countries after 1945 possessed neither the strength nor the desire to reassert their influence on the international scene successfully. Spent not only physically but psychologically as well, they simply were no longer up to playing a global role or trying to fix the direction of further Western development.

In addition, the course of contemporary events—especially the world wars and the rise of totalitarianism—had so magnified the scale and intensity of political strife by 1945 as to render obsolete the old-fashioned national state, the West's principal mode of political organization during the preceding modern era, as a vehicle for influencing international affairs. By the end of World War II, European countries like Britain and France no longer were large enough or their empires cohesive enough to compete successfully with the far bigger, far more consolidated continental countries like the United States and the Soviet Union, which had by then grown to maturity in certain areas of European settlement.

Consequently, the first postwar decade witnessed the

paradoxical spectacle of a swift and remarkable recovery of European economic strength paralleled by an abrupt and unceremonious termination of European global political predominance. American aid sufficed to initiate the region's economic restoration, but nothing could be done to initiate its political restoration, leaving the field of international relations to the United States and the Soviet Union.

The Cold War

The so-called cold war resulted; pitting a communist bloc of states dominated by the Soviet Union against a liberal-democratic bloc dominated by the United States in an openly hostile but rigorously restrained continuance of the struggle for political supremacy between rationalism and irrationalism.

This sequel to the political mortification of Europe first began to develop in earnest at the outset of World War II, when the Soviet Union allied itself with the Nazis against Britain and France. To be sure, when Hitler's armies invaded Russia in 1941, the communists frantically sought—and easily obtained—an alliance of convenience with the rationalist camp; but this did nothing to alter their fundamental opposition to it. Not unexpectedly, therefore, the Soviet Union soon reverted to a posture of open antagonism toward its nominal allies once Germany had been defeated.

This renewed animus manifested itself in widespread efforts to expand the communist sphere by exploiting Soviet military strength and postwar chaos. In eastern Europe, communist regimes were everywhere established under the protection, real or implicit, of Soviet occupation forces. In western Europe and the Near East, extant communist movements were encouraged to vie for political control. And in Asia, clandestine support was provided to foster armed communist uprisings. In short, no sooner had the German-led fascists been defeated in their attempt to wrest control of Western Civilization from the liberal democracies than the

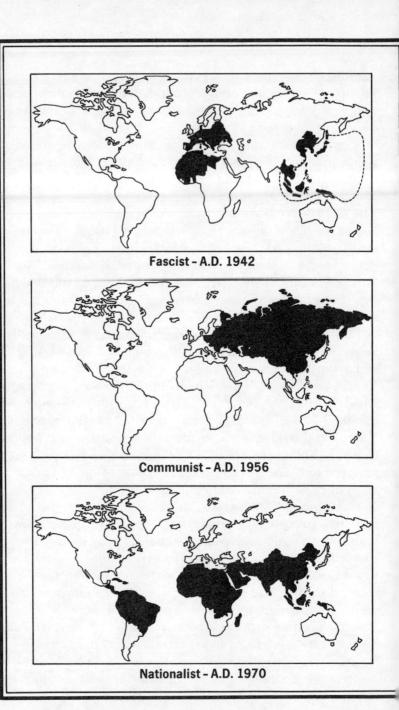

Fascist – A.D. 1942

Communist – A.D. 1956

Nationalist – A.D. 1970

Map 21. Challenges to Rationalism's Contemporary Hegemony

Russian-led communists appeared to be initiating another such attempt in the guise of an unconventional struggle to undermine, intimidate, and overthrow the rational political order without recourse to another major war.

The initial American response to this undertaking was nugatory; but by the winter of 1947-1948, after an interlude of self-delusion and disarmament, more decisive measures were hurriedly adopted to cope with the deteriorating international situation, particularly in Europe, and to force the communists back from what seemed the verge of sweeping success.

Simultaneously, the Americans increased their foreign aid, began to rearm, and initiated a political reorganization of the rationalist camp. The flow of economic assistance, primarily to western Europe, was increased to hasten the elimination of material shortcomings, thought to be one of the most fertile seedbeds of communist revolution. Rearmament was begun to enable the establishment of a far-flung military force capable of encircling the Soviet Union and frustrating its apparent expansionist tendencies. And political reorganization was initiated—in the form of a series of anti-Soviet alliances—to firm up rationalism's resistance and to coordinate its economic and military resurgence.

The expectation was that this combination of measures would soon not only frustrate communism's current endeavors but also dampen its avowed ambitions, thereby containing postwar irrationality within the boundaries it had already attained, and making possible the indefinite preservation of a rationalist-dominated status quo elsewhere in the world. In other words, the plan was to envelop the Soviet sphere with American-enabled prosperity, American-led armed forces, and American-inspired alliances, and thus prevent its further expansion without recourse to open warfare.

The plan worked in the Western world proper, but not elsewhere, certainly not in Asia. As an increasing number of American forces—both conventional and nuclear-armed

—were deployed, as the United States' many new allies were rearmed, as their economic recovery became assured, and as the rationalist countries began to make common cause through a host of new political and economic organizations such as the European Economic Community (Common Market) and the North Atlantic Treaty Organization (NATO), the communist sphere ceased to expand in the West, but not in the Far East. There, in 1949, China succumbed to communist revolution in spite of substantial American aid to the anticommunists; in 1950, Russian-backed North Korean troops invaded South Korea in spite of the presence of American armed forces there; and in 1954, communist insurgents took over North Vietnam by defeating American-supported French forces, presaging their kindred efforts to seize all of Indochina a decade later.

In sum, where memories of the destruction wrought by conventional warfare were still vivid, where the devastation likely to be wrought by nuclear warfare was clearly unacceptable, where postwar economic recovery was both dramatic and extensive, and where accompanying political and economic reorganization was meaningful, American countermeasures against communism quickly proved effective. But where calamities more destructive than conventional warfare—that is, epidemic and famine—were commonplace, where nuclear attack probably would not wreak prohibitive damage for want of vital urban and industrial targets, where poverty remained the economic norm in the postwar period, and where no significant degree of political or economic reorganization was sponsored by the rationalists after 1945, the tactics which were so successful in dealing with communism in the West proved deficient.

The United States initially responded to this deficiency (in the case of China) by simply letting events take their course and then endeavoring to contain the new communist regime that resulted—gigantic as it was—in the same manner as the

Soviet Union was being contained. American leaders decided that they could do little else in the face of so enormous and profound an upheaval so long in the making (since the early 1920s). But such a passive policy clearly would not suffice should communism attempt further expansion in Asia; and so, when it did, in Korea the year after China's conquest, the United States took advantage of more favorable circumstances to respond more vigorously. The form of response it chose, and thereafter made the cornerstone of its resistance to communism everywhere in the non-Western world, was simply to meet force with force—to counter the invasion from the north (and subsequent Chinese intervention) with sufficient conventional military might to produce an armed stalemate based on the preinvasion status quo.

The ploy worked, first in Korea and then elsewhere, stemming the spread of communism in the Orient for the next decade; and by doing so it made American foreign policy global and rationalism's sway secure, tacitly fulfilling the United States' primary postwar political objective. In other words, by stalemating the communists militarily in the non-Western world, just as they had stalemated them in the West by other means, the Americans made containment—whether by deterrence, economic improvement, or force of arms—the cornerstone of a globally effective anticommunist policy, a policy affirming liberal democratic rationality's determination to oppose and check communist irrationality the world over, just as it had fascist irrationality. And that affirmation, together with the mobilization of American might in support of it, confirmed the wartime reestablishment of rationalism's international political hegemony.

Evidently, then, the political collapse of Europe and the ensuing cold war did not result in the sudden triumph of communist irrationality, but rather in the restoration, under liberal democratic rationality's auspices, of a semblance of international political order. The Soviet Union's continuation of the irrational effort to capture control of Western development after 1945 served not to produce another bout of total war (as well it might have), but rather limited, yet decisive counteraction by the United States, counteraction that by the mid-1950s had stalemated the international political struggle in rationalism's favor and expanded the Pax Americana into a worldwide phenomenon.

The Systematic Revolution

Postwar developments outside the ideological-political sphere per se also contributed to the affirmation of rationalism's predominance under American auspices: in part by supplying the physical resources that enabled the restoration of western Europe and the successful waging of the cold war, and in part by shifting the emphasis of further rational achievement from politics back to economics. The most important of these developments were those that continued and accelerated the material transformation of Western life begun by the Industrial Revolution; this sequence of changes increased the pace of scientific discovery, technological development, and economic output to unprecedented levels simply by rendering them ever more rational, methodical, and systematic.

The United States, foremost among the latter-day rationalist countries, pioneered most of these changes during or just after World War II, and the resultant American experience was the harbinger of a fundamental Western-wide postindustrial upheaval—the Systematic Revolution—during the 1950s and 1960s. The primary ingredient in this revolution (as in the industrial one preceding it) was the more thorough application of reason, as revealed and elaborated by scientific discovery, to the basic processes of material life in the West, principally via the introduction of machine control or automation to regulate systematically the machine power adopted during the Industrial Revolution.

The foremost initial result of such automation was to improve the capabilities of the United States' economy in respect to other Western nations during the first decade after World War I so drastically as to give it undisputed preeminence and make the American life style it enabled the envy of all mankind (see figs. 19 & 20). Such preeminence and envy quickly prompted widespread emulation of the American system, thereby initiating the transformation of Western economic life as a whole—and, by indirection, of Western material life in its entirety—along similar lines after 1955.

The origins of this transformation, this Systematic Revolution, lay chiefly in the United States' essentially rational history of development, a history quite as much material as it was ideological. Like the origins of the Industrial Revolution in Britain, those of its successor in America were not simply the result of chance or circumstance but rather of generations of sustained effort by reasonable men to produce a more reasonable way of life.

The first major fruit of such effort in North America was the foundation of an eminently rationalistic federal republic, the United States, in the immediate aftermath of the American Revolution (1775-1783). Once established, the new nation underwent a half century of more or less unrestricted expansion in territory, population, and productivity. This expansion buttressed its material commitment to reason by increasing its physical strength, in accord with rationalistic precepts, to a par with the leading European countries and by preparing the way for even more rapid physical growth in years to come.

Before such growth could take place, however, the mounting ideological crisis induced by rapid postrevolutionary material expansion had to be resolved. The fundamental issue in that crisis was whether the country as a whole should persist in such expansion—whether it should continue to follow the northern states' lead in the direction of materialistic, liberal-democratic rationalism of the western European sort or veer off toward the kind of mythic, eastern European obscurantism that had begun to take root in the southern states. The question was settled abruptly, after decades of futile political compromise, by recourse to arms in the bloody, massive American Civil War from 1861 to 1865, a conflict won decisively by the northern United States.

Thereupon, the swift prewar pace of rationalistic development resumed, became increasingly materialistic, and carried the United States into a position of international economic leadership by 1900, a position based in part on the nation's renewed ideological dedication to reason, but even more so on the quantity of its productive output, the superiority of its manufacturing techniques, the efficiency of its organizational methods, and the discoveries of its scientific research.

Yet even after having reached this plateau of global material preeminence (and accompanying domestic prosperity), the Americans did not rest, particularly once they had been prompted to redouble their efforts at rationalistic economic development by the advent of World War I. Called upon to make a major economic contribution to the Allied war effort, they did so principally by mobilizing wholesale popular support—both within the labor force and among consumers—on behalf of such a contribution, and then utilizing that support to enable the intense concentration of American resources upon the provision of essential goods and services of ever more standard character in ever larger quantity.

Generally successful, this comprehensive program not only produced the required war materiel but also laid the basis for dramatic postwar increases in the United States' domestic prosperity and international power beyond prewar levels. For when continued at reduced intensity after the war, such promotion, concentration, standardization, and assembly-line mass production produced surprisingly good results in terms of peacetime economic growth. Indeed, by the end of the 1930s, notwithstanding the Great Depression, the continued development of the American economy along the lines first established in World War I had become the norm; and when further intensified by the onset of World War II, its relentless pace and impact began to initiate the Systematic Revolution in the United States (see figs. 19 & 20).

The advent of this latter-day upheaval was heralded by the further mechanization not only of the American economy but of American life as a whole, and by the accompanying deemphasis of liberal-democratic politics in favor of industrial economics as the focus of collective endeavor in the United States. New machinery of every kind was introduced throughout the American productive process during the early 1940s to provide more power and better control; and the additional output it generated sufficed not only to supply the United Nations' enormous wartime needs but also to meet the United States' own increasing requirements, both domestic and international.

Such stark material success, coming at a time when accustomed liberal-democratic political modes and methods were everywhere on the defensive, had a prodigious impact. In particular, it finally persuaded a great many Americans —most of them already half-persuaded by the United States' prior history of development—that industrialism rather than ideology was the key to the future. It convinced them that the United States and the rational cause it led could survive and prosper only by stimulating further scientific development and economic growth, that they could defeat the contemporary irrational bid for supremacy and reassert rational supremacy only by concentrating upon the further mastery of nature per se rather than of human nature.

Accordingly, once the wartime supermechanization of the American economy had begun to prove highly successful, its influence started to spread rapidly throughout the whole of American life. Increasing numbers of Americans embraced the tenets of automation and ultraindustrialism as their new credo and simultaneously forswore those of liberal democracy. And as they did, the United States became caught up in a sweeping, revolutionary transformation along materialistic, systematic lines.

The consequences of this upheaval began to manifest themselves fully during the first years of the postwar period. In the economic sector, systematization's onset was perhaps best characterized by the increasing integration of certain processes to improve the entire economy's performance markedly. Thus, as scientific research and technical innovation were more closely linked via management expertise to skilled fabrication and line assembly; and as the resultant products were more adeptly marketed by means of swifter transport, psychological advertising, and improved credit manipulation, the whole American system of production, distribution, and consumption flourished.

The specific evidence of this and of systematization's onset was to be seen in the outpouring of increasingly standardized goods from fewer production units. In particular, the deluge of increasingly standardized primary machines, such as vehicles, power tools, precision instruments, and regulatory devices, was symptomatic; for by enabling the easy, rapid overhaul and reequipment of the economy, it made the process of systematization all but self-sustaining.

In addition to such elemental machines, the latter-day transformation of the American economy also produced a host of mechanical conveniences for use by the general public. In fact, the proliferation of washers, refrigerators, telephones, radios, television sets, and, of course, automobiles was probably the most apparent consequence of the Systematic Revolution's advent in the United States. Equally significant but less noticeable than this flood of labor-saving, time-saving, and time-filling devices was the accompanying upsurge of such unprecedented mass services as credit buying, preventative medicine, audiovisual entertainment, and higher education. The supply and variety of staple consumer goods was also greatly increased.

But perhaps most important of all was the new American style of life that this deluge of goods and services hurriedly set about creating: a style of life based upon prodigious prosperity, unrestrained consumption, enormous waste, hectic speed, widespread leisure, increasing complexity, greater conformity, runaway organizational growth, accelerating scientific discovery, and moral-ideological atrophy. It was, in short, a life style determined by the mechanization of an entire people—by mass adoption of the bountiful machine as the cornerstone of civilized life.

Such were the short-term consequences of the Systematic Revolution's onset in the United States. Rapid further industrialization and the introduction of automation had combined with the nation's long prior history of rationalistic development to transform its economy into a veritable cornucopia. As a result of these changes, the United States was able to produce not only the extensive materiel required to prevail in World War II, maintain prosperity, and restore rationalism to a position of predominance in the postwar era, but also an excess sufficient to enrich the American people en masse. The British having devised the means by which Western man could master nature by pioneering mechanization, the Americans proceeded to apply them on behalf of Western mankind by pioneering methodization.

Thus, the American-led Systematic Revolution, like the British-led Industrial Revolution before it, was essentially a continuation of the West's revived development along rational lines; and as such, it proved decisive in preserving the rationalistic orientation of Western Civilization in the wake of the second Germanic regression. By placing increased reliance upon machine-powered, machine-controlled mastery of the physical world at the expense of ideology and politics, the Americans almost singlehandedly were able to resuscitate political security, economic prosperity, and social stability throughout much of the postwar world, particularly in the West. Having once discovered how to generate a surfeit of materiel, they were able to apply the fruits of their discovery, first to defeat the challenge of fascist irrationality, then to repair the destruction it had caused, and finally to cope with the challenge of communist irrationality. What is more, they enriched themselves en masse at the same time. In other words, by this combination of achievements, the mid-twentieth-century inhabitants of the United States continued the rational development, through material progress, of Western Civilization.

CHAPTER 17

LATTER-DAY UNREST, A.D. 1960-1970

The Emergence of the Underdeveloped Countries

Even as rationalism was being given a fresh lease on life by the American-led Systematic Revolution, a new conglomerate irrationality was beginning to coalesce in opposition to it. Based chiefly on the tenets of self-assertion, self-determination, and self-supervision, it sought to terminate the predominance of reason, curb material progress, and end the Pax Americana; and to make anarchy, existentialism, and nationalism preeminent in their stead. Consequently, as soon as it had attracted the support of large segments of the world's backward, poor, and disenchanted peoples, the rationalists were once again faced with a challenge; and not only the West but the world as a whole was plunged into the throes of renewed ideological-political strife (see map 21).

This latter-day resurgence of the contemporary crisis first

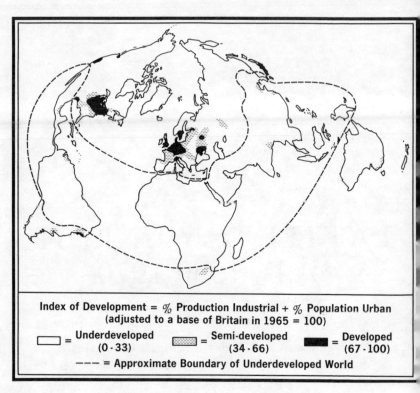

Index of Development = % Production Industrial + % Population Urban
(adjusted to a base of Britain in 1965 = 100)

☐ = Underdeveloped (0 - 33)   ▨ = Semi-developed (34 - 66)   ▧ = Developed (67 - 100)

--- = Approximate Boundary of Underdeveloped World

Map 22. Developed and Underdeveloped Regions
in the Postwar World

became apparent when non-Western nationalism emerged in
the economically underdeveloped portion of the world after
World War II. As it did so, it began to contest the hegemony of
Western imperialism there and expand the struggle for international political-ideological supremacy beyond the limits described by the cold war. Such nationalism manifested itself in
two principal forms, nativist and communist; and during the
first two postwar decades the former gave rise to the creation
of a whole battery of new countries in what had been the

European West's colonial sphere, while the latter prompted the recrudescence of China.

The new postcolonial states and the new China, as well as the new bifurcated, irrational order they formed together, were in large part the fruit of transplanted nineteenth-century Western obscurantism—in particular, of the concept of ethnic nationalism engrained in that ideology. This concept, like so much else in Western life, was introduced into Asia and Africa without conscious design by the imperialists of the late modern era; and ere long, the peoples of both continents began to call it their own. Gradually, they made its central notion—the right of national self-determination—the cornerstone of their increasingly antiimperial, anti-Western, antirational politics.

Thus, when Europe passed into political eclipse in the wake of World War II, national self-determination immediately became the dominant tenet in its restive overseas domain. This prompted, on one hand, the disintegration of the polyglot empires constituting that domain into a congeries of quarreling, clamorous, impoverished, pseudonational states; and, on the other, the reunification of China, fragmented by Occidental imperialism, into a giant among the underdeveloped countries.

Such an abrupt mid-century termination of the Western imperial status quo, established almost everywhere at the outset of the century, began with widespread popular resistance to continued European dominance. Where it was forcibly countered (as in French Indochina and the Dutch East Indies), such resistance quickly took the form of guerilla warfare. Just as quickly, it became apparent that this mode of conflict—pitting irregular, outnumbered, ill-armed native forces against well-armed contingents of European troops in insidious, drawn-out, military-psychological contests—was of a sort alien to latter-day Western experience. Consequently, in nearly every instance of anti-Western insurrection by such

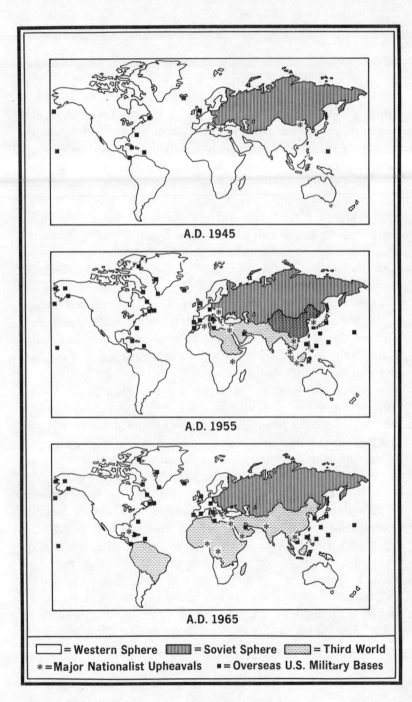

A.D. 1945

A.D. 1955

A.D. 1965

☐ = Western Sphere   ▦ = Soviet Sphere   ▨ = Third World
∗ = Major Nationalist Upheavals   ■ = Overseas U.S. Military Bases

Map 23. The Advent of the Third World

means, the native forces eventually won out, slowly wearing down their already debilitated opponents by means of sabotage, terror, infiltration, and other clandestine tactics until they prevailed by default.

But for the most part, the imperial powers, exhausted by World War II, did not oppose the anti-imperial upsurge by force of arms. Instead, they sought to cope with it by making piecemeal concessions and belated preparations for native self-government with one hand, and by trying to shore up their extant colonial regimes via administrative reform with the other. Later, as sufficient native antagonism surfaced and coalesced to override such token measures, the Europeans in most places simply permitted the old imperial order to give way. Pressed to get out, they usually did, often with almost humiliating haste.

In their wake, they left a collection of half-formed, half-functional native governments throughout Africa and southern Asia, a bloody civil war in China, and an all-pervading, now envious, now hateful attitude toward the West and things Western everywhere imperialism had intruded. In China, that attitude was shortly institutionalized in the state as the result of a communist triumph in the civil war, so much so that the new regime there soon proved to be more anti-Western in character—and more nationalistic—than Marxist, Leninist, or Stalinist. Elsewhere, the principal elements of the West's imperial heritage combined to produce a less vehemently anti-Western, but perhaps even more nationalistic, political order, which soon assumed the guise of a neutralist bloc (vis-à-vis the cold war). Together with China, the members of that bloc quickly came to compose a formidable third world of new, economically underdeveloped, politically bellicose Afro-Asian states. Individually bent on asserting their independence, these same states were also collectively determined to wrest control of global affairs from their former Western overlords—to substitute the hegemony of nationalistic irra-

tionality for that of liberal-democratic rationality, whatever
the means required to do so.

The Resurgence of the Contemporary Crisis

This upsurge of non-Western irrationality during the first
two postwar decades heralded the onset of a general revival of
unreason—and of the onrunning contemporary crisis of
Western Civilization—after 1960. For even as the rational-
irrational struggle was being expanded on the international
scene, from the dualism of the Soviet-American cold war to a
quadripartite contest also involving China and the Afro-Asian
bloc, so was it also being extended from the international to
the domestic arena by the rise of restive minorities within the
West. As this took place, the peoples of individual Western
countries, particularly the United States, were divided into
hostile, warring political factions similar to those that had so
long fragmented the community of nations; and the problem
of somehow mastering human nature as well as nature itself
was being mastered once again became preeminent in Western affairs.

The domestic unrest that helped produce this revival was
the result of a sudden proliferation of discontent among the
West's unassimilated peoples, that is, its nonwhites, its poor,
its young, and its disenchanted. Still debarred from full participation in Western life and denied its full benefits in the
wake of World War II, these minorities were incessantly bom-
barded by existentialist, nationalist, and anarchist propaganda demanding that they do something about it. Eventually, they responded by losing their patience and erupting in
strenuous protest during the 1960s.

Insisting that their unjust situation was a direct consequence of the unjust nature of the existing Western order or
so-called Establishment, they commenced to clamor and con-
spire for its complete transformation or overthrow, propos-
ing to establish in its place a new antiorder based on the

individual rather than society, on the tenets of selfhood rather than collectivity. To escape the manifest limitations Western law, community, and government imposed upon them, they sought to institute the imagined freedoms of anti-Western self-assertion, self-determination, and self-supervision. Seemingly unable to find contentment within the bounds of the postwar period's restored rationalistic status quo, they undertook to fragment it into an irrationalistic chaos.

That is, as the minorities of the West grew increasingly dissatisfied with peripheral prosperity and circumscribed citizenship in a time of burgeoning wealth and expanding civil liberty, they became steadfastly more unreasonable in their ideological orientation and began to emulate the successful revolutionary tactics of their third-world counterparts. Convinced in the course of rationalism's postwar recovery that the further development of Western Civilization along such lines would bring them no relief, they simply turned increasingly to violence and exploded in rebellion halfway through the sixties, a rebellion calculated to promote a general Western-wide reversion to conditions akin to those of Germanic barbarism.

They were given powerful if unwitting assistance by sizable segments of the Western majority. Influenced by the brew of anti-Americanism, isolationism, antimaterialism, and existentialism that came to a boil in western Europe just after World War II and quickly overflowed throughout the West, a good many nonminority inhabitants of the liberal democracies had by the sixties lapsed even further into negative attitudes toward rationalism than their parents had a generation earlier. Disgusted with the onrunning international political struggle, distressed by the continuing economic transformation, and despairing for the individual in an increasingly collective world, ever larger numbers of Westerners began to question the fundamental character of Western life. They wondered whether the prosperity was worth the pollution, the equality worth the mediocrity, the control worth the regimentation, the might worth the menace; whether the leisure compensated for the boredom, the convenience for the dependence, the utility for the danger, the security for the unease.

More specifically, they expressed deepening doubt as to whether the epitome of rationalism's fruits and failures, the American way of life, could—or should—any longer be upheld as the Western model. They asked whether a life style at once restless and yet stable, restrictive and yet free, wasteful and yet efficient, troubled and yet self-confident was aptly suited to the times or merely a jumble of contradictions; whether it was in fact an appropriate means of rational response to the irrational challenge emanating from a bifurcated, half-underdeveloped, half-developed world, or only a confused, irrelevant, perhaps equally irrational contemporary mode of living. Also, they wondered if that same mode of living might not be starting to break down of its own accord, given the accelerating tempo of domestic discord in the United States. And by nurturing such doubts members of the majority created an atmosphere in which the minority impulse toward antirational upheaval could flourish, thereby encouraging its rapid growth and confirming the resurgence of the contemporary crisis.

Rationalism's Countermeasures

Western rationalism (and Western communism insofar as it contained rational elements) sought to cope with this resurgence in both its domestic and international guises by essentially two means: economic development and military force (or the threat of it), the same two means employed in defeating fascism and winning the cold war. The economic approach, being the more reasonable of the two, was initially the preferred one; and, accordingly, great efforts were made at the outset of the latter-day irrational resurgence to foster not only the continuance of rapid material progress in the West but also the widest possible dissemination of its fruits and techniques throughout the world.

Internationally, these efforts were begun during the first decade after World War II, when the United States supplied $25 billion in aid to western Europe (discussed above in Chapter 16). Once recovery there was well under way, the main flow of such economic assistance—now western European and Soviet as well as American—was redirected into the underdeveloped region; and by 1965 the West had supplied it with about $90 billion. Domestically, meanwhile, extraordinary expenditures to combat the upswing of irrationality within the Western world itself equaled perhaps $100 billion, most of which was used to raise minority living standards on a short-term basis.

Indeed, nearly all the sums mentioned—those expended abroad as well as at home—were dispersed to achieve short-term objectives; and as a result most of the entire enormous outlay was in vain. Too often spent to satisfy the immediate needs or demands of the recipients rather than to equip them to satisfy themselves in time, nearly all the $200 billion and more supplied by Western rationalism during the first two postwar decades to stifle resurgent irrationality went for naught. Used to purchase food, housing, health care, and arms rather than to implement population control, education, and industrialization, its net effect was neither remedial nor palliative.

As this failure of economic development became increasingly apparent, its sponsors began to rely ever more heavily upon military means in an effort to cope with resurgent, burgeoning unreason. Internationally, this tactic of last resort combined with the cold war to produce an arms race and an upsurge of militarism after 1960 unprecedented in the history of the world. Domestically, it helped induce conjointly rising indices of violence and repression, particularly in the most highly developed Western countries. But in neither sphere did the turn to force prove any more effective in curbing irrationality than had the attempted economic development.

Indeed, it only served to strengthen the very tendencies it was meant to weaken, accelerating rather than retarding the development of both international strife and domestic unrest. Internationally, the rationalists' increasing recourse to force prompted the further mechanization of limited warfare, the adoption of nuclear ballistic missile attack as the new mode of total war, and the ever more frequent use of the former and threat of the latter to conduct foreign relations. Furthermore, by doing so, it only served to make the contest for supremacy among nations more ruthless, more inhumane, more expensive, and more destructive—all without giving the rationalists any worthwhile advantage, since their military innovations proved worthless in coping with continued guerilla insurgency. Likewise, on the domestic scene their intensification of police power and of the military's role in civilian life accomplished little. Without doing anything significant either to ameliorate minority protests or to deal effectively with their increasingly incendiary modes, these impulses served only to help generate further disruptive unease among the majority of the population, in regard to both revolution and repression.

The quintessential example of the damage done to the rationalists' own cause by their embrace of force as a means of coping with resurgent unreason was provided by the Vietnam War, the climactic act of the revived contemporary crisis; and by its repercussions in and for the United States, the preeminent rationalist country. The war was effectively begun in 1965 when the Americans sought to intervene against an increasingly successful third-world revolt being staged in Indochina by nationalistic communists using guerilla tactics. It amounted to a major effort by the leading rationalist power to effect an exemplary defeat of resurgent irrationality in its most menacing guise, chiefly by recourse to armed force. But although the Americans brought powerful conventional military pressure of the most advanced sort to bear toward that end for five long years (and provided extensive economic assistance as well), no such defeat was forthcoming. Rather, their expenditure of more than $100 billion and nearly half a million casualties (of which over 40,000 were fatalities and 120,000 disabilities) produced only a disastrous quagmire of slaughter, ruin, disgrace, and stalemate, in which the United States—and through it, rationalism as a whole—became stuck. As indecision on the battlefield prompted ever more indiscriminate destruction of friend and foe alike; as the generals' arrogance degenerated into the GIs' atrocities; and as the homefront's initial solidarity was rent by sustained, increasingly widespread protest against continuation of the war, America and the rationalistic cause it championed suffered major damage.

In short, the Vietnam War simply made clear the fact that, as of 1970, the rationalistic response to the irrationalistic revival of the contemporary crisis in the 1960s had not succeeded, permitting unreason to remain in the ascendant. Neither rationally generated wealth nor technique nor force had sufficed to curtail or contain irrationality's militant latter-day upthrust either within or without the West, even though that upthrust was everywhere rooted in poverty, backwardness, and weakness. The continuing breakdown of confidence in rationalism, together with the coincident revolt against its hegemony, had simply proved more powerful than the countermeasures devised to cope with them, enabling the third world's nationalists and the West's discontented minorities to mount a potentially successful challenge to the postwar rationalist hegemony established by the United States.

The Continuing Dominance of Reason

Nonetheless, American-led rationalism still remained predominant as the 1970s began; and throughout the West, particularly in the United States, reason's adherents continued to outnumber its detractors. The strongest evidence of this was to be seen in the eminently reasonable, if much delayed, American reaction to its futile involvement in Vietnam. Slowly but surely, through incessant debate and deliberate assessment of the war's effects both in Indochina and the United States, a majority of Americans concluded that U.S. intervention had been a mistake. They reluctantly accepted the view that, however worthwhile its purpose (and even this was disputed), the undertaking simply exceeded the real limits of the United States' and rationalism's power—and perhaps their ethics as well. Having gradually come to recognize that the roots of the conflict in Indochina were both highly complex and deeply embedded in the region's environment and past, they reasonably concluded that any swift resolution of it, however well-intended or powerfully imposed, was impossible.

Indeed, by 1970, large numbers of rationalists both in the United States and elsewhere throughout the West had concluded that what was true in Vietnam was, in fact, true the world over, debarring the possibility of finding any quick or easy means of coping with resurgent irrationality in a comprehensive manner. Coupling that conclusion with mounting evidence of unreason's intrusion into their own countries' internal affairs, many of these same rationalists further concluded that large-scale efforts to stifle or contain irrationality on the international scene ought to be curtailed so as to concentrate the brunt of such effort upon the Western domestic scene. Thus, after five years of futile American intervention in Indochina and burgeoning unrest within the United States, these conclusions had by 1970 begun to influence and reshape Western policy toward resurgent unreason—particularly that policy's American vanguard.

Consequently, as the decade of the seventies opened, rationalism appeared to be entering upon a period of international retreat and domestic retrenchment, a period less indicative of any general abandonment of reason as the guiding principle of Western Civilization than of adjustment to certain disconcerting consequences of its postwar predominance. In particular, the United States seemed to be on the verge of giving up its quarter-century-old pose as the international champion of the rational cause by curtailing its activities as global reformer and gendarme and turning inward in search of remedies for its growing domestic difficulties. Having proved unable to rectify social discontent, fulfill political expectations, extend economic prosperity, or otherwise implement the rationalist program on a truly grandiose international scale, the Americans gave every indication that they were about to quit trying and to refocus such efforts largely within their own borders—to sacrifice the Pax Americana abroad in order once more to attempt to fulfill the American Dream at home.

Such indications by no means meant that rationalism was on the verge of being displaced as the West's fundamental credo. In spite of all the misgivings, doubts, and disaffections expressed concerning American life in particular and Western life in general; and in spite of all the evident shortcomings that combined to initiate the gradual eclipse of rationalism's American-established postwar hegemony, Western faith in reason as the ultimate vanguard of civilized advance remained relatively intact in 1970.

Indeed, at the height of the renewed irrational onslaught, the American life style epitomizing that faith continued to excite the envy and admiration not only of Westerners but of men everywhere—and, accordingly, to serve as the model for civilized development the world over. Having enabled sweeping material improvements in American life and, indeed, Western life as a whole; and having fostered a fundamental American commitment to resolution of the contemporary crisis—by domestic reform if not by foreign intervention —that style at the end of the sixties remained mankind's most successful and vigorous mode of existence. As such, as the route most likely to lead directly from an uncertain present to a better future, as the surest avenue from the West's hard-won commitment to rationalism to a more rational world in general, it continued to set the pace of Western Civilization's development in 1970.

Reason had persisted, in spite of the ideological onslaught of obscurantism during the nineteenth century and the physical blows of two world wars in the twentieth. Notwithstanding the repeated challenges to which it was subjected from the very outset of the contemporary era down to its juncture with the present, rationalism had managed to preserve a recognizable dominance over the majority of Western mankind, if not over mankind as a whole. Assailed by the second Germanic regression, the Russian Revolution, the advent of totalitarianism, the political collapse of Europe, the onset of the cold war, the resurgence of petty nationalism, the spread of discontent amidst affluence, and much more, the inhabitants of the West, for the most part, had continued to dream noble dreams, to cherish positive ideals, and to nurture material wants more than they had doubted, despaired, or longed for death; and they continued to perceive that the best way to fulfill such dreams, realize such ideals, and satisfy such wants was to persist in their allegiance to reason.

Consequently, the continuing effort to realize the rational objectives first clearly defined by the Romans—to achieve freedom from both the authentic tyranny of nature and the artificial tyranny of man through rationally directed organization—remained the chief hope and central purpose of human endeavor in the West as of 1970. The age of reason ushered in at the outset of the modern era continued to unfold, as its initial, ideological epoch—begun in the Reformation and climaxed during the Enlightenment—was succeeded by a second, materialistic epoch born in the Industrial Revolution and moving toward its apogee in the Systematic Revolution. The rationalism of politics had yielded its preeminence to that of science, but rationalism as a whole, speculative as well as applied, had survived as the basis of Western Civilization's further advance.

The uncertainties and shortcomings of the contemporary

era—in particular, the failure to achieve a significant degree of rational control over man—had not changed the orientation of Western development. The dream of reason omnipotent continued to exercise its allure, the rational history of the West to unfold.

Part V

Conclusion

The Long-Term Upswing of Civilized Development

Western Civilization began as a struggle to organize human life more rationally and persists as such: only the focus and scope of the effort have changed in the course of its five-thousand-year history. Nonetheless, the principal theme of that history has been one of long-term upswing. For whereas rational civilized endeavor was at the outset composed of the efforts of a few people in a few Mesopotamian hamlets to somehow better organize the rudimentary details of their rudimentary lives, it now entails the efforts of hundreds of millions of people throughout the world to better organize all the complex details of their complex lives, having grown from the puny handiwork of a few pioneer agrarians into the chief preoccupation of a large part of mankind.

During the initial or ancient era of this growth, the inhabitants of the Near East gave Western Civilization its original and primary impetus toward rational organization, first in agriculture, then society and culture, and finally politics and arms. Their achievements in agriculture remained unexcelled throughout the remainder of the era; those in society and

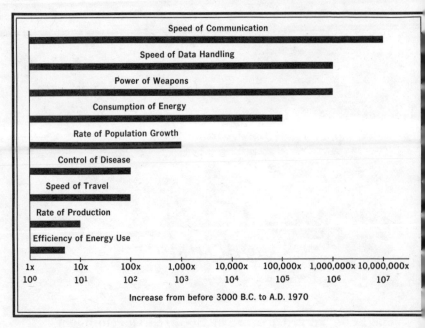

Fig. 21. Indexes of Western Civilization's Long-Term Impact

culture—especially in culture—provided the raw material
from which the Greeks, by consolidation and refinement,
created the classical forms that climaxed ancient civilized development in that direction; and those in politics and arms
served as the norm until improved upon by the Greeks and
Romans, especially the latter. Indeed, ancient Western Civilization was, in effect, Near Eastern Civilization, until the Romans arose to make it a Mediterranean-wide phenomenon
through their innovations in political and military organization, innovations that led to the unification and pacification of
virtually the entire Western world. Having achieved unity and
peace, the Romans also sought to bring prosperity and equality to much of the West; and in so doing they completed the
Romanization of ancient Western Civilization by rendering
their own primary civilized objectives those of Western mankind as a whole.

Consequently, when the Roman Empire ultimately collapsed under the strains of economic weakness and barbarian invasion, ending the ancient era of Western Civilization and beginning the medieval, the basic Roman ideals of unity, peace, prosperity, and equality persisted as that civilization's principal directing force. And it was in the guise of a quest to uphold or restore this Roman heritage that the objective of rational organization was preserved in the midst of the post-Roman Germanic regression to barbarism throughout western Europe. Likewise, when rational organization was gradually revived in practice as a comprehensive Western phenomenon—first by the revolutionary consolidation and improvement of western European agriculture, and then, after futile efforts at Western-wide religious unification, by the development of national dynastic states—it was done by harmonizing Germanic or Celtic usage with Roman precedents and objectives.

As a result, by the twilight of the medieval era, a Roman restoration of sorts had been effected in that portion of the Roman Empire overrun and semibarbarized by the Germans, giving rise there to a new Germanic-Roman mode of Western Civilization. By the fifteenth century, this western European way of life, on the basis of indigenous developments, had already managed to exceed Roman economic achievements and devise alternative (if fragmentary) means of political organization, even as it simultaneously adhered to the Roman ideals of material prosperity, social equality, and universal peace as its primary objectives. But in order to press ahead toward the achievement of these objectives, the people of western Europe at that juncture had to forsake Christian spirituality, the prevalent medieval ideology, in favor of Roman materialism, its ancient equivalent; and that reorientation, begun by the Renaissance and climaxed by the Reformation, ended the medieval era and started the modern.

The secularization of western Europe symbolized by this abandonment of Christianity was largely completed during the first two modern centuries (the sixteenth and seven-

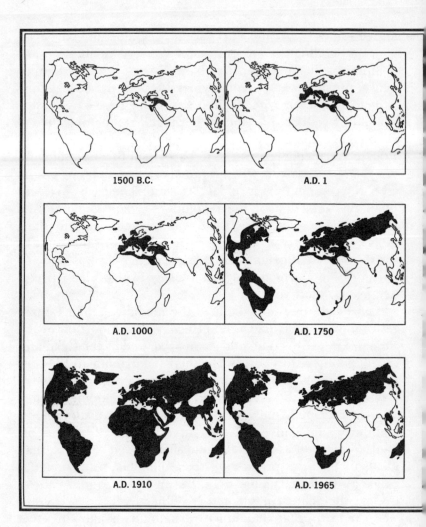

Map 24. The Territorial Extension of Western Dominion

teenth), which were characterized by the firm reestablishment of materialism as the West's preeminent ideology, the stabilization of the material prosperity born of the medieval agricultural revolution, and the direction of Western Civilization's further development along economic and scientific lines. Unfortunately, these same two centuries were *not* characterized by the reestablishment of peace or the development of greater equality, those other primary objectives of the West's Roman heritage; and that deficiency produced social and political revolution throughout western Europe and in its North American colonies during the third modern century (the eighteenth) with the aim of realizing those objectives. This Democratic or Rational Political Revolution achieved only partial short-term success and soon degenerated into a long-term struggle between the advocates of Roman (or rational) and Germanic (or irrational) modes of sociopolitical organization—a struggle that was to persist right down to the end of the modern era and on into the contemporary. However, the Democratic Revolution was paralleled by a highly successful Industrial or Rational Economic Revolution based on the application of rapidly developing scientific knowledge to production and distribution; and that transformation accelerated the rate of material progress in western Europe and North America beyond all prior expectations, thereby establishing such progress as a cornerstone of latter-day Western Civilization. Unfortunately, the rational preeminence enabled by the Industrial Revolution was so undercut by the social, political, and cultural success of resurgent obscurantism that, as the modern era drew to a close, the Western world found itself heading toward a general crisis—a crisis of direction.

That crisis, which ushered in the contemporary era, began early in the twentieth century, when the obscurantists, led by the Germans, plunged the West into total war in an effort to seize control of Western Civilization from the rationalists, and so initiated another regression toward barbarism, like the one

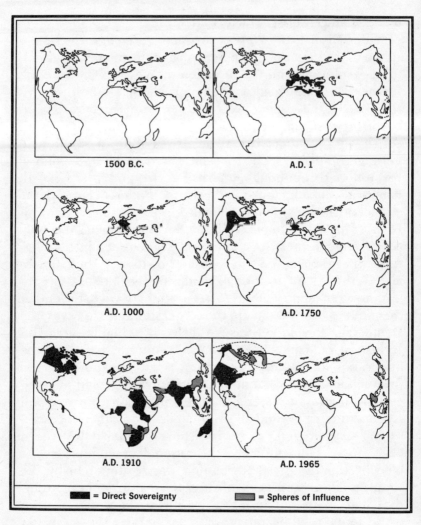

Map 25. The Growth of Dominant Western Political Units

that followed Rome's collapse. Not until the mid-twentieth century, when the German camp had been dealt the second of two resounding military defeats, was this reversal of civilized development halted and renewed rational advance begun (under American leadership). Even then, the struggle for sociopolitical predominance between rationalism and ir-rationalism continued, as first Soviet communism and then third-world nationalism arose to challenge the American-led rationalist sway and perpetuate the contemporary crisis. Nonetheless, reason persisted as the dominant force in West-ern Civilization, since the majority of the West's inhabitants continued to strive, in practice, toward Roman rather than Germanic objectives—toward the tangible benefits of ration-ally directed organization rather than the elusive expectations of untrammeled individualism.

Civilized Achievements to Date

Evidently, then, the direction of Western Civilization's de-velopment has not changed significantly in the course of its five-thousand-year history. Today, as in 3000 B.C., the main thrust of Western civilized endeavor is toward a more rational order of things based on greater material prosperity and social equality; only the scale and appreciation of the effort have changed, the former by expansion from within strictly Mesopotamian limits to include not only the entire West but the world as a whole, and the latter by the gradual genesis of a civilized consciousness among the West's inhabitants and im-itators. In short, Western mankind for five millennia has had a fixed set of objectives—a mission, if you will. And in pursuit of that mission's fulfillment, in pursuit of an order at once more bountiful and more equalitarian, the people of the West have, largely by rational means, transformed their own way of life and have begun to transform that of all the rest of the earth's people as well.

The positive aspects of this transformation—the achieve-ments of Western Civilization—have for the most part been

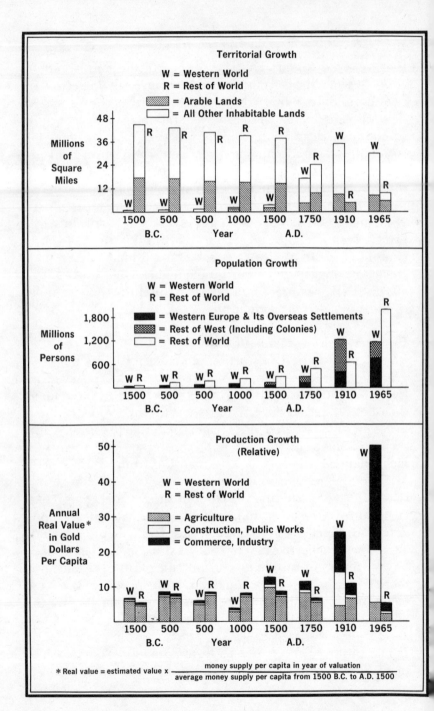

Fig. 22. Indexes of Western Civilization's Long-Term Development

derived from the development of science and industry. That is, they have been by-products of the ever more intensive and extensive human comprehension and control of nature, achievements made possible by the onrunning discovery and application of rational organizational methods to master the physical world.

On the material side, such methods have resulted in an all-important increase in production in the West during the civilized epoch—more than tenfold on a per capita basis —while it has remained virtually stagnant elsewhere in the world. This increase, enabled chiefly by the modern shift from agriculture to industry and commerce as the primary means of production, has sufficiently enriched the people of the West to lift them from subsistence to affluence, in spite of a quadrupling of their numbers during the modern era. Such unprecedented prosperity has, in turn, made possible a multiplicity of improvements in popular living standards and the quality of everyday life, improvements exemplified by the extension of Western life spans and by the elimination of Western slavery and peasant serfdom.

The mental strides made as a result of the rationalization of Western mankind's approach to nature have also prompted important material improvements in Western life, a few notable examples being the development of visual-electric communication, the elimination of epidemic disease, and the widespread adoption of synthetics such as plastic. In addition, the same mental advances have done much to promote significant nonmaterial improvements such as greater personal freedom, the elevation of intellectual standards, the spread of learning, and the growth of scientific understanding and technique. In other words, the rationalization of Western thought probably has done as much to improve human existence in the West as any strictly concrete developments that have paralleled it.

Consequently, Western Civilization's achievements to date are summed up not only in improved living conditions but

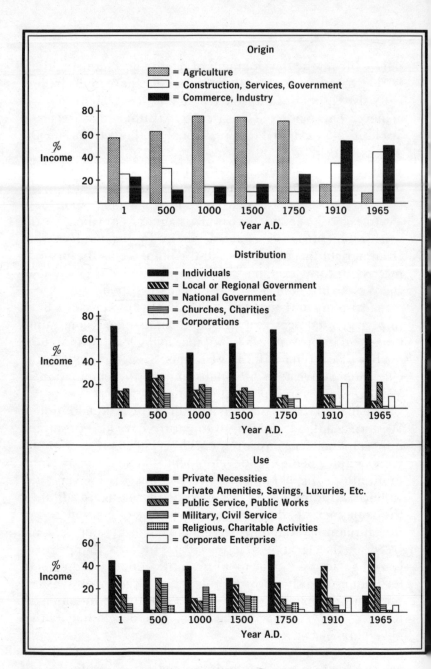

Fig. 23. Long-Term Changes in the West's Income Patterns

also in an improved outlook on life—in Western man's mood of optimism and sense of mastery, as well as in his comfortable material circumstances. Insofar as the people of the West have succeeded in their five-thousand-year-long undertaking to improve human life rationally, they have done so by transforming themselves quite as extensively as they have transformed their surroundings, by changing their interior as well as their exterior existences for the better. In short, they have been able to lift themselves up from barbarism just to the extent that they have been able to remold both their environment and themselves.

Civilized Failures to Date

The principal shortcomings of Western Civilization have been neither individual nor circumstantial but rather associative, that is, matters of collective human organization and enterprise. The most important has been the long-term failure to establish international peace, save for two or three centuries under the Roman Empire. Nor has the ideal of equality ever been genuinely fulfilled in the West, of late chiefly due to the prevalence of major inequities in the distribution of wealth and income. In addition, Western culture has largely been destroyed in the course of the modern and contemporary struggle for ideological-political supremacy. Finally, the danger of intense organization for unreasonable rather than rational purposes has lately become pronounced—as exemplified by the rise of contemporary totalitarianism. In short, the inhabitants of the West still have not been able to master the difficulties of getting along with one another, of collectively coping with collective human nature, in a rational manner.

The foremost instance of this lingering inability, and the most long-lived, has been the aforesaid failure to achieve peace, a failure intimately connected since Roman times with the rise of nationalism. By reconstructing the shattered structure of Western politics after Rome's fall along the ethnic lines

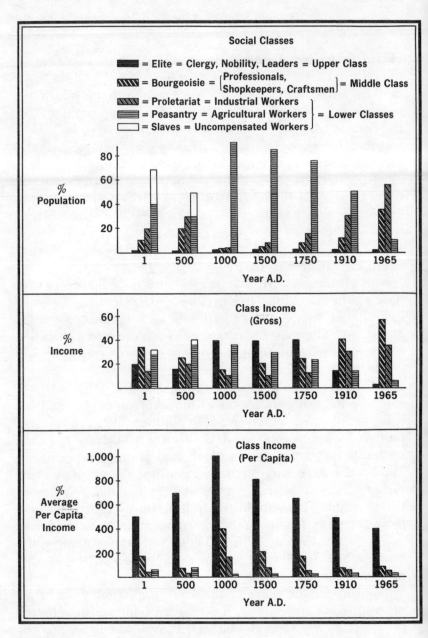

Fig. 24. Long-Term Changes in the West's Social Structure

laid down by the barbarian invasions, the inhabitants of western Europe in effect abandoned the Roman notion of a peaceful human commonwealth and instead embraced the Germanic alternative of incessant tribal antagonism, from which the modern international order of hostile national states was evolved. Consequently, not even the establishment of Western political hegemony over much of the globe during the modern era served to promote the spread of peace, which has remained a subcontinental phenomenon generally limited in its extent by national boundaries.

Equality, like peace, has also long been an unfulfilled objective of Western Civilization, and for much the same underlying reason—the legacy of the Germanic invasions. By placing renewed emphasis upon elitism, the barbarian onslaught sufficiently buttressed inequality to preserve it right down to the present, this in spite of increasingly widespread, popularly inspired economic, social, and political efforts to destroy it. To be sure, inequality has been severely curtailed—from an all-pervasive class structure as old as Western Civilization itself to an essentially economic matter—but its antithesis, genuine equality, nonetheless remains only an ideal throughout much of the Western world.

Culture, by contrast, has lately been reduced from a reality to an ideal in the West by elite exploitation and mass indifference, again largely as a result of the Germanic heritage, since the sacrifice was made on behalf of nationalism and the other forms of political-ideological irrationality reintroduced by the Germans into the mainstream of Western life. Seized upon as a convenient means of mobilizing popular support, first for the creation of elite-run dynastic national states and then for their preservation in the face of rationalistic popular revolution, the established modes of Western aesthetic expression were so mangled and debased in the process as to be rendered worthless save as adjuncts to obscurantism; and as a result Western culture has in recent times simply ceased to exist as a meaningful component of Western Civilization.

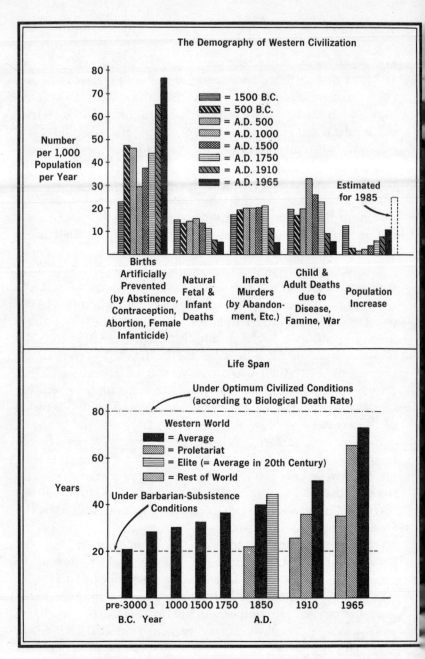

Fig. 24. Long-Term Changes in the West's Social Structure

Ideological-political irrationality, the prime mover in the eradication of culture, has also played a signifcant role, together with the irrational abuse of scientific technology, in bringing on the most recent instance of a basic failure in Western Civilization—namely, the latter-day organization of Western life to a degree and toward ends that have begun to exceed the dictates of both reason and necessity. As ideologues, politicians, and scientists alike have become increasingly incapable, yet increasingly desirous, of extending their sway by accustomed means, they have simply begun to rely more and more upon the sheer impetus of further organization via the latest scientifically revealed methods to achieve it. Consequently, the character and impact of latter-day organization in the West have become steadily more technical, mindless, and pointless, rendering such organization increasingly a phenomenon of drift toward further unnecessary regimentation rather than the hub of further Western development. This phenomenon, antipathetic to the very foundations of Western Civilization rather than an extension and reinforcement of them, is the latest untoward consequence of the Germanic onslaught that destroyed Rome.

Indeed, the essence of Western Civilization's failures to date has been its inability to cope with the Germanic heritage, while continuing to pursue the Roman—the inability to identify barbarian notions clearly and either assimilate-and-civilize or isolate-and-destroy them in order to preserve their civilized counterparts. And since the majority of such notions apply to person-to-person or associational relationships, the West's failure to cope with them has been largely a failure to establish the same significant, civilized degree of rational control over man's interaction with other men as over his interaction with nature and himself.

On balance, therefore, Western Civilization has thus far proved to be a process of mastering environment and self rather than, as is commonly supposed, of mastering relations among men. Rational organization has sufficed to establish far better control over nature and human consciousness than previously existed, but not over human society. The achievement of genuine civility in men's affairs still remains an objective to be fulfilled in Western life. In fact, it constitutes the principal task presently facing the heirs to Western Civilization, the main obstacle that must be overcome if the West's long-term advance in the direction of human betterment is to be continued. The prior course of that advance has taught the inhabitants of the West how to get along reasonably well with the natural world and with themselves: it remains to be seen if they can also learn how to get along reasonably well with each other, and so perpetuate the rational history of Western Civilization.

Bibliography

Readers interested in further study of the rational history of Western Civilization may find some of the following books worthwhile. Those in **boldface** are the most important and useful. Those marked with an asterisk (*) are available in paperback; those marked with a zero (0) are available in hardcover; those marked with a cross (x) are available in a reprint; and the rest, although out of print in the United States, can be obtained in facsimile. Most of the titles listed will be found in any metropolitan library; and at least a few of them should be present in even the smallest public collection.

The selection offered below deliberately excludes biographies, fiction, studies in foreign languages, and most multivolume works, especially anthologies, collections, series, and the like. For these and other additional titles, the reader is referred to the extensive lists appended to many of the works cited below, and to the host of historical bibliographies that have been published as separate entities. Two of the latter, which together provide a readily available, annotated survey of the corpus of Western history, are:

American Historical Association. *Guide to Historical Literature*. G. F. Howe *et al*., eds. New York, 1961.

0 McGarry, D. D., and White, S. H. *Historical Fiction Guide* . . . . New York, 1963.

I. SOURCES
A. Descriptive

1. Ancient
     0 **Loeb Classical Library. Cambridge, Mass., 1912 ff.**
2. Medieval, Modern, and Contemporary
     * **Anvil Book Series. New York, n.d. ff.**

B. Statistical

1. Geography
     Palmer, R. R. et al. Atlas of World History. Rev. ed. New York, 1968.
2. Chronology
     0* Steinberg, S. H. *Historical Tables, 58 B.C.-A.D. 1965*. 8th ed. London, 1966.
3. Population and Production
     0* **Cipolla, C. M. The Economic History of World Population. 5th ed. Harmondsworth, England, 1970.**
     Woytinsky, W. S., and Woytinsky, E. S. World Population and Production . . . . New York, 1953.
4. Resources, Wealth, and Income
     Doane, R. R. *World Balance Sheet: A Comprehensive, Inventoried Examination . . . of the World's Physical Resources . . . .* New York, 1957.
     * Studenski, P. *The Income of Nations*. Part 1: *History*. Abr. ed. New York, 1958.
5. General
     x Frank, T., ed. *An Economic Survey of Ancient Rome*. 6 vols. Baltimore, 1933-1940. Reprint. New York, n.d.
     0 Cave, R. C., and Coulson, H. H., eds. *A Source Book for Medieval Economic History*. Milwaukee, 1936.
     Mitchell, B. R., and Deane, P. *Abstract of British Historical Statistics*. Cambridge, England, 1962.
     x U.S. Bureau of the Census. *The Statistical History of the United States from Colonial Times to the Present*. 3 vols. Washington, D.C., 1949-1960. Reprint. 3 vols. in 1. Fairfield, Conn., 1965.

II. SECONDARY WORKS
(in chronological order)

A. THE FORMATIVE OR ANCIENT PHASE

1. The Near Eastern Origins, 3000-500 B.C.
    0 **Starr, C. G. A History of the Ancient World. New York, 1965.**
    0 Clark, G. *World Prehistory: A New Outline*. 2d ed. Cambridge, England, 1965.
    0 Cole, S. *The Neolithic Revolution*. London, 1965.
    * Curwen, E. C., and Hatt, G. *Plough and Pasture: The Early History of Farming*. New York, 1953.
    0* Frankfort, H. *Birth of Civilization in the Near East*. Bloomington, Ind., 1951.
    0* Childe, G. *New Light on the Most Ancient Near East*. 4th ed. New York, 1957.
    * Olmstead, A. T. *History of the Persian Empire*. Chicago, 1948.
2. The Greek Transition, 500-200 B.C.
    0 **Botsford, G. W., and Robinson, C. A., Jr. Hellenic History. 4th ed. New York, 1956.**
    x* Rostovtzeff, M. I. *Greece*. J. D. Duff., trans. E. J. Bickerman, ed. New York, 1926. Reprint. New York, 1963.
    0 Toynbee, A. J. *Hellenism*. Oxford, England, 1959.
    0 Starr, C. G. *Origins of Greek Civilization, 1100-650 B.C.* New York, 1961.
    * Adcock, F. E. *The Greek and Macedonian Art of War*. Berkeley, Calif., 1957.
    0 **Cary, M. A History of the Greek World from 323 to 146 B.C. Vol. III of Methuen's History of the Greek and Roman World. 2d ed. London, 1951.**
    0 Rostovtzeff, M. I. *Social and Economic History of the Hellenistic World*. 3 vols. Oxford, England, 1941.
3. The Roman Hegemony, 200 B.C.-A.D. 200
    0 **Scullard, H. H. et al. A History of the Roman World. Vols. IV-VII of Methuen's History of the Greek and Roman World. 2d ed. London, 1953-1963.**
    0 Jolowicz, H. F. *Historical Introduction to the Study of Roman Law*. 2d ed. Cambridge, England, 1952.

Sherwin-White, A. N. *The Roman Citizenship*. Oxford, England, 1939.

0 Homo, L. P. *Roman Political Institutions*. M. R. Dobie, trans. 2d ed. New York, 1950.

Stevenson, G. H. *Roman Provincial Administration* . . . . 2d ed. New York, 1949.

0 Powell, T. G. E. *The Celts*. New York, 1958.

x Parker, H. M. D. *The Roman Legions*. 2d ed. Cambridge, England, 1928. Reprint. Cambridge, 1958.

0 Adcock, F. E. *The Roman Art of War Under the Republic*. 2d ed. New York, 1963.

Waddy, L. *Pax Romana and World Peace*. London, 1950.

4. The Roman Collapse, A.D. 200 500

0 **Mattingly, H. Roman Imperial Civilization. London, 1957.**

0* Clarke, M. L. *The Roman Mind*. Cambridge, Mass., 1956.

0 Edelstein, L. *The Idea of Progress in Classical Antiquity*. Baltimore, 1967:

* **Haywood, R. M. The Myth of Rome's Fall. New York, 1959.**

0 Rostovtzeff, M. I. *Social and Economic History of the Roman Empire*. 2d ed. 2 vols. P. M. Frazer, ed. Oxford, England, 1957.

Frank, T. *An Economic History of Rome*. 2d ed. Baltimore, 1927.

Heitland, W. E. *Agricola: A Study of Agriculture and Rustic Life in the Greco-Roman World*. Cambridge, England, 1921.

Charlesworth, M. P. *Trade-Routes and Commerce of the Roman Empire*. 2d ed. Cambridge, England, 1926.

Drachmann, A. G. *The Mechanical Technology of Greek and Roman Antiquity*. Copenhagen, 1963.

Bailey, C., ed. The Legacy of Rome. Oxford, England, 1923.

0* **De Burgh, W. G. Legacy of the Ancient World. 3d ed. 2 vols. New York, 1960.**

B. The Resurgent or Medieval Phase

1. The Germanic Regression, A.D. 500-800
   Arragon, R. F. The Transition from the Ancient to the Medieval World. New York, 1936.
   x* Bury, J. B. *The Invasion of Europe by the Barbarians*. London, 1928. Reprint. New York, 1963.
   0* **Owen, F. The Germanic People. New York, 1959.**
   * Easton, S. C., and Wieruszowski, H. *The Era of Charlemagne: Frankish State and Society*. Princeton, N.J., 1961.
   * **Ganshof, F. L. Feudalism. P. Grierson, trans. New York, 1952.**
   x* Dawson, C. H. *Religion and the Rise of Western Culture*. New York, 1950.
   0* Southern, R. W. *The Making of the Middle Ages: A Short History*. New York, 1953.
   0 **Baynes, N. H. The Byzantine Empire. London, 1926.**
   0* Diehl, C. *Byzantium: Greatness and Decline*. N. Walford, trans. New Brunswick, N.J., 1957.
   0* Lewis, B. *The Arabs in History*. 3d ed. New York, 1958.
   * **Gibb, H. A. R. Mohammedanism: An Historical Survey. 2d ed. Oxford, England, 1962.**
2. The Economic Transformation, A.D. 800-1100
   x **Dopsch, A. The Economic and Social Foundations of European Civilization. London, 1937. Reprint. New York, 1969.**
   0 Orwin, C. S., and Orwin, C. S. *The Open Fields*. 3d ed. Oxford, England, 1967.
   Neilson, N. Medieval Agrarian Economy. New York, 1936.
   0* Bennett, H. S. *Life on the English Manor: A Study of Peasant Conditions, 1150-1400*. Cambridge, England, 1937.
   Poston, M. M., and Rich, E. E., eds. *Trade and Industry in the Middle Ages*. Vol. II of *The Cambridge Economic History of Europe*. Cambridge, England, 1952.
   0* White, L. *Medieval Technology and Social Change*. Oxford, England, 1962.
   * Mundy, J. H., and Riesenberg, P. *The Medieval Town*. Princeton, N.J., 1958.

    * **Pirenne, H. Economic and Social History of Medieval Europe. I. E. Clegg, trans. New York, 1937.**

3. The Christian Mission, A.D. 1100-1300

    0 **Ullmann, W. The Growth of Papal Government in the Middle Ages . . . . 3d ed. London, 1970.**

    x* Newhall, R. A. *The Crusades*. 2d ed. New York, 1963. Reprint. Magnolia, Mass., n.d.

    Wright, R. F. *Medieval Internationalism: The Contribution of the Medieval Church to International Law and Peace*. London, 1930.

    0* Taylor, H. O. *The wemergence of Christian Culture in the West: The Classical Heritage of the Middle Ages*. 3d ed. New York, 1929.

    0* Von Simson, O. G. *The Gothic Cathedral* . . . . 2d ed. Princeton, N.J., 1962.

    * **Baldwin, M. W. The Medieval Church. Ithaca, N.Y., 1953.**

    * Painter, S. *Medieval Society*. Ithaca, N.Y., 1951.

    * **Strayer, J. R. Western Europe in the Middle Ages: A Short History. New York, 1955.**

4. The Cultural Renaissance, A.D. 1300-1450

    0 **Artz, F. B. The Mind of the Middle Ages, A.D. 200-1500. 3d ed. New York, 1958.**

    * **Ferguson, W. The Renaissance. New York, 1940.**

    0 Bolgar, R. R. *The Classical Heritage and Its Beneficiaries*. Cambridge, England, 1954.

    Kristeller, P. O. *The Classics and Renaissance Thought*. Cambridge, Mass., 1955.

    x* ————. **Renaissance Thought: The Classic, Scholastic, and Humanist Strains. 2d ed. New York, 1961. Reprint. New York, n.d.**

    * Panofsky, E. *Renaissance and Renascences in Western Art*. Stockholm, 1960.

    Gould, C. *An Introduction to Italian Renaissance Painters*. New York, 1957.

    x Mather, F. J. *Western European Painting of the Renaissance*. New York, 1939.

    0* **Huizinga, J. The Waning of the Middle Ages: A Study in the Forms of Life, Thought, and Art in France and the**

   Netherlands in the 14th and 15th Centuries. London, 1924.

5. The Dynastic Revival, A.D. 1450-1550

 x **Thompson, J. W. Economic and Social History of Europe in the Later Middle Ages (1300-1530). New York, 1931. Reprint. New York, 1960.**

 * Stephenson, C. *Medieval Feudalism.* Ithaca, N.Y., 1942.

 * Painter, S. *The Rise of the Feudal Monarchies.* Ithaca, N.Y., 1951.

  Lyon, B. D. *From Fief to Indenture: The Transition from Feudal to Non-Feudal Contract in Western Europe.* Cambridge, Mass., 1957.

 x **Figgis, J. N. Political Thought from Gerson to Grotius, 1414-1625 . . . . 2d ed. Cambridge, England, 1916. Reprint. New York, 1960.**

 * Myers, A. R. *England in the Late Middle Ages (1307-1536).* Harmondsworth, England, 1952.

  Grant, A. J. *The French Monarchy, 1483-1789.* Cambridge, England, 1905.

 0* Elliott, J. H. *Imperial Spain, 1469-1716.* New York, 1963.

 0* **Cheyney, E. P. The Dawn of a New Era, 1250-1453. New York, 1936.**

C. THE TRIUMPHANT OR MODERN PHASE

1. The Religious Fragmentation, A.D. 1550-1650

 0 **Green, V. H. H. Renaissance and Reformation: A Survey of European History Between 1450 and 1660. 2d ed. New York, 1964.**

 0 **Grimm, H. The Reformation Era, 1500-1650. 2d ed. New York, 1965.**

  Elliott-Binns, L. *History of the Decline and Fall of the Medieval Papacy.* London, 1934.

 x Flick, A. *Decline of the Medieval Church.* 2 vols. New York, 1930. Reprint. New York, n.d.

 x* Mosse, G. L. *The Reformation.* 3d ed. New York, 1963. Reprint. Magnolia, Mass., n.d.

x Kidd, B. J. *The Counter-Reformation, 1550-1600*. London, 1933. Reprint. Kentfield, Calif., n.d.

0x* Wedgwood, C. V. *The Thirty Years War*. London, 1938. Reprint. New York, n.d.

x Murray, R. H. *The Political Consequences of the Reformation*. London, 1926. Reprint. New York, 1960.

* **Pauck, W. The Heritage of the Reformation. 2d ed. New York, 1968.**

2. The Western European Ascendancy, A.D. 1650-1750

0 **Reynolds, R. L. Europe Emerges: Transition Toward an Industrial World-Wide Society, 600-1750. Madison, Wis., 1961.**

x* **Beloff, M. The Age of Absolutism, 1660-1815. New York, 1954. Reprint. New York, 1966.**

0 Clark, G. N. *The Seventeenth Century*. 2d ed. Oxford, England, 1947.

x* Smith, P. *A History of Modern Culture, 1543-1776*. 2 vols. New York, 1930-1934. Reprint. Magnolia, Mass., n.d.

Hall, A. R. The Scientific Revolution, 1500-1800. 2d ed. London, 1962.

0 Van Bath, B. H. S. *The Agrarian History of Western Europe, A.D. 500-1850*. New York, 1963.

Packard, L. B. *The Commercial Revolution, 1400-1776*. New York, 1927.

* Parry, J. H. *Europe and a Wider World, 1415-1715*. London, 1949.

x* Sorel, A. *Europe Under the Old Regime*. F. H. Herrick, trans. New York, 1947. Reprint. New York, n.d.

3. The Democratic Revolution, A.D. 1750-1815

0 **Gay, P. The Enlightenment: An Interpretation. 2 vols. New York, 1967-1969.**

* Hill, C. *Puritanism and Revolution: The English Revolution of the 17th Century*. New York, 1964.

x Trevelyan, G. M. *The English Revolution, 1688-1689*. 2d ed. London, 1946. Reprint. Magnolia, Mass., n.d.

0* **Palmer, R. R. The Age of the Democratic Revolution: A Political History of Europe and America, 1760-1800. 2 vols. Princeton, N.J., 1959-1964.**

0* Wright, E. *Fabric of Freedom, 1763-1800* [*The American Revolution*]. New York, 1961.

0 **Lefebvre, G. The French Revolution. 2 vols. E. M. Evanson, trans. (vol. 1), and J. H. Stewart and J. Friguglietti, trans. (vol. 2). New York, 1963-1964.**

0* Brunn, G. *Europe and the French Imperium, 1799-1814*. New York, 1938.

x* Nicholson, H. *The Congress of Vienna: A Study in Allied Unity, 1812-1822*. London, 1946. Reprint. Magnolia, Mass., n.d.

4. The Industrial Revolution, A.D. 1815-1890

0 **Cole, G. D. H. Introduction to Economic History, 1750-1950. 2d ed. London, 1965.**

x Sée, H. *Modern Capitalism: Its Origins and Evolution*. M. M. Knight, trans. New York, 1928. Reprint. East Orange, N.J., 1968.

x Wolf, A. *A History of Science, Technology, and Philosophy in the 16th, 17th, and 18th Centuries*. 2d ed. 2 vols. London, 1950-1952. Reprint. Magnolia, Mass., n.d.

0* **Deane, P. The First Industrial Revolution. Cambridge, England, 1965.**

* Ashton, T. S. *The Industrial Revolution, 1760-1830*. London, 1948.

0 Henderson, W. O. *Britain and Industrial Europe, 1750-1870* . . . . 2d ed. Leicester, England, 1965.

0* ————. *The Industrial Revolution on the Continent, 1800-1914*. London, 1961.

x **Knowles, L. C. A. Economic Development in the Nineteenth Century: France, Germany, Russia, and the United States. London, 1932. Reprint. East Orange, N.J., 1968.**

5. The Modern Culmination, A.D. 1890-1910

0* **Williams, R. The Long Revolution. New York, 1961.**

0 **Woolf, L. After the Deluge (Principia Politica): A Study of Communal Psychology. 3 vols. London, 1931-1953.**

0 **Hallowell, J. H. Main Currents in Modern Political Thought. New York, 1950.**

* Viereck, P. *Metapolitics: The Roots of the Nazi Mind (From the Romantics to Hitler)*. 2d ed. New York, 1961.

* Wilson, E. *To the Finland Station . . . [Roots of the Leftist Mind (From the Utopians to Lenin)]*. Garden City, N.Y., 1940.

0 Watkins, F. *The Political Tradition of the West: A Study in the Development of Modern Liberalism*. Cambridge, Mass., 1948.

Bernal, J. D. *Science and Industry in the Nineteenth Century*. London, 1953.

0 **Taylor, A. J. P. The Struggle for Mastery in Europe, 1848-1918. Vol. I of The Oxford History of Modern Europe. Oxford, England, 1954.**

0 **Moon, P. T. Imperialism and World Politics. New York, 1925.**

* Remak, J. *The Origins of World War I, 1871-1914*. New York, 1967.

0* Hayes, C. J. H. *A Generation of Materialism, 1871-1900*. New York, 1941.

D. THE UNCERTAIN OR CONTEMPORARY PHASE

1. The Second Germanic Regression, A.D. 1910-1945

Kohn, H. Force or Reason: Issues of the Twentieth Century. Cambridge, Mass., 1937.

* Dehio, L. *Germany and World Politics in the Twentieth Century*. London, 1959.

x Dickinson, G. L. *The International Anarchy, 1904-1914*. London, 1926. Reprint. New York, n.d.

0* **Baldwin, H. W. World War I: An Outline History. New York, 1962.**

0* **Moorehead, A. The Russian Revolution. New York, 1958.**

0 Churchill, W. S. *The World Crisis*. Vol. VI: *The Aftermath*. New York, 1929.

* Lewis, W. A. *Economic Survey, 1919-1939*. London, 1949.

0* Arendt, H. *The Origins of Totalitarianism*. New York, 1951.

0 Armstrong, J. A. *The Politics of Totalitarianism*. New York, 1961.

0* **Snyder, L. L. The War: A Concise History, 1939-1945. New York, 1960.**

2. The American Hegemony, A.D. 1945-1960

0* **Steel, R. Pax Americana. New York, 1967.**

x **Fischer, E. The Passing of the European Age: A Study of the Transfer of Western Civilization and Its Renewal in Other Continents. 2d ed. Cambridge, Mass., 1948. Reprint. New York, 1967.**

0* Postan, M. M. *An Economic History of Western Europe, 1945-1964*. London, 1967.

0 Holborn, H. *The Political Collapse of Europe*. New York, 1951.

0* La Feber, W. *America, Russia, and the Cold War, 1945-1966*. New York, 1967.

0 Blackett, P. M. S. *Atomic Weapons and East-West Relations*. Cambridge, England, 1956.

0 Lindsay, M. *China and the Cold War*. Melbourne, 1955.

* Ekirk, A. *The American Democratic Tradition: A History*. New York, 1963.

Clough, S. B. *The American Way*. New York, 1953.

0* **Giedion, S. Mechanization Takes Command . . . . Oxford, England, 1948.**

0* **Brooks, J. The Great Leap: The Past Twenty-five Years in America. New York, 1966.**

3. Latter-Day Unrest, A.D. 1960-1970

* **Gatzke, H. W. The Present in Perspective: A Look at the World Since 1945. 3d ed. Chicago, 1965.**

0 **Emerson, R. From Empire to Nation: The Rise to Self-Assertion of Asian and African Peoples. Cambridge, Mass., 1960.**

0* Ward, B. *The Rich Nations and the Poor Nations*. New York, 1962.

0 Benham, F. C. *Economic Aid to Underdeveloped Countries*. New York, 1961.

0 Cooper, C. L. *The Lost Crusade: America in Vietnam*. New York, 1970.

0* Bell, D. *The End of Ideology: On the Exhaustion of Political Ideas in the Fifties*. Glencoe, Ill., 1960.

Rauschning, H. The Revolution of Nihilism. New York, 1939.

0 Popper, K. R. *The Open Society and Its Enemies.* 2 vols. 5th ed. Princeton, N.J., 1965.

0 Seton-Watson, H. *Neither War nor Peace: The Struggle for Power in the Postwar World.* London, 1960.

Youngson, A. J. *Possibilities of Economic Progress.* London, 1959.

Rapoport, A. Science and the Goals of Man: A Study in Semantic Orientation. New York, 1950.

E. Conclusion

0 **McNeill, W. H. The Rise of the West: A History of the Human Community. Chicago, 1963.**

Lecky, W. E. H. *History of the Rise and Influence of the Spirit of Rationalism in Europe.* 3d ed. 2 vols. New York, 1914.

Seagle, W. *The History of Law.* 2d ed. New York, 1946.

0 **Randall, J. H. The Making of the Modern Mind. 2d ed. Boston, 1940.**

0* Collingwood, R. G. *The Idea of Nature.* Oxford, England, 1945.

* Forbes, R. J., and Dijksterhuis, E. J. *A History of Science and Technology.* 2 vols. Baltimore, 1963.

0 Van Doren, C. *et al. The Idea of Progress.* New York, 1967.

0 **Clough, S. B. European Economic History: The Economic Development of Western Civilization. 2d ed. New York, 1968.**

x* **Barnes, H. E. An Intellectual and Cultural History of the Western World. 3d ed. 3 vols. New York, 1963. Reprint. Magnolia, Mass., n.d.**

0 Latourette, K. S. *History of Christianity.* New York, 1953.

0 Sabine, G. H. *History of Political Theory.* 3d ed. New York, 1961.

Beales, A. C. F. *The History of Peace.* New York, 1931.

0* Fuller, J. F. C. *A Military History of the Western World.* 3 vols. New York, 1955.

Finally, for an interpretation of Western Civilization's rational history opposite to the one presented in this text, an interpretation that views it as a mistaken retreat from the promise of spirituality into the death grip of materialism, readers should consult:

* **Berdyaev, N. The Meaning of History. New York, 1936.**

Acknowledgments

Figures

None of the figures presented derive directly from previously published illustrations. Rather, they are all based on data extracted piecemeal from a variety of historical sources, the foremost of which are listed in the bibliography.

For example, Figure 6, "Composition of Elites and Masses in the Roman Empire," is based primarily on data from the following:

Boak, A. E. R. "The Roman Magistri in the Civil and Military Service of the Empire," *Harvard Studies in Classical Philology*, XXVI (1915), 73-164.

Cheesman, G. L. *The Auxilia of the Roman Imperial Army*. Oxford, England, 1914.

Lacey, R. H. *The Equestrian Officials of Trajan and Hadrian: Their Careers*, ... Princeton, N.J., 1917.

de Laet, S. J. "La composition de l'Ordre Equestre sous Auguste et Tibère," *Revue Belge de Philologie et d'Histoire*, XX, nos. 3-4 (1941), 509-531.

———. "Le rang social du Primipile à l'époque d'Auguste et de Tibère," *L'Antiquité Classique*, IX (1940), 12-23.

———. *De samenstelling van der Romeinschen Senaat gedurende de eerste eeuw van het Principaat (28 vóór Chr.-68 na Chr.).* "Ryksuniversiteit te Gent: Werken uitgegeven door de Faculteit van de Wijsbegeerte en Letteren," vol. 92. Antwerp, 1941.

Lambrechts, P. *La composition du Sénat Romain de l'accession au trone d'Hadrien à la mort de Commode (117-192).* "Ryksuniversiteit te Gent: Werken uitgegeven door de Faculteit van de Wijsbegeerte en Letteren," vol. 79. Antwerp, 1936.

Mattingly, H. *The Imperial Civil Service of Rome.* Cambridge, England, 1910.

———. "The Property Qualifications of the Roman Classes," *Journal of Roman Studies,* XXVII (1937), 99 ff.

Parker, H. M. D. "The Officers of the Legion," ch. vii in *The Roman Legions.* Oxford, England, 1928.

Taylor, L. R. "Freedmen and Freeborn in the Epitaphs of Imperial Rome," *American Journal of Philology,* vol. 82 (1961), 113 ff.

Maps

The basic geographic outlines of all the maps presented have been redrawn from previously published maps, as follows:

Maps 1, 3, 4, & part of Map 6:
National Geographic Society. *Europe.* Atlas Plate 30. Washington, D.C., 1962.
Map 2:
———. *The World.* Washington, D.C., 1970.
Map 5 & part of Map 6:
———. *Africa.* Atlas Plate 54. Washington, D.C., 1960.
Remainder of Map 6:
[Anon.] "Spread of Metal Technology from Central Asia to Europe . . . ," (after a map in C. Singer, E. J. Holmyard, and A. R. Hall, *A History of Technology,* vol. I [New York, 1954]), in S. N. Dicken and F. R. Pitts, *Introduction to Human Geography* (New York, 1963), p. 381.
Maps 7 & 11:

Denoyer-Geppert Co. *South and Central Europe*. Carto-craft Desk Outline Series, no. 18036. Chicago, n.d.

Inset of Map 7:

[Anon.] "The Habitable World According to Ptolemy, about 150 A.D.," (after Nordenskiöld, from an edition at Rome, 1490), in R. R. Palmer *et al.*, eds., *Atlas of World History* (Chicago, 1957), p. 10.

Map 8:

[Anon.] "Medieval Commerce and Trade Routes," in Palmer, *Atlas of World History*, p. 53.

Map 9:

[Anon.] "Europe . . . ," in E. B. Espenshade, Jr., ed., *Goode's World Atlas*, 12th ed. (Chicago, 1964), p. 107.

Map 10:

Willatts, E. C. "Fragmentation and Dispersal of Land Holdings . . . ," (from Government of Palestine, Dept. of Statistics), reprinted in Dicken and Pitts, *Introduction to Human Geography*, p. 215.

Map 12 & part of Map 17:

[Anon.] "North Atlantic Ocean with Eastern North America and Europe," in C. H. Dietz and O. S. Adams, *Elements of Map Projection* . . . , U.S. Dept. of Commerce, Coast and Geodetic Survey, Special Publication no. 68, 5th ed. (Washington, D.C., 1945), App., Plate I.

Map 13:

University of Chicago Press. *Europe, Southern, and the Levant*. Goode's Series of Base Maps, No. 124. Chicago, 1919.

Maps 14 & 22:

Tremblay, J. P. "Colonization: 17th Century," in J. R. Strayer, H. W. Gatzke, and E. H. Harbison, *The Course of Civilization*, vol. I (New York, 1961), pp. 576-577.

Map 15:

[Anon.] "Atlantic Ocean [Cosmo Series: Atlantic]," in G. D. Hudson, W. Yust *et al.*, eds., *Britannica World Atlas*, 2d ed., rev. (Chicago, 1960), p. 6.

Map 16 & part of Map 19:

[Anon.] "Europe about 1560," in Palmer, *Atlas of World History*, p. 66.

Remainder of Map 17:

[Anon.] "United States . . . ," (after U.S. Dept. of Commerce, Bureau of Census), in Espenshade, *Goode's World Atlas*, p. 59.

[Anon.] "Eastern and Southern Asia about 1775," in Palmer, *Atlas of World History*, pp. 130-131.

Maps 18, 24, & 25:

Raisz, E. "Key Map: Outline of the Continents . . . ," in W. S. Woytinsky and E. S. Woytinsky, *World Commerce and Governments: Trends and Outlook* (New York, 1955), p. 1.

Remainder of Map 19:

[Anon.] "Eurasia: The Growth of Civilization to 200 A.D.," in Palmer, *Atlas of World History*, pp. 18-19.

Map 20:

[Anon.] "Revolutions in the Atlantic World," in Palmer, *Atlas of World History*, pp. 86-87.

[Anon.] "Population," in *The Shorter Oxford Economic Atlas of the World*, prepared by the Economist Intelligence Unit and the Cartographic Dept. of the Clarendon Press, 2d ed. (New York, 1959), pp. 104-105.

[Anon.] "The War in Eastern Europe . . . ," in V. J. Esposito, ed., *The West Point Atlas of American Wars*, vol. II (New York, 1960), section 2, map 23.

Maps 21 & 23:

[Anon.] "World . . . ," (after U.S. Navy Hydrographic Office), in Espenshade, *Goode's World Atlas*, p. 44.

Information shown on the maps in addition to basic geography was extracted piecemeal from a variety of historical sources and atlases, the foremost of which are listed in the bibliography.

For example, Map 7, "The Roman Empire," is based primarily on information from the following:

[Anon.] "Europe, Showing Barbaric Migrations in the Fourth and Fifth Centuries," in *Hammond's Historical Atlas* (New York, 1948), p. H-8.

[Anon.] "Roman Empire about 400 A.D. and the Barbarian Invasions," in Palmer, *Atlas of World History*, pp. 42-43.

[Anon.] "Roman Empire about 120 A.D.," in Palmer, *Atlas of World History,* pp. 38-39.

[Anon.] "The Roman Empire at Its Greatest Extent about 117 A.D.," in *Hammond's Historical Atlas,* p. H-5.

[Anon.] "Roman Republic in the Time of Caesar and Cicero," in Palmer, *Atlas of World History,* pp. 34-35.

Bartholomew, J. "Roman Empire . . . A.D. 1-300," in *Encyclopaedia Britannica,* 1929 ed., 1961 rev. XIX, pp. 500-501.

Gray, V. "Later Roman Empire," in C. G. Starr, *A History of the Ancient World,* pp. 568-569.

————. "Roman Empire under Augustus," in Starr, *A History of the Ancient World,* pp. 562-563.

Stalker-Miller, T. "The Roads of the Romans," in V. W. Von Hagen, *The Roads That Led to Rome* (Cleveland, 1967), pp. 18-19.

Tremblay, J. P. "The German Problem: 1st and 2nd Centuries A.D.," in Strayer, Gatzke, and Harbison, *The Course of Civilization,* vol. I, p. 112.

————. "The Roman Empire at Its Height: A.D. 117," in Strayer, Gatzke, and Harbison, *The Course of Civilization,* vol. I, p. 124.

Index